AF650948

COVID-19 PANDEMIC IN INDIA

About the Editors

Prof. (Dr.) M.R. Biju, currently working as Dean, School of Social Sciences and Professor of Public Administration and Policy Studies, Central University of Kerala, Kasaragod. He has served the full term as Dean, School of Social Sciences (2017-2020), School of Legal Studies (2019-2022) and also a short span as Dean, Academic (2020). Prof. M.R. Biju is one of the widely cited writers in the field of Social Sciences with 161 citations and H-index of 6 and i10 index of 3.

Prof. Biju is the Editor of *South Asian Journal of Socio-Political Studies* (*SAJOSPS*), a UGC Listed Journal (No. 34425 dated 11.01.2017 with an impact factor of 3.1028). He is also serving as Editor-in-Chief of *International Journal of Political Science* (*IJOPS*). He is a prolific writer on socio-political and developmental issues.

He has published Thirty Four (34) books, One hundred and Seventy-Five (175) research papers, Seventeen (17) book chapters and 11 (Eleven) Seminar Proceedings. All the books were published by leading publishing houses in New Dehi. He has delivered 78 (Seventy-Eight) Invited Lectures,16 (Sixteen) Key note addresses and reviewed over Nine Hundred books for *South Asian Journal of Socio-Political Studies.*

His teaching and research experience, spanning over three decades, includes several achievements such as completion of three major research projects funded by Ministry of Panchayati Raj, Government of India and University Grants Commission, New Delhi and the post-doctoral fellowship awarded by the UGC in 2004-07. He has also successfully guided doctoral students of the University of Kerala. Seven students are currently pursuing their doctoral studies under his supervision at CUK. He is consistently making professional academic contributions in the capacity of an Associate Board Member of *Economics and Management*, a prestigious journal published by the Technical University of Liberce, Czech Republic; as the Director and Member Secretary of the Asian Institute of Development Research (AIDR); and as a life Member of several Academic and Professional Bodies.

M.R.B. Anantha Padmanabha is currently serving as Deputy Editor of *South Asian Journal of Socio-Political Studies.* He has to his credit a sizeable number of publications in reputed research journals and he has presented papers in National Seminars and Conferences. He is a Doctoral Student in International Relations and Politics at Central University of Kerala, Kasaragod.

COVID-19 PANDEMIC IN INDIA
Impact and Assessment Studies

Edited by
M.R. Biju
M.R.B. Anantha Padmanabha

CONCEPT PUBLISHING COMPANY PVT. LTD.
NEW DELHI - 110059

© Editors

All rights reserved. No part of this work may be reproduced, stored, adapted, or transmitted in any form or by any means, electronic, mechanical, photocopying, micro-filming recording or otherwise, or translated in any language, without the prior written permission of the copyright owner and the publisher. The book is sold subject to the condition that it shall not, by way of trade or otherwise, be lent, resold, hired out, or otherwise circulated without the prior publisher's written consent in any form of binding or cover other than that in which it is published.

The views and opinions expressed in this book are editor/author(s) own and the facts reported by them have been verified to the extent possible, and the publishers are not in any way liable for the same.

ISBN: 978-93-5594-670-6

First Published 2025

Published and Printed by

Concept
Since 1974

Concept Publishing Company Pvt. Ltd.
A/15-16, Commercial Block, Mohan Garden
New Delhi-110059 (India)
T: +91-11-41101460
E: publishing@conceptpub.com, *W*: www.conceptpub.com

Cataloging in Publication--Courtesy: D.K. Agencies (P) Ltd. <docinfo@dkagencies.com>

COVID-19 pandemic in India : impact and assessment studies / edited by M.R. Biju, M.R.B. Anantha Padmanabha.
pages cm
Contributed articles.
Includes bibliographical references and index.
ISBN 9789355946706

1. COVID-19 Pandemic, 2020- --Economic aspects--India. 2. COVID-19 Pandemic, 2020- --Social aspects--India. 3. India--Economic conditions--21st century. 4. COVID-19 Pandemic, 2020- --Government policy--India. I. Biju, M. R., 1965- editor. II. Anantha Padmanabha, M. R. B., editor.

LCC RA644.C67C68 2025 | DDC 362.196241440954 23

Preface and Acknowledgements

The COVID-19 pandemic has had a significant impact on India, both in terms of public health and the economy. As of August 2021, India has recorded over 32 million cases and over 4,00,000 deaths due to COVID-19. The pandemic has put a strain on the country's healthcare system, with hospitals struggling to cope with the surge in patients. The Indian government has implemented various measures to contain the spread of the virus, including lockdowns, travel restrictions, and vaccination drives. However, the efficacy of these measures has been limited by factors such as vaccine hesitancy, inadequate healthcare infrastructure, and a lack of resources in rural areas. The pandemic has also had a significant impact on the Indian economy. The lockdowns and restrictions have resulted in a sharp decline in economic activity, with many businesses shutting down and workers losing their jobs. The informal sector, which employs a large portion of the Indian workforce, has been particularly hard hit. The Indian government has implemented various measures to mitigate the economic impact of the pandemic, including stimulus packages and loan moratoriums. However, the economic recovery has been slow, with many businesses continuing to struggle. The COVID-19 pandemic has had a significant impact on India, both in terms of public health and the economy. While the government has implemented various measures to contain the spread of the virus and mitigate the economic impact, the road to recovery remains long and challenging.

Against this backdrop, this handy volume presents Fourteen chapters on varied aspects and issues connected with the management of COVID-19 pandemic viz. managing COVID-19 in the Islamic Republics of South Asia, its implications on Society, Polity and Economy of India, COVID-19 and its impact on the Human Rights of Vulnerable Groups, Food Security, *Atma Nirbhar Bharat* and its accomplishment, CSR practice to tackle Covid pandemic, Gender perspectives in managing COVID-19, Role of Women in PRIs and SHGs, Covid Management Experiments in Kerala, bilateral relations in Sino-India, India and Australia, Consumer Behaviour in Automobile Sector and Consumer Experiences etc. Before conclude, the volume editors, would like to add that through these research papers and articles from the academics and researchers, they have tried to explore and examine a few fundamental issues confronted with the management of COVID-19 during the pandemic days. Apart from their presentations, the contributors have submitted solid and practical suggestions to revitalise the system, which may be useful for the students, researchers, practitioners and policy-makers in the field. These prefatory remarks remain incomplete without expressing our gratitude to those who have been kind enough to help us in the preparation of this volume. First of all, we would like to thank our esteemed contributors to this anthology of articles. Similarly, we are extremely thankful to Shri Ashok Kumar Mittal, Managing Director of Concept Publishing Company Pvt. Ltd., New Delhi who brought out the volume in an elegant form.

M.R. Biju
M.R.B. Anantha Padmanabha

Introduction

The COVID-19 pandemic has had a significant impact on India, both in terms of public health and the economy. As of August 2021, India has recorded over 32 million cases and over 4,00,000 deaths due to COVID-19. The pandemic has put a strain on the country's healthcare system, with hospitals struggling to cope with the surge in patients. The Indian government has implemented various measures to contain the spread of the virus, including lockdowns, travel restrictions, and vaccination drives. However, the efficacy of these measures has been limited by factors such as vaccine hesitancy, inadequate healthcare infrastructure, and a lack of resources in rural areas. The pandemic also had a significant impact on the Indian economy. The lockdowns and restrictions have resulted in a sharp decline in economic activity, with many businesses shutting down and workers losing their jobs. The informal sector, which employs a large portion of the Indian workforce, has been particularly hard hit. The Indian government has implemented various measures to mitigate the economic impact of the pandemic, including stimulus packages and loan moratoriums. However, the economic recovery has been slow, with many businesses continuing to struggle. The COVID-19 pandemic has had a significant impact on India, both in terms of public health and the economy. While the government has implemented various measures to contain the spread of the virus and mitigate the economic impact, the road to recovery remains long and challenging.

Against this backdrop, this handy volume presents fourteen chapters on varied aspects and issues connected with the management of COVID-19 pandemic viz. managing COVID-19 in the Islamic Republics of South Asia, its implications on Society, Polity and Economy of India, COVID-19 and its impact on the Human Rights of Vulnerable Groups, Food Security, *Atma Nirbhar Bharat* and its accomplishment, CSR practice to tackle Covid pandemic, Gender perspectives in managing COVID-19, Role of Women in PRIs and SHGs, Covid Management Experiments in Kerala, bilateral relations in Sino-India, India and Australia, Consumer Behaviour in Automobile Sector and Consumer Experiences etc.

Content of the Volume

In the inaugural chapter, Debasish Nandy presents a comparative study in managing COVID-19 pandemic based on the experiments and experiences in the Islamic Republics of South Asia. According to the contributor, the pandemic COVID-19 has posed an immense challenge to South Asia. To him, COVID-19 affected three Islamic republics of South Asia, such as Pakistan, Afghanistan, and the Maldives. This study presents a detailed investigation on the managerial techniques of state authorities in the handling of COVID-19. In the study, the author questions whether the South Asian Islamic Republics have shown responsibilities in managing COVID-19 or not? He adds that in some cases, the bias attitudes of local administration have been shown in treating a particular community during the COVID-19. The COVID-19 has brought forward the vulnerability of public health of these states. No doubt, this study will shed light on the affected economies of the respective Islamic Republic of South Asia. Justification for this include firstly, are the Islamic Republics of South Asia have duly fulfilled their responsibility equally in dealing with all sections of the society to combat COVID-19? Secondly, Is the state the only actor for rescuing its people in a pandemic? Thirdly, Are the financial and infrastructural factors crux of the

COVID-19 challenges? The present study has been carried out based on two research methodologies—(1) content analysis, and (2) observation method. The present study is carried out based on both primary and secondary sources.

In Chapter Two, Sujit Lahiry examines the implications of COVID-19 pandemic on the society, polity and economy of India. According to the author, the COVID-19 pandemic has unfolded as one of the most major and greatest humanitarian crises in the contemporary world. Though it started with China, it soon spread to US and Europe, and subsequently to Asian countries, like India. It brought in its wake major upheavals and trajectories of devastation for India, causing enormous infections, starting with 550 infections on March 23, 2020; and now, the corona virus infections in India has crossed 1,05,12,835 and 1,51,783 deaths as on January 14, 2021. Further this study critically analyses the origin of the COVID-19 pandemic, US-China blame-mongering, and how the Indian state led by Modi has tackled this COVID-19 pandemic, and what are the social, political and economic implications of COVID-19 pandemic in India. It seems to this author that the Modi government has not been fully successful in saving both lives and livelihood of the citizens of India, and has aggravated the problems of poverty, especially for the migrant workers. This chapter also offers some constructive suggestions for the Modi government to control the COVID-19 pandemic and maintain a balance between health security and economic security.

Raj Kishore Pradhan and Rahul Kumar make a critical enquiry in Chapter Three on the aftermath of COVID-19 and evaluate how it can be developed as an opportunity to boost Indian economy. According to the authors, Indian Economy has been going through a challenging time. The dream period from 1991 to 2013 is now over. In-between it has faced a lot of challenges like Global financial market crisis in 2008 and persistent slow down from 2017, which is aided by present COVID-19 pandemic. It has created havoc in our economy which has witnessed record negative growth of our GDP and also loss of employment. But in hindsight it has created huge opportunity for record growth as we have discussed earlier. The objective of this study according to the authors is to highlight how it will become huge boon for our economy. This chapter is explorative by nature and secondary sources have been used as the source of information.

In Chapter Four, Tanvi Yadav and Nagendra Ambedkar Sole present, an academic enquiry into the impact of COVID-19 lockdown on the Human Rights of Vulnerable groups and the Role of Judiciary. According to the authors, COVID-19 brought the health emergency along with the socio-economic crisis in the whole world. In India, the government gave attention to COVID-19 by giving Indian citizens a surprise lockdown. The surprise immensely affects the lives of vulnerable groups of society. They face humiliation, hunger, and violence. The persisting inequalities become the cause of the deplorable condition of these groups. The authors further add that the government took action irresponsibly without any preparation for healthcare, shelter, and food. Numerous human rights violence against women, minorities, marginalized workers, and indigenous people occurred, primarily due to their socio-economic vulnerability. The chapter also explores the government failures and the role of judiciary in lockdown.

Nithya N.R. in her study tries to presents a chapter on The COVID-19 Management Practices in the State of Kerala. In this chapter, the author investigates the experiences and accomplishments of Kerala in its battle against COVID-19. To her, the State of Kerala is known all-over the world as an educationally advanced part of the country which has many outstanding achievements in the field of education, health, habitat, land reforms etc., generally constitutes what is widely known as 'Kerala Model of Development'. Much of the uniqueness of the Kerala model of Development is contributed by the pre-eminent achievements of Kerala in the education and health sectors. Modern economic theory says that this combination of underdevelopment and high standard of living is impossible. How has Kerala done it? There were a large number of factors helping the evolution of the 'model' from the demand side. Social equality is one of the hallmarks of Kerala Model. Today we are passing through a most turbulent crisis in the form of Corona virus, which originated from Wuhan, China. As great global crisis of this century, it affected almost all countries of the world in one way or the other. All of governments of the world are striving hard to contain the spread of COVID-19 viral infections. Kerala state in south part of India has become a model state in the fight against COVID-19. The state government's prompt response to COVID-19 can be attributed to its experience and investment made in emergency preparedness and outbreak response in the past during Kerala floods in 2018 and especially, the NIPAH outbreak in 2019. Many developed nations are in awe of the achievements of Kerala in its fight against COVID-19 pandemic. What really is the Kerala model of Health? How Kerala is responding to Corona virus? What can the rest of the world learn from Kerala's experience? Is Kerala's strategy is successful in its fight against COVID-19 pandemic? These are some of the questions that the researcher would like to answer through this chapter. However, the chapter concludes that rebuilding the village economy, revamping primary healthcare system and village panchayats etc. can effectively curb and contain any pandemic.

COVID-19 and Food Security Challenges in South Asia is the Central Theme of Discussion in Chapter Six presented by Santhosh Mathew. To him, No doubt, the COVID-19, has a long-lasting impact on every aspect of life. COVID-19 is the world's hazardous. Every part of the world has been affected by COVID-19. This kind of hazardous has not seen the world communities after the Second World War. A large number of peoples are affected and died by COVID-19 pandemic. The ratio is growing rapidly day by day. South Asia is severely vulnerable to COVID-19, because of the density of the population, and lack of medical facilities, and the limited capacity of the economy to mitigate the challenges. As a developing region South Asia's economy was badly affected by this pandemic. It is a big challenge for South Asia and its county to face this challenge, economic challenge as well as a governance challenge.

In Chapter Seven, Iftekhar Alam presents his thoughts and ideals on accomplishing *Atmanirbhar Bharat* or Self-Reliant India amidst COVID-19 pandemic. Here the researcher made a noble attempt to examine the government policies on Social Entrepreneurship. According to Alam, *Atmanirbhar Bharat* is a noble attempt to realise the past glory of our country which existed ever since ancient India till the colonization of the country happened. The clarion call given by our Hon'ble Prime Minister to be self-reliant or *Atmanirbhar* is resonated in converting challenges into opportunities, concomitantly reviving the Indian economy. Government policies to propel the Economic Patriotism, Techno-nationalism, bolstering manufacturing ecosystem and conducting translational research in the country have potential to realise the Self-reliance movement in India. The prospects of Social Entrepreneurship & Start-ups to convert challenges faced during pandemic into opportunities to generate income, livelihood promotion, strengthen local economy, check the migration and explore the unexplored areas for growth and sustenance can have overwhelming impact on *Atmanirbhar Bharat Abhiyan*.

Consumer behaviour in the Automobile industry and its impact of COVID-19 is the core of discussion in Chapter Eight which is contributed by Lijo Mon L. According to author, due to the emergence of globalization and liberalization, there is a stiff competition among the automobile industries which are focusing attention in capturing the Indian markets during this pandemic situation of COVID-19. At present automobiles have become a common need and almost a necessity product. This sweeping change leads to increase in demand for different types of automobiles. Automobile financing is a common facility provided by banks and non-banking finance companies which include the people in the purchase of automobiles. Public in this situation is more conscious about health, giving it the first priority. Here the researcher has tried to attempt a study on the impact of COVID-19 on consumer behaviour in automobile industry. 200 samples were drawn for the purpose of study by using convenient sampling method. The study reveals that maximum of respondents made their self-decision before making a purchase. It was extracted from the responses that when a buyer enters a showroom to purchase a product, then most of the time he is with the frame of mind for the product he is going for, the buyer does his homework and comes down with a frame of mind to go for the product.

Consumer practices of companies to tackle the Coronavirus pandemic is the study presented by D. Divya Prabha in Chapter Nine. According to the author, the coronavirus outbreak is first and foremost a human tragedy, affecting hundreds of thousands of people all-around the globe in more than 198 countries. As it has a growing impact on the global economy, the world is gearing up to tackle this crisis of unforeseen magnitude and governments issue healthcare advisories and quarantine the infected. From the business front, the Covid Pandemic have begun painting a bleak picture of broken supply chains, disrupted manufacturing, empty stores and flagging demand. Even though the companies all around the globe are facing an economic slowdown, companies are stepping up to support their stakeholders in all possible ways as a part of their corporate social responsibility. This chapter analyses the activities undertaken by the Multinational companies around the world to support the society to combat and recover from this coronavirus pandemic.

Changing gender practices in managing COVID-19 and the Role of Panchayati Raj Institutions and Self Help Groups is the topic of Discussion in Chapter Ten by Smita Nayak. The study is based on the State of Odisha. According to the researcher, the three-tier Panchayati Raj structure also strengthened the process of decentralized governance in India and 73rd Constitutional Amendment brought radical changes towards paving path for women's empowerment through perpetuating the spell of reservation for women in all key positions of PRIs. The women Panchayat leaders were specially empowered in Odisha as the state took pioneering steps in spearheading women's empowerment. Odisha is also reckoned as an exemplary state for rapid growth of SHG movement augmenting women's empowerment. In this chapter, the researcher delves deep into the issues of changing Gender perspectives in view of management of COVID-19 revamped through convergence of women Panchayat representatives and leaders of Women Self Help Groups in sample districts selected specifically for the study.

The disproportionate impact of COVID-19 on Indian Society is discussed in a detailed manner by Imtiyaz Ahmad Wani and Akumarthi Nageswara Rao in Chapter Eleven. To them, COVID-19 (Corona virus) has rapidly affected our day to day life. Presently, the impacts of COVID-19 in daily life are extensive and have far reaching consequences. COVID-19 pandemic is shaking fundamental assumptions about the human life course in societies around the world. COVID-19 has led to a dramatic loss of human life worldwide and presents an unprecedented challenge to public health and the world of work. The economic and social disruption caused by the pandemic is devastating millions of people into extreme poverty and millions of enterprises face an existential threat. Significant economic impact has already occurred across the globe due to reductions in income, reduced productivity, loss of life, business closures, trade disruption and decimation of the tourism industry. The COVID-19 pandemic has disrupted every aspect of our lives. Even before the onset of the crisis, the social and economic integration of young people was an ongoing challenge. People cannot carry on with their usual jobs or occupations. The existing situation of unemployment worsens. Incomes fall or cease. Economically better-off people manage with varying degrees of difficulty, but people from the lower economic sections become almost destitute. With very less or no money-in-hand people are on the verge of starving. Their weakened physical condition increases their susceptibility to disease. This study aims to provide a comprehensive analysis of the social, economic and psychological impact of the COVID-19 outbreak on the Indian society and investigate the global preventive measures taken to reduce the transmission of COVID-19.

Sujit Kumar Datta in Chapter Twelve illustrates the changing pattern of Sino-Indian Relations in the post-COVID era. According to the author, when two big neighbouring countries of comparable national power are vying for influence in South Asia and strategic space, competition is bound to occur. Geographically, India is supposed as a South Asian provincial supremacy, but a nearer appearance exposes that it is in an unfavourable location *vis-à-vis* China in that region. The most crucial factor is that the Indian government does not have more of the political, financial, and martial capabilities to track the South Asian regional power determinations than their neighbour's for the long run. So, all the South Asian small states could continuously show the China card to balance India's effect in their countries. However, these disagreements have evolved from confrontation to the mixed elements of competition and cooperation in the current period. Sino-Indian relations in South Asia has undergone a transformation with momentum toward collaboration on several South Asian regional issues over the last two decades. With Chinese inspiration in the South Asian region is rising day by day, it is vital that India not to fall behindhand in the South Asian area, but preserve a stable dominance in that region. In brief, this chapter will articulate the construction of a valuable analytical outline for the investigation of the transformation of Sino-Indian relationship in South Asia in the post-COVID era, revealing the importance of external factors in influencing Sino-Indian bilateral and multilateral interactions throughout the adjustment of the order of their political and strategic preferences.

Bimalendu Ghosh submits a study in the Chapter 13 on the bilateral relations between India and Australia. It is an academic enquiry from the post-Cold War period to COVID-19. According to Ghosh, India and Australia have various commonalities, which provide as a foundation for closer cooperation and multifaceted interaction. Before independence, Australia and India were both part of the British Empire. Both are members of the Commonwealth of Nations, founding members of the

United Nations, and members of regional organisations including the Indian Ocean Rim Association for Regional Cooperation and ASEAN Regional forum. Both are strong, vibrant, secular and multicultural democracies. Both have a free press and an independent judicial system. They also share political, economic, security, lingual and sporting ties. As a result of British colonisation, cricket has emerged as a strong cultural connection between the two nations, as well as the English language. Recently, military cooperation between Australia and India is growing that includes the regular joint naval exercise AUSINDEX, security dialogues as Quadrilateral Security Dialogue (Quad). The two countries now share many security concerns, including the growing impact of China on the strategic environment. Thus, in coming years, India is likely to become one of Australia's most important partners in the region. The rise of India will make it one of Australia's most important economic relationships and a key diplomatic collaborator. Australia has recognised India as an important new strategic partner. India too is beginning to see Australia as one of several new security partners in the Indo-Pacific region in specific and economics and politics in general. The Australian market is one of the partners of strategic importance to India as it provides immense avenues to establish a foothold in the emerging East-Asian markets. Therefore, this has become an important component of India's strategic economic priorities as a part of its Act East Policy. In this perspective, this chapter provides an overview of developments in the relationship between India-Australia from post Cold-War to COVID-19 Era. The chapter then explores in detail the many potential areas for enhanced cooperation between them and finally includes observations on prospects for the relationship.

In the concluding chapter, Anjali A. and Bijith George Abraham present a research outcome on the consumer shopping experiences in Kerala during the pandemic phase. The study is based on Krishna Stores in the state. In their study, the authors observe that the pandemic COVID-19 has come as life changer for everyone worldwide. One such change is that of people's outlook on life and living, especially consumer behaviour towards shopping preferences. With the restrictions, the choice of most modern shopping centres was seen last on consumers' list. This chapter attempts to expose the rebirth tactics adopted by traditional *Kirana* Stores from the demand-based perspective of consumers during the pandemic phase. Altogether 300 responses were gathered from different regions of Kerala to capture the change in consumer perception towards shopping preferences and understand the re-emergence of the *Kirana* stores. Factor analysis and logistic regression model was used to identify the pertinent factors favouring the shopping preference. The service offered by the *Kirana* stores as part of revival strategy is reflected in their adaptability, quality, safety, digitalization, quick delivery, personalized services, and tie-up with online delivery partners helped them regain the customers' faith.

Before conclude, the volume editors, would like to add that through these research papers and articles from the academics, researchers have tried to explore and examine a few fundamental issues confronted by the society, polity and economy of India during the Covid pandemic days which may be useful for the students, researchers, practitioners and policy-makers in the field.

M.R. Biju
M.R.B. Anantha Padmanabha

Contents

List of Contributors

Akumarthi Nageswara Rao (Dr.), Professor, Department of Political Science, Maulana Azad National Urdu University, Hyderabad. **Email:** akumarthirao@gmail.com

Anjali A. (Dr.), Assistant Professor, SCMS Cochin School of Business, Cochin, Kerala. **Email:** aafin3@iimk.ac.in

Bijith George Abraham (Dr.), Associate Professor, Marian Institution of Management, Marian College (Autonomous) Kuttikkanam, Idukki, Kerala.
Email: bijithabraham@gmail.com / beithabraham@gmail.com

Bimalendu Ghosh (Dr.), Assistant Professor in Political Science, Kanchrapara College, Kanchrapara, 24 Parganas (N), West Bengal. **Email:** bimalendughoshkc@gmail.com

D. Divyaprabha, Associate Professor, Department of International Business, PSG College of Arts & Science, Coimbatore.
Email: divyaprabha@psgcas.ac.in

Debasish Nandy (Dr.), Professor, Department of Political Science, Kazi Nazrul University, Kalla Bypass, More, Asansol, Paschim Barddaman, West Bengal. **Email:** debasish762010@yahoo.com

Iftekhar Alam (Dr.), Assistant Professor, Department of Social Work, Pondicherry University, Puducherry.
Email: iftemsw@pondiuniversity.ac.in

Imtiyaz Ahmad Wani (Dr.), Lecturer, Department of Sociology, Government Degree College Khansahib, Budgam Kashmir.
Email: iftemsw@pondiuniversity.ac.in

Lijo Mon L. (Dr.), Assistant Professor, Department of Commerce, Mar Ivanios College (Autonomous), Thiruvananthapuram. **Email:** lijomonl95@gmail.com

Nagendra Ambedkar Sole (Dr.), Department of Public Policy, Law and Governance, Central University of Rajasthan, Ajmer, Rajasthan. **Email:** ambedkarsn@gmail.com

Nithya N.R. (Dr.), Assistant Professor, Department of Political Science, University of Kerala, Thiruvanthapuram. **Email:** nithyatpm@keralauniversity.ac.in

Rahul Kumar (Dr.), Statistical Assistant, Tobacco Board, Ministry of Commerce & Industry, Govt. of India, Guntur, Andhra Pradesh. **Email:** rajkishore81@gmail.com

Raj Kishor Pradhan (Dr.), Senior Statistical Officer, NSO (FOD), Ministry of Statistics & PI, Govt. of India, Sambalpur, Odisha. **Email:** rajkishore81@gmail.com

Santhosh Mathew (Dr.), Associate Professor, Centre for South Asian Studies, Pondicherry Central University, Puducherry. **Email:** santhoshveranani@gmail.com

Smita Nayak (Dr.), Head, PG Department of Political Science, Utkal University, Bhubaneswar. **Email:** nayaksmitha1992@gmail.com

Sujit Kumar Datta (Dr.), Associate Professor, Department of International Relations, University of Chittagong, Bangaladesh. **Email:** datta.ir@cu.ac.bd

Sujit Lahiry (Dr.), Professor of Political Science, Panjab University Regional Centre, Sri Muktsar Sahib, Punjab. **Email:** sujitlahiri29@gmail.com

Tanvi Yadav (Dr.), Assistant Professor of Law, Department of Law, National Forensic Science University, Delhi Campus, Outer Ring Road, Industrial Area, Sector 3, Rohini, Delhi. **Email:** tanvi110391@gmail.com

1

Managing COVID-19

A Comparative Study of Islamic Republics of South Asia

Debasish Nandy

Introduction

How Pakistan, Afghanistan, and the Maldives have handled the COVID-19 that will be critically analyzed in this study. I have chosen four different types of countries in terms of the nature of the state, and economy. I would make a comparative study on the responsibility of these four different states critically. In the era of globalization, the question of the responsibility of the states has revolved around the intellectuals. The common perception about the state now is less responsible state due to the interference of MNCs, and other private agencies in most of the sectors. The idea of global governance is an outcome of globalization, and the concept of the welfare state has been challenged. For, the Third World states, whether the very concept of world government would be useful or not that has been questioned by eminent scholar of International Relations, Professor Jayantanuja Bandyopadhyaya. He said, "the inadequacy of their domestic power base makes it imperative for them to seek the assistance and protection of a democratic world government for ensuring development and welfare of their people"

(Bandyopadhyaya, 2002). However, the South Asian states are not immune from the effect of globalization. The overwhelming involvement in state affairs by the non-governmental agencies raised several questions. Most of the debt-laden and vulnerable South Asian states are often reluctant to fulfilling their due responsibilities for their inability or don't care attitudes. The nature of the state often does matter. For a military state or puppet state or terrorist state or a vulnerable state, the issue of state responsibility is a utopian idea.

The nature of the social fabric and vibrancy of civil society is very important in this regard. The governments of some South Asian states often make them delinked with the people intentionally. It is also true that in a crisis period, it is very difficult to overcome the crisis without citizens' response. The social security emphasis on voluntary citizen involvement rather than on top-down governmental solutions (Linnell, 2014: 68). Participation in civil society and voluntary organizations has made a positive change in many western societies. The will to engage in pro-social efforts to assist fellow members of the society very much needs to overcome the crisis (Rodríguez, Trainor, & Quarantelli, 2006). The citizens of a country are primarily responsible for protecting their own lives and property and then they will try to assist others abiding by the advisories given by the government. The pandemic situation cannot be overcome by the government alone without the equal response and cooperation of the citizens. The backward societies like Pakistan and Afghanistan and some parts of India are unconsciously disappearing in fighting with the pandemic COVID-19. We cannot avoid corporate social responsibility. Often it has been found that the corporate houses are intentionally avoiding their committed social responsibility. The national and transnational companies often forget Corporate Social Responsibility to confronted economic and social challenges (Idowu, Vertigans, and Burlea, 2017). It has been proven in the pandemic COVID-19 that the state is still the prime responsible institution to bail out its citizens from the crisis. Although there is a lot of criticism about the state's responsibility, yet there is no alternative to the state. Technically speaking, it is necessary to establish coordination among different levels of the government to overcome the crisis. This study attempts to make a comparative study of the selected South Asian states regarding their responsibility in combating COVID-19.

The Pakistani Experience

Pakistan is a state without nationalism. Despite being an Islamic state it has failed to secure human rights for all. Political violence is a language of Pakistani politics (Ullah, 2014). Pakistan is considered a failed state for restless ethnic conflicts, intra-religious clashes, terrorism, religious orthodoxy, and military intervention. Being a democratic country with a federal structure, Pakistan has not been yet to fundamental rights and human rights for the citizens nor able to ensure equal opportunity to all ethnic groups. Over the years, the federal government of Pakistan has witnessed several ethnic conflicts for pro-Panjabi policy and pampering of the Sunni community. The process of Islamization in every sector of society collapsed its democratic structure. Pakistan has gone through military regimes after several intervals. The economy of Pakistan is very vulnerable due to many reasons. The developmental activities are immensely hampered for many reasons. The internal conflict is the major reason. The extremist policies are imposed on Shia and Ahamedia communities. According to T. Paul, "Pakistan's ongoing war-making efforts have deeply affected its prospects for emerging as a tolerant, prosperous, and unified nation-state. This has major implications not only for Pakistan but also for global and regional security orders" (Paul, 2014).

Pakistan has been highly affected by a deadly coronavirus. Thousands of people have been highly infected, and the economy of Pakistan has been slow-downed. The Pakistan government announced a lockdown in March 2020, when the situation went out of control. All educational institutions were closed down. The domestic and international flights were grounded. Primarily, the attitude of the government was so much reluctant. The negligence of the government has been manifested when it denied evacuating the citizens from abroad. The inhuman attitudes of the government with COVID-19 patients were highly neglected by the global community. If we talk about the human rights and human security of Pakistan, then it can be easily stated that Pakistan is the worst example of human exploitation, and human rights violations. However, due to domestic compulsion, the Pak government had lifted the lockdown on May 9, 2020. After lifting the lockdown, the COVID-cases have rapidly increased due to the least caring attitude of the common masses. The entire healthcare system was broken down due to the overwhelming pressure of COVID patients. Testing kits were not available in Pakistan. Due to the infection of countless health workers from the very beginning, the failure of health management of the Pakistan government was reflected. When the Pakistan government decided to lift the lockdown, then Prime Minister Imran Khan addressed the Pakistani people in saying that they must live with the virus. The voice of the Supreme Court of Pakistan was very surprising.

The apex court of Pakistan ruled that COVID-19 is 'not a pandemic' and ordered the stakeholders for reopening shopping malls. The role of a religious master, like *ulema*, was very orthodox. They urged the faithful to fill up mosques for Eid prayers. I am mentioning the role of these institutions and states pillars to understand the nature of Pakistan's state. The people of Pakistan, could not be secured by the government economically, socially, religiously, and medically also. The government of Pakistan never gives priority to human security before the military, ISI, and religious factors. Many people of Pakistan relied on the words of leaders and experts to make critical health decisions. This outbreak is not only a public health crisis but also a public communication crisis.

Impact on Healthcare and the Role of the Government

The COVID-19 has immensely affected the public healthcare system of Pakistan. The healthcare system in Pakistan is very weak.

Some standard hospitals and medical centres are situated in big cities. The health security issue is closely related to social security. The Pakistan government spends only 2 per cent of its GDP which is much lower than the global average of 11 per cent. Social security and public health are notably weak in Pakistan. The World Health Organization (WHO) recommends and encourages the member states to spend at least 5 per cent of their GDP on public health. The developed member countries are spending more than the suggested percentage of their GDP. But, for the least developing countries, like Pakistan, it is far from the suggested percentage. In the case of Pakistan, it spends the lowest amount on developing public health and education. In FY 2006-2007, the governmental expenditure on healthcare was 0.5 per cent of the GDP (Ahmed and Shaikh, 2008). The inadequacy in health sector budgeting compelled the citizens to be more dependent upon the private healthcare system.

The indigenous medical equipment is unavailable in Pakistan. Due to the overwhelming pressure of coronavirus-infected patients, government hospitals cannot accommodate more patients due to a shortage of beds and ventilators. In Karachi, there are 15 hospitals (including private and government) that are dealing with COVID patients. The total number of ventilators in all of these hospitals is 136. In Lahore, there are 539 beds and 200 ventilators are available for patients infected by COVID-19 (*The Times of India*: 2020). The Pakistan government has spent $298.94 million to purchase medical equipments. The government of Pakistan has taken some initiative to make awareness among the people for healthcare to combat the pandemic situation. The local governmental agencies have announced for maintaining social distancing and using masks as mandatory. The government had also enforced some directives to the local government for sanitizing. To promote public awareness, the government has taken several programmes on sensitization. The particular governmental agencies have regularly sent a message to the people for making awareness. The health department has tried to identify the coronavirus-affected areas to conduct rapid tests.

Impact on the Economy

To sustain, Pakistan will have to overcome the current economic hardship. They have assumed that Pakistan's economic growth will be reached around 1-2 per cent in the next year and the government's revenue will be hugely reduced. Due to negative economic growth, the State Bank of Pakistan has decided to reduce interest rates by 2 per cent. The government has decided to cut down the expenses of selected sectors. To rejuvenate some selected sectors, the government has taken some generous steps by declaring some relaxation on taxes and providing subsidies. The State Bank of Pakistan has declared a temporary economic refinance facility to encourage new investments. The government has also announced a special package for small entrepreneurs. The government of Pakistan has offered to establish new hospitals and medical centres by offering low-interest loans for five years. As Pakistan is a federal state, that is why the provincial government has some special provisions to deal with the deadliest situations in their ways. The coordination between the federal and provincial have been found to combat the coronavirus. The economic status of Baluchistan, NWFP, and FATA is not at par with Sindh and Punjab. So, all provinces have not been able to ensure subsidy to their needy provincial people. Sindh is the first state which announced curfew and lockdown in major cities to stop the spreading of infections. The Northwest Frontier Province has also declared a partial lockdown to stop social interaction. The provincial governments have also announced some special packages for the economically backward classes.

Discriminatory Attitudes Towards Religious Minorities in Food Distribution

Constitutionally Pakistan is the Islamic Republic, but practically, it is a multi-religious country with Islamic factionalism. When the entire world has been fighting with COVID-19 unitedly, then in Pakistan, governmental discriminations have been found in treating religious minorities. Religious intolerance has been manifested in Sunni Muslim-dominated Pakistan. The coronavirus has been referring to as the **'Shia virus'** to make more social pressure on the socially cornered minority Shia community. During the pandemic, an allegation has been raised against the Sunni-owned ration shop for pressurizing Christians to recite the *karma* for getting ration. The same attitudes were shown towards Hindus. Some government distribution centres had denied giving ration to the Hindus despite showing the national identity card. This is the hard fact of Pakistan, where the state agencies or allied agencies often do discriminatory acts towards the religious minority. The governmental policy of exclusion has been implied in society also. In many places, relief was distributed by private foundations and trusts. These organizations often deny assisting non-Muslim people to provide aid (Mirza, 2020).

During the pandemic situation, the Hazara Shias were victimized due to the government. The government has tagged them as non-Muslim which is why they are socially isolated. In a democratic country is it expected that any public notice can be issued for a particular community in a discriminatory manner? As far as public health is concerned, no public notice can be issued to isolate any particular community by the government. The police authority of Baluchistan has announced the Hazara Shia community to confining themselves within the home. On another notice, issued by the Water and Sanitization Authority of Baluch Government on March 13, it was said that the two Shia-majority inhabited towns namely Marriabad, and Hazara will be treated isolated. The Shia people of these two cities were restricted to go outside of their homes during the amid of pandemic. Interestingly, other communities were remained free to go outside. However, to establish itself as a self-dependent county, the Pakistan government should abandon the policy of exclusion and ethnoreligious division policy within the state. It should be more aware of its economic development and self-reliance.

The Experience of Afghanistan

Afghanistan has failed to maintain human security. For Afghanistan, human security always exists in a volatile situation. The war-torn Afghan society is suffering from the inadequacy of human rights. There are several reasons behind the fragile human security in Afghanistan (1) Lawlessness, unstable government, absence of governability, restless political and social unrest, (2) Taliban militancy, (3) Violence against women, (4) Ethnic conflicts and civil wars, (5) Bombing and firing by external forces (Nandy, 2019:64). The relative autonomy of Afghanistan has been immensely questionable. Afghanistan got underway following the Soviet pull-out in February 1989, the forces which the CIA and ISI had gathered for the *jihad* begun realizing their importance for *jihad* elsewhere (Gul, 2009: 215). What Afghanistan is today, the responsibility of superpowers is highly questionable for that. The concept of peace has been a utopian dream for Afghan people. The government has no role in peacebuilding in Afghanistan. Since the Soviet invasion in 1979, thousands of Afghan people had left the country for saving their lives and took shelter in neighbouring Pakistan, Iran, and some central Asian countries, like Tajikistan, Uzbekistan etc. Due to economic vulnerability and non-stop civil wars and external wars, Afghan people use to take shelter in developed countries also. The inability and irresponsibility of the state are found in the case of Afghanistan in protecting human security. Since the invasion of the USSR in 1979, Afghanistan has been a place of restless conflicts, and a pawn of the global cheeseboard for exercising of power of global powers.

In 2001, a United States-led military coalition invaded Afghanistan to fight against the al-Qaida and Taliban groups. Afghanistan consisting of 38 million people, out of this figure, 1.11 million has already been internally displaced, and 1.7 million people had taken shelter in Pakistan, Iran, Tajikistan, and other countries due to civil wars, terrorism, food crisis, unemployment. The Taliban group is brutally attacking not only government offices, foreign diplomatic missions, but also educational institutions, and hospitals. The BBC News has reported that in May 2020, a deadly terrorist attack was conducted at Ataturk Children's Hospital, and another attack was done on a maternity hospital in Kabul. These incidents are not exceptional which probes the challenge of the human security of Afghanistan (https://www.bbc.com/news/world-asia-52631071). The healthcare system of Afghanistan is very much fragmented and weakened. The capacity of the government in spending money on public health is minimal. The government of Afghanistan spends a little amount on healthcare due to insufficient budgetary allocation. However, in recent times, the government has initiated to development of the health system with external financial assistance. Now, per 10,000 people, 1.9 per cent of physicians and 9.4 per cent of skilled healthcare professionals have been allocated. Indian doctors and nurses are working in Afghanistan for providing advanced healthcare. The major challenge to President Hamid Karzai was to stop civil wars and decade-long terrorism.

Impact on Several Sectors

As human security is immensely questionable in Afghanistan, that is why human assistance is immediately needed for 14 million people. The state authority is unable to arrange humanitarian assistance for all of them, that is why external assistance has been pleaded by the government. During the last couple of years, the international community has been worried about the peace, and development of Afghanistan (Sarkar, 2012: 16). The development and peace of a country cannot be ensured or installed from the outside. The response of the society and aspirations of the countrymen are essentially needed for that. Despite receiving external assistance, a humanitarian vulnerability has not been removed in Afghanistan. The most vulnerable among the vulnerable like rural poor, minority groups, internally displaced people, and returned refugees from the neighbouring countries. The COVID-19 has been introduced as an additional hazard with internal conflict, poverty, and repeated natural disasters (OCHA, 2020). For an economically challenged, orthodox, and unconscious state, it is quite a difficult task to combat the COVID-19.

Since February 2020, the COVID-19 crisis has fuelled due to the returning of thousands of Afghan refugees, and migrants from Iran, Pakistan, and Turkey. These reversed people had carried the coronavirus and reached different provinces by public transport without maintaining the minimum directives of WHO. The government agencies of Afghanistan are usually very casual about public hygiene, sensitization, and healthcare. In the case of COVID-19, the same attitudes of the government were found. Lawlessness has been an integral part of Afghan society, which caused the spread of COVID-19. Afghanistan is an uncertain country in the true sense. The inhuman, and barbaric actions of the Taliban have been restarted in the pandemic situation which violated its earlier promises the government in maintaining the ceasefire. The Taliban had conducted several terrorist attacks during the pandemic situation. At least 55 attacks were conducted by the Taliban from March 2020 to August 2020. Taliban had also promised to help the governmental initiatives with international organizations to fight against the COVID-19, but ultimately the Taliban chose its old way of violence. This is a problem for a war-torn, and terrorist-affected country to take any step towards the welfare project despite huge challenges. Due to the escalation of violence, the Afghan government has to face double jeopardy in the pandemic situation.

The World Bank has approved $ 400 million to the Afghan government to fight against COVID-19. The Afghan government has received assistance for handling the COVID-19 from Abu Dhabi, Germany, and other countries that had assisted Afghanistan to combat COVID-19, but mismanagement of funds at different levels of the government has been found. Another alarming concern is a low social hygienic sense among the people, and due to health illiteracy, the infections have rapidly increased across the country. The shortage of food is not a new phenomenon for Afghanistan. As I have mentioned that the Taliban is always a problem for Afghanistan which has been more complicated during the pandemic due to the release of 933 Taliban prisoners from different prisons of Afghanistan.

The Governmental Initiatives

The Afghan government has taken some measures to control the pandemic situation. (1) The government has tried to make awareness among the people to use masks, sanitization, and social distancing. (2) The government has initiated testing the suspected COVID patents in government hospitals with its limitations. (3) Some quarantine centres and isolated wards have been made by the government. The Kabul-centric healthcare system could not mitigate the required public health demand for all provinces. (4) The working hours in the government health centres have been increased, and shifting duty charts were made for the doctors and health staff. (5) The government advisory was given to the people. The aged employees and pregnant women were advised to do work from home. (6) The government offices were asked to avoid the gathering of more people. (7) New budget allocation was made for fighting with coronavirus offices (UNDP, 2020).

For fighting with coronavirus, Afghanistan is not in a position to arrange isolation centres for the majority of infected people. The country has only 991 beds for COVID patients. Kabul has a capacity of 50 tests for COVID-19 per day. It is quite difficult to afford foreign testing kits for the common people. The situation of provincial governments is very worst. Afghanistan has a total of 172 hospitals. The well-trained doctors, healthcare staffs, and nurses are inadequate in Afghanistan. There are only 9·4 skilled health professionals and 1·9 physicians per 10,000 citizens in Afghanistan. The physicians are disproportionately distributed across the country (Shah, Karimzadeh, Tareq, Hamid, Sayed, and, Tien, 2020). The overdependence on foreign countries in healthcare and other infrastructural developments is to be reduced by the government. The state management strategies are to be introduced by the Afghan government. In the post-COVID-19 world order, it would be very difficult to receive foreign assistance from any economically vulnerable states, as most of the donor countries already cut up their budgetary allocation for the aid due to the acute financial crisis. The Afghan government should move to explore its sources in handling the further crisis.

The Maldivian Experience

The Islamic Republic of Maldives is a vulnerable state in every sense. The tourism-dependent economy has to face an acute financial crisis. It is the least developed country, as it depends on tourism, and fishery being as its main source of income (Bussa, 2017). As the state economy is overly dependent on tourism that is why it has immensely weakened the economy. International assistance has been received by the Maldivian government from various sources. The Maldivian president Ibrahim Mohamed Solih was democratically elected with a lot of promises in 2018. The state government led the economy of the Maldives to have a stronghold in society. The role of private sectors in the Maldivian economy is not significant due to the lack of indigenous industries. The influence of the Chinese government and companies has been drastically changed the economic autonomy of the country since 2012. A huge amount of Chinese liquid assistance has been received by the Maldives over the last few years. The complex financial conditions have been imposed on the Maldivian government, but when the question of social responsibility comes, the Chinese government is used to keep mute itself. Maldives has pleaded for getting financial assistance from the different international agencies and countries as well to procure personal protective equipment (PPE) and medical supplies. The World Bank has approved a fast-track aid package of $7.3 million to strengthen the preparedness of the country

Healthcare Facilities

The healthcare system of Maldives is very vulnerable. The Indira Gandhi Memorial Hospital in Male is the biggest in the country. Due to a shortage of money, doctors, nurses, and backwardness in medical research Maldives is struggling with the healthcare system. The population of Maldives is sacredly living in different islands.

Most of the islands have no medical facility, and the transportation system merely depends upon waterways. It is a less populated country. As per the record of 2018, the total population of Maldives is 5,16,000. Less population has given an extraordinary facility to the Maldives. Several islands and the resorts are uninhabited which are providing space for isolation or quarantine facilities. However, facilities for the test and treatment of COVID-19 patients are available only in the capital city. A limited number of ambulances are available in the country. The total number of ventilators in the Maldives is 97. After observing the situation, the National Health Emergency was declared in the country (Sultana, 2020). According to the report of the Health Emergency Operations Plan (HEOP), the primary objective of this plan is to strengthen the health sector and to take emergency preparedness to handle epidemics and pandemics; and other types of emergencies which have a substantial impact on people's health and society (HEOP, 2018). To tackle the COVID-19, from the very beginning the thermal screening facilities were set up at all international airports and seaports to identify passengers with possible symptoms, who would require isolation. Subsequently, a temporary ban was imposed on travellers and flights from the most affected countries in March. The issuance of visas for foreigners was suspended from March 27, 2020 (Sultana, 2020).

The Maldivian government has decided to produce foodgrains and vegetables in uninhabited islands to reduce dependency on other countries. Due to the acute financial crisis for the pandemic, the government of Maldives has decided to cut the salary of the government employees. With a limited capacity, the government has also announced some generous financial assistance for the fishermen, farmers, small, and medium-scale businessmen. The Maldivian government declared a special financial package of 2.5 billion MVR. Through the experience of the pandemic situation and acute financial crisis and shortage of foods, the Maldivian government decided to reduce its imports of staple foods, and overdependence on tourism. The tourism-based economy struck at the lowest point, so alternative sources of revenue generation will be to find out by the Maldivian government. The government has decided to give vacant land to those people who are interested in cultivation. To continue unimpeded imports during the crisis, the government has decided to establish state shipping lines in March 2020. The pandemic COVID-19 has given an unfolded experience to all states, which compelled those state authorities to explore new managerial perspectives of the state. The Maldivian government has also learned new things and tried to manage the crisis in a new manner. The Maldivian government has fallen in double jeopardy in the pandemic situation due to the overwhelming pressure imposed by China. The Maldives had taken a huge amount of loans during the regime of Abdulla Yameen.

The debt-burden economy of Maldives has been newly challenged by China by asking to repay the loan. In this unexpected crisis, it is very difficult for the Maldives to repay the Chinese loan. The Maldivian new government has started to re-establish friendly relations with India, making the country under the pressure from China. The Maldivian government has received enormous assistance during the COVID-19 crisis in the form of food, goods, and medical equipment. Now it is a great challenge to the Maldives to manage India and China in a balanced manner. The new managerial strategies are to be formulated by the government, which will be an additional lesson of COVID-19 for the Maldives. The Maldivian Government has been quite proactive in fighting against COVID-19. The government has started to explore new alternatives to be self-dependent. However, being a vulnerable state, the Maldives has been dealing with COVID-19 very well in comparison with other South Asian states.

Concluding Remarks

The responsibility of selected South Asian states is different in their performance. The experience of India is widely different from the other states. Being the regional power and core state of South Asia, the responsibility goes beyond the state boundary. The nature of civil society, rate of literacy, social awareness, and corporate social responsibilities are interrelated and essential in combating major crises, like COVID-19. The state managerial skill is not the same for all countries. The issue of corporate social responsibilities does not apply to non-globalized states, like Afghanistan. Countries like Maldives, and Afghanistan which are overdependent on external supports and supply will have to rethink indigenous production and the medical system. For Afghanistan, there are so many challenges that are difficult to overcome. The war-torn, economically vulnerable, and socially fragmented Afghanistan will have to develop its civil society and its resources. Pakistan stands for a military state which concentrates on the war-making process with an outlook of social exclusion. The shortcomings of the government's distributive policy are recognizable. The attitudes of the governmental agencies towards COVID-19 patients were not only reluctant but also inhuman in many cases. The responsibility of the state is not a mechanical thing; a humanitarian outlook is very much needed for it. The new managerial perceptions have been fixed by the states of South Asia as per their capabilities.

The responsibility of South Asian states in combating coronavirus is extensively different. Based on the entire study and observation, a few recommendations can be done—(1) The capacity of all states in the healthcare system is to be increased, (2) Self-dependency in healthcare, economy, and foods are to be ensured by Afghanistan, Pakistan, and the Maldives, (3) The new managerial perspective is to be developed by each country as per their capacity for handling such type of pandemic situation, (4) The attitude of the government towards a particular religious community in Pakistan is very discriminatory. The humanitarian and impartial governmental policies are to be implemented in Pakistan, and (5) The role of corporate houses should be more responsible. The state governments will compel the big corporate houses to perform cooperate social responsibility.

References

Adhikari, S. (2013). "Health, Nutrition and Care for Senior Citizens of Nepal in Twenty First Century." *JHAS. 3*(1) 73-75.

Ahmed, J., and Shaikh, B.T. (2008). "An All Time Low Budget for Healthcare in Pakistan". *Journal of the College of Physicians and Surgeons in Pakistan. 18*(6), 389-390.

Bandayopadhyaya, J. (2002). *World Government: For International Democracy and Justice.* Howrah: Manuscript India, 131-132.

Bhandari, A., and Jindal, C. (2018, February 7). The Maldives: Investments Undermine Democracy. Indian Council on Global Relations.https://www.gatewayhouse.in/chinese-investments-in-the-maldives/

Bussa, L. (2017). *India-Maldives Relations.* Avni Publications, 62.

Dhar, V. (2020, May 24). COVID-19 effect: Time for Made-in-India tag to go global. *Financial Express.*

Chatterjee, A. (2017). "Rethinking Human Security from a Theoretical Perspective." In Madhuparna, G. (Ed.) *Non-Traditional Security: Problems and Prospects,* pp. 25-26, Avenel Press.

Gul, I. (2009). *The Al Qaeda Connection: The Taliban and Terror in Pakistan's Tribal Areas,* pp.120-125, Penguin Books.

Goldfinch, S., and Joe, W. (2010). "Two Myths of Convergence in Public Management Reform." *Public Administration, 88*(4), 1099-115.Doi.org/10.1111/j.1467-9299.2010.01848.x.

Idowu, S.O., Vertigans, S., Burlea, S.A. (2017). *Corporate Social Responsibility in Times of Crisis,* pp.1-2, Springer International.

Linnell, M. (2014). "Citizens' Response in Crisis: Individual and Collective Efforts to Enhance Community Resilience." *An Interdisciplinary Journal on Humans ICT Environment, 10*(2), 68-94. doi: 10.17011/ht/urn.201411203311.

Ministry of Health, Republic of Maldives. (2018). *Health Emergency Operations Plan* (*HEOP*). http://origin.searo.who.int/maldives/documents/health-emergency-operations-plan-maldives-2018.pdf.

Mirza, J.A. (2020). "COVID-19 Fans Religious Discrimination in Pakistan." *Diplomat.* April 28.

Mondal, K. and Mou M.D. (2020). *Socio-economic and Political Impact of Coronavirus in India: Challenges and Prospects,* pp. 15-20. Independently Published.

Mooney, J., Timo, H., and Dominelli, L. (2020). "COVID-19: A New Challenge for Social Work." In Lena D. Timo *et al.* (eds.), *COVID-19 and Social Work: A Collection of Country Reports,* pp. 34-35. COVID-19 Social Work Research Forum.

Nandy, D. (2019). "Democracy, Civil Society and Human Security in a War-torn State: A Case Study of Afghanistan." In P. Pal (ed.) *India in South Asia: Challenges and Opportunities*, pp. 50-67. Kunal Books.

Paul, T.V. (2014). *The Warrior State: Pakistan in the Contemporary World*, pp. 84-85, Random House Publishers India Private Limited.

Rodríguez, H., Trainor, J., and Quarantelli, E.L. (2006). "Rising to the challenges of a catastrophe: The emergent and prosocial behaviour following Hurricane Katrina." *The Annals of the American Academy of Political and Social Science*, 604, 82-101.

Sarkar, S. (2012). *In Search of a New Afghanistan*. Niyogi Books.

Shah, J.K.S., Ali A., Tareq, M., Hamid, M., Sayed, U., Zahid, S., and Tien H.N. (2020). "COVID-19: The Current Situation in Afghanistan." *The Lancet Global Health*, *8*(6), 20, 30124-8. doi: 10.106/S2214-109.

Sultana, G. (2020, April 20). Maldivian Response to COVID-19. Manohar Parrikar Institute for Defence Studies and Analysis, New Delhi. *The Economic Times* (2020), April 23.

Ullah, H. (2014). *Vying for Allah's Vole: Understanding Islamic Parties, Political Violence, and Extremism in Pakistan*. Cambridge University Press.

UNDP (2020, July 22). *Afghanistan COVID-19 Impact: Short Term Disruptions and Policy Consideration.* file:///C:/Users/XYZ/Desktop/UNDP-socio-economic%20impact% 20 assessment - afghanistan-Brief2.pdf

United Nations Office for the Coordination of Humanitarian Affairs Humanitarian Response Plan Afghanistan 2018-2021 (2020), (OCHA). https://reliefweb.int/report/afghanistan/ afghanistan-humanitarian-response-plan-2018-2021-2020-revision-december-2019

https://www.bbc.com/news/world-asia-52631071, accessed on 8th August, 2020.

2

COVID-19 Pandemic and Its Implications on Society, Polity and Economy in Contemporary India

Some Critical Reflections

Sujit Lahiry

Introduction

It is now being widely speculated that the Coronavirus pandemic first originated in the Wuhan city of Hubei province in China towards the end of December 2019. It was later on referred to as the COVID-19 Pandemic by the World Health Organization (WHO), a specialised agency of the United Nations (UN) specialising in health matters. Later on, it spread to all the developed countries as well as developing and underdeveloped countries of Asia and Sub-Saharan Africa. As on January 14, 2021, about 9,22,80,089 people have been infected and 19,77,264 deaths have taken place globally because of the coronavirus pandemic. The most powerful superpower in the contemporary world, the US has witnessed 2,33,94,020 coronavirus cases and more than 3,90,454 deaths have taken place because of coronavirus pandemic in the US. While, the US stands tall as the number one country and India stands at the second position among the states affected by the coronavirus pandemic among all the countries of the world. These statistical figures only reflect the fact that despite the tall claims of both these states ruling elites, they have failed to ensure the health security of its citizens. The coronavirus pandemic has affected all countries and has adversely affected the economies of all countries, be it in North or South. However, some countries, like China, South Korea have dealt with this pandemic in a much better form and their economy has also not got ruined. How has India responded to this coronavirus crisis through its policy announcements made by Prime Minister Modi?

This chapter analyses the COVID-19 pandemic and its ramifications on society, polity and economy in contemporary India. This chapter has accordingly been divided into four sections. The first section deals with the COVID-19 pandemic and the consequent US-China war and blame-mongering against each other. The second section explains and analyzes a critical reflection of the COVID-19 pandemic's ramifications on society and polity in contemporary India. In doing so, I will critically analyse how the Modi government's policies threaten the secular fabric of the nation, threats posed by Modi government's policies to the federal polity and autonomy of the states. How COVID-19 pandemic has adversely affected the economy of our nation has been analysed in the third section. The fourth and concluding section analyses the policy challenges before us and what kind of policies need to be reworked to deal with the COVID-19 pandemic.

COVID-19 Pandemic and Global Politics

Needless to mention here, that the WHO is guilty of first spreading this message that the coronavirus does not spread through air, but at a later time in the month of April 2020, the WHO said that this coronavirus spreads through air. One fact which can be stated here is that this pandemic, now also called as an epidemic reflects the failure of the scientific community to devise an effective medicine and anticipate its causes and consequences. The US President Donald Trump initially totally roughed up the idea of this coronavirus disease and even went on to say further that this disease will just disappear within a few days. However, the reality is quite contrary to what Trump said and the COVID-19 pandemic has affected all countries—be it developed, developing and the under-developed countries. Subsequently, Trump was proved wrong and the US now stands at the top of the worst affected coronavirus cases. Let me go a little back to the developments taking place in India. In India, the first coronavirus case was reported in Kerala on 30th January, 2020. Kerala Chief Minister Pinarayi Vijayan immediately stepped into action and went in for active testing, contact-tracing and simultaneously also advocated the policies of isolation and quarantining. It was primarily because of his laudable efforts, that the coronavirus cases were contained in Kerala. What can be very convincingly argued is that neither Trump, nor Modi took cognizance of this pandemic seriously and this led to aggravation of the coronavirus pandemic. At the same time, nothing concrete came out of the Trump-Modi summit, except the mutual reiteration of each other's friendship and cooperation and promotion of business relations. An additional point which should be mentioned here is that both Trump and Modi belong to the same ideological spectrum, i.e., the Far-Right. It must be mentioned here that the US needs India only for controlling its vast domestic market for export of branded consumer goods and products.

At a similar level, the US and China are in a bitter spate of acrimony over the outbreak of the coronavirus pandemic. While, the US along with 100 other countries have blamed China and accused China of not sharing requisite information about the coronavirus pandemic; China, on the other hand, has denied these allegations and accused the US of playing politics over this issue. China had argued that it did not have any knowledge about this coronavirus disease and had also never refrained from suppressing any information about this global COVID-19 pandemic. And, after 100 out of the 194 countries of the World Health Assembly had expressed their displeasure against China, China has welcomed any international investigation into this issue. On 30th May, 2020, the US has moved out of the World Health Organization, saying that it would stop all funding of the WHO. This step of the US President Donald Trump is nothing unusual, as Trump has earlier also retreated out of several international agreements, like, Iran nuclear deal, climate change agreement, etc. These developments suggest two fundamental trends which are developing in contemporary world politics. The first one is the possibility of a new cold war over trade and hegemony between these two global super powers, i.e., the US and China. Secondly, it also signals the end of US unipolarity and the gradual trend towards a multipolar world. In other words, China has declared that it is not willing to be a subversive ally of the US—with which it does not share any ideological moorings. A perspective commentator has this to say about the Chinese steps taken amid the COVID-19 pandemic.

Unlike during the 2004 tsunami disaster in Asia or the 2014 Ebola outbreak in Africa, the US neither showed signs of leadership nor willingness to fight the pandemic. This has afforded China additional space to demonstrate leadership in resolving shared global challenges through multilateral mechanisms and the provision of public goods.

China has engaged the ASEAN, and other regional groupings such as the Arab League, Central and Eastern European states with "17+1" mechanism, Shanghai Cooperation Organization's (SCO) secretariat, and the ten Pacific Island states, in this endeavour. The Trump administration, on the other hand, froze the funding to the World Health Organization (WHO) at this critical juncture, which would have serious repercussions for countries in Africa and the Asia-Pacific, while China announced additional $30 million grant to the WHO in addition to the $20 million made earlier.

Further, China has been providing coronavirus test kits, masks, gloves, protective gears, and ventilators to over 120 countries, in addition to sharing doctors and healthcare professionals to 13 countries, which may have positive impact on China's image. Moreover, to address the issue of faulty equipments, China has strengthened quality control mechanisms at the factories and initiated customs inspection of every shipment (Gnanagurunathan, 2020).

Regarding a comparison of the Chinese and US economies, the commentator further noted:

> The coronavirus-ravaged global economy is in a pause, and the prospects look bleak. Yet, Chinese factories have already started bellowing post-virus containment. The Chinese economy is expected to grow by 1.2 per cent, while the US economy is likely to contract by 5.9 per cent in 2020.
>
> ...On the other hand, despite a $ 2.3 trillion financial package, domestic infighting over lifting of lockdowns, and inward looking, anti-free trade ideas like 'America First' of the present US administration leaves limited space for speedy recovery and generate fuel for growth. While the Two Sessions meetings, held on May 21-22, announced a stimulus package of $ 506 billion focusing on 'new infrastructure' such as 5G and new energy vehicles (NEV), which will help stabilise and accelerate the Chinese economy in the post-COVID-19 recovery phase compared to the US, and if proven effective, China will have the lever to move the global economy (Gnanagurunathan, 2020).

Thus various studies discussed above eventually prove that China has been successful not only in recovering at least a sizeable part of its economy despite the onslaught of COVID-19 pandemic, but will quite decisively replace the US dominant hegemonic position and emerge as the hub of new super power. What can be convincingly argued is that most of the world powers were busy engaged in trivial politics circumscribed by their own domestic national interests as well as concerns regarding their global power position in the contemporary world rather than what should have been a concerted effort to curb this COVID-19 global pandemic. As Emma R. Norman (2020) has argued that:

The tough lessons learned from the exercise smarted considerably and exposed large crisis response weaknesses in several areas. Frustrations were encountered surrounding the simulated international climate and lack of cooperation, diplomatic divisions, cross-national political tensions and instabilities, national security issues and agendas, national economic considerations, national healthcare capacity, the projected speed of vaccine development, who would pay for vaccine development and how vaccines would be distributed once acquired, unequal international access to vaccine sharing, and many others.

COVID-19 Pandemic and Its Ramifications on Society and Polity in India

Let us now look at the political ramifications of COVID-19 Pandemic in India. On March 28, 2020, P.M. Modi announced the formation of 'Prime Minister's Citizen Assistance and Relief in Emergency Situations Fund' (PM Cares Fund) to deal with any kind of emergency situations, like the present global coronavirus pandemic. In this public charitable trust, the Prime Minister is the Chairman of the Trust and it comprises of three other members—the Defence Minister, the Home Minister and the Finance Minister. However, there is neither any member from the Opposition parties, nor any independent academics and experts. Under the garbs of PM-Cares Fund, all donations made under it have been directly controlled by the Modi government. Renowned historian Ramachandra Guha has tweeted, "why a new fund when a Prime Minister's National Relief Fund already exists? And why the self-aggrandizing name, PM-CARES? Must a colossal national tragedy also be (mis)used to enhance the cult of personality?" (Guha, 2020). CPI (M) general secretary Sitaram Yechury has opined that instead of PM-CARES, it would be more appropriate to use the term, INDIA-CARES (Yechury, 2020).

At a similar level, what has happened is the overgrowing dependence of the states on the Centre for all assistance to contain the coronavirus pandemic. Moreover, the Centre has not yet released the assistance to be provided to the states on the GST (Goods and Services Tax) dues. In other words, the states have become begging bowls before the Centre for their own money (Guha, 2020a). Leave alone cooperative federalism, even the principles of bargaining federalism is not working between the Centre and the States under the Modi era. And, the situation is pretty dismal in the case of non-BJP ruled states, like West Bengal, Punjab, Rajasthan and Kerala. As a result, the states are going through a very bad phase. This fact becomes aptly clear from Punjab Finance Minister, Manpreet Badal's statement elaborated below:

> that of the Rs. 88,000 crore revenue receipts estimated by the state during the financial year 2020-21, only Rs. 66,000 crore would now be generated in the light of the curfew/lockdown, losing revenue of Rs. 22,000 crore. With GST collections to be much lower during the year and the Centre yet to clear a significant amount of the state's pending GST arrears, things would continue to worsen in the coming months (*HT*, 2020, April 17, p. 1).

The Central Government has released the GST arrears of December 2019, January 2019, January and February 2020 (*HT*, 2020, June 06, p. 11), but has still not released the GST arrears to Punjab for the month of May, June, July and August 2020 till now, thereby creating a huge revenue deficit for Punjab. And, recently, the Central Government has expressed its inability to pay GST arrears to the states. Further, it can be argued that why all money and donations should be made only in Prime Minister's National Relief Fund and PM-CARES Fund? The donations can also be given to Chief Minister's Relief Fund, since the Chief Ministers of the respective states are at the forefront of the battle against COVID-19 pandemic. A cursory look at the work done by the Chief Ministers of Punjab, Kerala, Rajasthan and West Bengal in controlling the coronavirus pandemic will testify my argument.

Punjab under the visionary leadership of Chief Minister Captain Amarinder Singh was the first state to impose lockdown and curfew, even much before it was announced by Modi. Kerala is probably the first state which went in for very aggressive and random testing of the citizens for coronavirus. Moreover, the Chief Ministers of all the states, especially Punjab along with other states, like Kerala, Rajasthan, West Bengal and Chattisgarh have initiated several social welfare measures for the benefit of the poor and needy sections of society as well as the lakhs of migrant workers stranded in their respective states.

At a similar level, the Modi government is functioning in a highly authoritarian and autocratic manner, whereby the question of federalism and political autonomy of the states are being thrown into oblivion. If we look at the lockdown strategy initiated by the Indian state, one can easily infer that in the first three lockdowns, Modi worked in a highly authoritarian manner, and made all decisions himself, leaving little room for the states to manoeuver their own strategies. On March 24, 2020, at 8 p.m., Modi announced three week curfew from March 25, 2020 midnight, just giving four hour notice to all the Indians. At the same time, all trains, buses, flights—both domestic and international, were snapped, leaving many Indians stranded away from their home state. Along with all these, all business, economic activities, educational institutions as well as the private factories and industries were shut down. Naturally, the poor and deprived sections of society, like, migrant workers, rickshaw-pullers, domestic help, slum dwellers, and the daily wagers—all of them were deprived of their livelihood and were left to fend for themselves. Neither the Modi government, nor the corporate sector which he patronizes did anything for these marginalized sections of society. Added to all these, even the small scale industries, MSMEs, petty shopkeepers all were shut down and they also fired their employees. This automatically led to huge loss of jobs and livelihood for all these categories of people working in the unorganized sector.

All Indians were advised to stay home, stay safe and practice social distancing. The alternative suggested was to 'work from home'. Naturally, this works wonderfully well for top level officers, who had access to all resources, internet, information technology, etc. But, what about the labourers, migrant workers, daily wagers, who live hand-to-mouth and were left to live a miserable and despicable existence. Now if we take up the question of social distancing, these unorganized workers are living in one-room cramped houses, slums, where they cannot have any access to social distancing. On the other hand, the Modi government and his MPs and MLAs advocated ill-conceived, irrational, unscientific and superstitious beliefs like, 'thali bajao', 'diya jalao', 'gaumutra and gobar lagao' (use cow urine and cow-dung), 'go-corona-go' and the 'concomitant puja-path', to contain the coronavirus disease.

In the meantime, the Modi government in India had put a ban on the export of hydroxychloroquine, a key drug to cure the coronavirus pandemic on March 25, 2020. Subsequently, the Trump administration talked of retaliation against India on April 5, 2020, if India does not agree to lift the ban on export of hydroxychloroquine to the US. And following the US snub and retaliation, the Modi government lifted the ban and allowed the export of hydroxychloroquine to the US on April 6, 2020. This was followed by India allowing the export of hydroxychloroquine to Brazil also. This essentially reflects the poor statesmanship of the Modi government, which has surrendered before the US capitalist and imperialist structure. Further, it can be argued that India does not manufacture this drug hydroxychloroquine indigenously and is dependent for the active pharmaceutical ingredients on primarily China (Jayakumar, 2020).

In the subsequent two lockdowns, some easing of restrictions had been made and Modi formally had a meeting with the chief ministers of all the states. But, here also, it was actually an eyewash as Modi allowed only the BJP-led Chief Ministers of their respective states to put their perspectives on the COVID-19 Pandemic and others, i.e., the non-BJP Chief Ministers sat there as mere spectators. It was only in the fourth lockdown, that some selected

Chief Ministers of non-BJP ruled states were also allowed to speak. Now, Modi is trying to decentralize his powers and leaving it to the states to decide on their own and their future course of action to deal with the COVID-19 pandemic. However, this had been done with an ulterior motive, as the Modi government has failed to fully ensure the lives and livelihood of its citizens.

Impact of COVID-19 Pandemic on the Indian Economy

What can be the possible implications of the COVID-19 Pandemic on the Indian economy? A major US think tank, *Congressional Research Center* in its Report analyzing the impact of COVID-19 on Indian economy has argued, "Foreign investors have pulled an estimated USD 26 billion out of developing Asian economies and more than USD 16 billion out of India, increasing concerns of a major economic recession in Asia" (*Outlook,* 2020). Even the Moody's Investor Services has downgraded India's sovereign credit rating to Baa3 from Baa2, the lowest investment grade and predicted slower growth and consistent stress in India's economy, amid COVID-19 Pandemic (*HT*, 2020, June 2, p. 11). Now, the question arises that why there is slower growth and what are the reasons behind it? This question has been beautifully analyzed by Arun Kumar, a renowned economist in the following manner:

> Generally, world over, production is carried out in large- and small-scale industrial units. In India, there is also the medium and cottage industry, or the unorganised sector. The large and medium industrial sectors by definition have a lot of capital and machines while the rest have minimal resources. A working capital is needed to buy raw materials and inputs, and to pay workers their salaries. At the start of a business, to buy machinery and to construct factory buildings, among others, loans are taken from banks. The smaller units get loans from private lenders, or have to invest their own savings. In a nutshell, businesses work with a lot of debt on which they pay interest.

> An interest is paid out of revenue generated from sales. So, if sales stop, repayment of loan or payment of interest becomes difficult, and businesses begin to fail. Such loans from the banks turn into non-performing assets (NPAs). However, if production continues when sales have stopped, more inputs are needed and more unsold products accumulate, so more working capital is required and more interest has to be paid. As a result, losses increase, and companies stop production in a lockdown (Kumar, 2020).

Another issue which has caught attention of academics and policy-makers is the economic impact of COVID-19 on the poor and deprived sections of society. The poor and marginalised sections of society, like the slum-dwellers, migrant labourers, beggars, rickshaw pullers, daily wage earners, are at the receiving end of the coronavirus pandemic. What we are witnessing in India is the mass exodus of migrant labourers and daily wage earners from metropolitan cities to their respective native villages in the absence of any regular sources of income and livelihood. The poor, and especially the workers in the unorganised sector are the worst hit. Two issues are of central concern in the issue of migration—displacement and rehabilitation of the poor and marginalized sections of the society. In India, only 7 per cent of the workforce is working in the organized sector, whereas 93 per cent of the workforce is working in the unorganised sector. The two-month long lockdown has completely ruined the back of the small and big industries, and has thrown lakhs of workers unemployed. According to a study of the Centre for Monitoring Indian Economy (CMIE), released before the Lok Sabha elections in April-May 2019, unemployment rate in India was at an all-time 45 year high of 6.1 per cent. What is alarming is that in the latest figures released by CMIE as of January 13, 2021, unemployment rate in India stood at 8.3 per cent. While, urban unemployment stood at 8.3 per cent, rural unemployment stood at 8.4 per cent. In a similar study by International Labour Organisation (ILO), it is estimated that about 400 million Indians will lose their jobs in the unorganised and informal sector, and will sink deep into poverty (*The Economic Times*, 2020, April 8; and *Hindustan Times*, Chandigarh, April 9, 2020: 11). These figures only show the poor state of the Indian economy in the current conjecture under the Modi government. Definitely, this should sound alarm bells for the Modi government, which is completely apathetic to the poor, marginalized and deprived sections of the society.

However, notwithstanding the Central Government's response to COVID-19, the Punjab government has taken some laudable steps to stem off this crisis in recent times. The Punjab government by providing free ration to the poor and underprivileged sections of society and free food to the migrant workers and labourers and is trying its best to ameliorate their conditions of hunger and deprivation. Further, Captain Amarinder Singh, the Punjab Chief Minister, has also given 10 kg wheat, 2 kg *dal* (lentils) and 2 kg sugar to 15 lakh poor people, who are not covered under the PDS (Public Distribution Scheme) in Punjab.

The various developed countries, like US, China, Italy, Spain, France, Germany, are spending 10 to 15 per cent of their GDP, to fight the COVID-19 pandemic. While, the US has committed $2 trillion stimulus package, China has invested $ 170+ billion package, United Kingdom has committed 330 billion pound package, Germany has committed $610 billion, France has invested $335 billion loans, Spain has committed $220 billion plan, Australia has committed $ 83 billion stimulus, Italy has committed $28 billion rescue plan, Malaysia has invested $6.6 billion, UAE has invested $27.2 billion, Thailand has committed $17.6 billion, South Korea has invested $9.8 billion and Saudi Arabia has invested $13.3 billion (*Hindustan Times*, March 27, 2020, p. 7). Even a small and tiny country in South Asia, Bangladesh has committed to invest $ 8 billion to fight the coronavirus pandemic (*The Statesman*, April 5, 2020).

The complete apathy of the Modi government towards the plight of all the above mentioned types of workers can be seen in the fact that most of these migrant workers are trying to return to their native villages on foot, by cycle, without any food, water, and means of transportation. Needless to mention here that most of these workers are also often being beaten up by the police machinery and the situation is pretty dismal in the states of Uttar Pradesh and Bihar. At a similar level, while the Modi government has written off the loans of the big corporates, it turns a blind eye to the pathetic situation of the farmers all over India, many of whom are now committing suicides or are being forced to live in penury. The farmers all over India, because of lockdown and curfew were compelled to dump their produce in the absence of any means of transportation. Thereby the farmers could not sell their produce and are compelled to live in sub-standard existence. Thereby, it had further aggravating the agrarian crisis in contemporary India.

In May 2020, the Modi government has announced a COVID-19 package of Rs. 20 lakh crore, which he claimed constitutes 10 per cent of GDP. But a careful and critical study of this package reveals that the actual package is only of Rs. 4 lakh crore, which is only merely 2 per cent of India's GDP (Singhvi, 2020: 10). As this commentator further elaborates, "The efficacy of collateral-free loans of up to Rs. 3 lakh crore or government guarantees is questionable when it comes to those units which are reeling under debt. They will remain liabilities in the books, liable to be repaid, and can, thus, hardly be termed as part of the fiscal stimulus" (Singhvi, 2020:10). The argument is simple: the lack of consumption and demand in the economy is the basic problem. If people don't have money in their hands, what is the utility of production? Therefore, there is an urgent need to revive demand and give money to the poor and underprivileged sections, so that consumption can be revived and together, all these steps will give a boost to the economy.

Except for Rs. 40,000 crore for NREGA, no provision has been made anything in the Covid Relief Package announced by Prime Minister Modi. Even with regard to NREGA, there is no clear policy pronouncement about how this will be distributed among all the states. It is a common knowledge that the ruling party—i.e., BJP in India will give much more funds for NREGA to the BJP-ruled states, rather than the opposition ruled states, and especially the Congress party-led states. Whatever policy pronouncements and allocations have been made in Modi's Covid Relief Package is in the form of giving loans to MSME and small scale factories, shops and businesses loans at cheaper rates of interest. But, a fundamental question which arises here is that if there is no demand, what will these small scale industries and MSMEs do with loans? The Prime Minister Modi talks of 'Atmanirbhar Bharat Abhiyan' (Self-Reliant India Mission), and even in the last six years had talked about 'Make in India'. However, there is no concomitant policy pronouncement on how to be a 'self-reliant India'. Further, just contrast this with what his other policy pronouncements, like 'Digital India' and 'Start-Up India'. In contemporary times, all these enterprises have collapsed because of lockdown and curfew. Further, we all know that 'Digital India' and 'Online Education' caters to only 10 per cent of the population of 130 crore in India. The remaining 90 per cent of the population are left far behind and are left to fend for themselves. The Modi government caters to the interests of the handful of big corporates, who are funding indirectly the BJP's election campaign and party activities in the various states of India.

And all these had aggravated the problem of poverty and hunger in India. In the *Global Hunger Index 2019* Report, published by *Concern Worldwide*, it has been revealed that India stands at 102nd spot, way below Pakistan (94) and Bangladesh (88), out of 117 countries. *Global Hunger Index* (GHI) is based on indicators, like, "undernourishment, child stunting, child wasting and child mortality to calculate the levels of hunger and undernutrition", and India's score of 30.3 reflects the fact that India's level of hunger is of serious concern. Look, this was the data in the third quarter of 2019, and recent data will reveal even more acute cases of poverty, hunger and malnutrition in the times of COVID-19 era.

Added to all these developments, the BJP governments in the various states of Uttar Pradesh, Madhya Pradesh, Gujarat and

Karnataka have abolished the labour laws in their respective states. These BJP governments have increased the working hours of the workers from eight hours to 12 hours, and also pronounced at the same time that the workers would not be paid overtime dues for their four extra hours of work. This tantamount to depriving the workers of their due rights, and constitutes a violation of their human rights. These violations have been pointed out by ILO (International Labour Organization), various human rights bodies, like PUCL, PUDR; as well as the Geneva Convention of Human Rights and Universal Declaration of Human Rights (UDHR). Further, it may be noted that these labour laws have been achieved in independent India after a long and arduous struggle for emancipatory politics.

On May 1, 2020, the Modi government after relentless and strong protests by the opposition parties, and especially the Congress Party as well as visuals showing the despicable plight of the migrant workers on print and electronic media, who have started walking back hundreds and thousands of kilometres on foot, started Shramik Special trains to transport the migrants back to their home state. But, no sooner it started, the politics of 'who will pay for the tickets' of these migrant workers started. The Modi government said that the Railways will pay for 85 per cent of the fare and the States will bear rest of the fare. But, the question is from where will the state governments mobilise resources, when because of lockdown and curfew, their economy is in tatters and the Central Government has not released even their legitimate due, what to talk about additional funds for the pandemic (something which I have elaborated earlier). The President of the Congress Party, Mrs. Sonia Gandhi was magnanimous in her approach, when she said that the Congress Party will bear the expenses of migrants travel to their native places back home. But, the Congress Party faced tremendous opposition from some BJP-ruled state governments in this regard. After many activists and lawyers made a petition before the Supreme Court regarding the pathetic condition of migrant workers, the Supreme Court took *suo motu* (on its own) cognizance of the problem and held that on 28th May, 2020 that the migrant workers should not be asked to pay for their travel and they should be provided food, water and all other facilities. And, in the latest direction, the Supreme Court has also asked the Central and state governments to provide transport, welfare programmes, including job opportunities for the migrant workers and report back to the Court within a fortnight (*Hindustan Times*, June 10, 2020: 1).

The Modi government seems to be totally biased towards pro-capitalist and pro-bourgeoisie class and has provided several incentives to them, like Ambani's, Adani's, Goenka's, etc. I will prove my argument with some of the recent developments taking place in India. After easing of some restrictions during lockdown 4.0, the Modi government has provided special treatment to the super-rich and privileged upper-middle class. The Modi government is bringing in Indians stranded in different parts of the world and had also decided to put them in five star hotels during the quarantine period. Thus, while, the Indian state is providing lavish treatment to these super neo-rich crony capitalist class, on the other hand, it is totally obliterating the worker's rights. Even during the lockdown period, the Modi government has brought in Indians staying in different cities of the world and they were brought back in even without proper testing and social distancing norms as specified by the WHO (World Health Organization) and ICMR (Indian Council of Medical Research).

Conclusion

This last and concluding section sets out some of the policy prescriptions for the Modi government to emulate in order to save both the lives and livelihood of the countrymen—the most sacred and important duty of the ruling government in contemporary India. First and foremost, the Modi government should provide direct cash benefit to the poor and underprivileged sections of the society. In other words, there should be a Universal Basic Income. Secondly, the Modi government needs to provide ration to all the informal workers—whether they have a ration card or not. The

Modi government should provide ration of five kg rice/wheat and minimum two kg pulses per person to all the members of the family for a minimum of the next six months. Thirdly, the Modi government needs to provide unemployment allowance to all the 93 per cent workers in the unorganised sector, who have lost their jobs and livelihood because of the COVID-19 pandemic. Fourthly, the Modi government should increase the allocation of Rs. 40,000 crore to NREGA from the fetters of limitation, as the Congress Party has advocated, and then distribute this amount to all the states, so that the migrant population who have returned back home are able to get some means of jobs, which can ensure their survival. The migrant populations are not beggars, and they have a right to live a decent life with dignity. Fifthly, apart from NREGA, other alternative sources of jobs and livelihood need to be identified by the Modi government, so that poverty and destitution can be averted.

Sixthly, the farmers need to deserve a better deal. While, the Modi government has written off the loans amounting to thousands of crores of rupees of many big corporates; the government needs to write off the loans of much smaller amount of the farming community. Further, agriculture is a state subject (*HT*, 2020, June 6, p. 2) and the Centre should not impose its own hegemonic policies for the agrarian economy on the respective states in India. For example, the Modi government should immediately withdraw 'The Farming Produce Trade and Commerce (Promotion and Facilitation) Ordinance, 2020', so that farmers can continue to receive Minimum Support Price (MSP) of their agricultural production. It will lead to greater corporatisation of India's agricultural sector. What will happen is that the foreign multinational companies as well as big Indian companies engaged in agri-business will compel the farmers, and especially small farmers to sell their produce at cheaper rates and these corporate agricultural entities will create a cartel of their own, whereby they will create a monopoly of their own and control the agricultural production in India. It will lead to greater commodification of the agrarian economy in India. The smaller and marginal farmers will gradually be wiped out of this agrarian market created by the Modi government and they will be compelled to live a below subsistence life, and gradually move into abject poverty and hunger. Therefore, all concerted action should be made to start a movement against the anti-farmer policies of the Modi government.

Lastly, the Modi government should put greater emphasis on the healthcare sector. The COVID-19 pandemic has exposed the hollowness of our poor public healthcare system in India. The situation is pretty dismal in the rural countryside, with very poor infrastructural facilities to deal with the health security amid the COVID-19 pandemic. Let me remind all of us of the fact that the healthcare industry was thrown open to the private corporate sector in 2001, during Prime Minister Atal Bihari Vajpayee's tenure, thereby bringing in private multinational hospitals, like Apollo, Max, Fortis, etc. The Indian state should try to build up the healthcare infrastructure and increase the healthcare spending as percentage of its GDP in India. Further, the Modi government should now ensure that the COVID-19 vaccine should be given free of cost to the poor and underprivileged sections of society in India.

Therefore, the Modi government should try to have a dialogue and interaction with all the chief ministers of states, academia, civil rights activists, policy analysts and then try to formulate an appropriate policy for the vast majority of the Indians. To conclude, one can say that the COVID-19 pandemic is here to stay for a long time. What I emphasize is that we need to make a balance between health security and economic security—jobs and livelihood in such a manner, that both maintain a precarious and healthy balance.

References

"Centre's agri marketing reforms attack on federal structure: Capt" (2020). *Hindustan Times,* Chandigarh, June 6: 2.

"CMIE—Unemployment Rate in India" (2021). January 13. [https://unemploymentinindia. cmie.com, accessed 13 January, 2021].

"Delhi Violence—Explainer: What do we know about the communal violence that left 53 dead in Delhi in February 2020?" (2020). *Scroll.in,* May 11.

[https://scroll.in/article/ 955251/explainer-what-do-we-know-about-the-communal-violence-that-left-47-dead-in- Delhi-in- february-2020, accessed 11 May, 2020].

"Foreign Investors Pull Out $ 16 Billion from Indian Economy Amid COVID-19: Report" (2020). *Outlook*, May 20.[https://www.outlookindia.com/website/story/business-news-foreign-investors-pull-out-16-billion-from-indian-economy-amid-COVID-19-report/353143, accessed 31 May, 2020].

"Global Stimulus Plans: How India Should Think Big" (2020). *Hindustan Times,* Chandigarh/Punjab, March 27: 7.

Guha, Ramachandra (2020). "Guha's T.V. Interview—On Record with Ramchandra Guha—Corona Se Jyada Mushkil Communal Virus Ko Harana", aired on *Swaraj Express*, April 14. [https://tr-cam.com'QysglQaFebE,accessed 14 April, 2020].

Guha, Ramachandra (2020). "PM-Cares fundraising initiative self-aggrandising", *Deccan Herald*, March 31. [https://www.deccanherald.com/national/pm-cares-fundraising-initiative-self-aggrandising-ramachandra-guha-819628.html, accessed 20 April, 2020].

Gnanagurunathan, A.D. (2020). "Breaking Down the China-US Tussle for Global Order Amid COVID-19",*The Wire*, May 31. [https://thewire.in/diplomacy/breaking-down-the-china-us-tussle-for-global-order-amid-COVID-19, accessed 31 May 2020].

Hindustan Times, Chandigarh (2020). June 10: 1.

Hindustan Times, Chandigarh (2020). June 6: 11.

Hindustan Times, Chandigarh/Punjab (2020). April 17: 1.

"India—Global Hunger Index 2019" (2019). [https://www.globalhungerindex.org, accessed 9 April, 2020].

Jayakumar, P.B. (2020). "Coronavirus: Trump calls Modi for hydroxychloroquine, but Indian makers at China's mercy", *Business Today*, April 7. [https://www.businesstoday.in/latest/trends/coronavirus-trump-calls-modi-for-hydroxychloroquine-but-Indian-makers-at-chinas-mercy/story/400208.html?utn, accessed 29 May, 2020].

Krishnan, Murali (2020). "Migrants can't be made to pay for travel: Apex court", *Hindustan Times,* Chandigarh, May 29: 1.

Kumar, Arun (2020). "COVID-19 Crisis: Understanding the State of Economy during and after the Lockdown", *Economic and Political Weekly*, 55(19), May 9. [https://www.epw.in/engage/article/COVID-19-crisis-understanding-state-economy-during-and-after-lockdown, accessed 10 May, 2020].

"Moody's cuts India rating by one notch" (2020). *Hindustan Times,* Chandigarh, June 2: 11.

Norman, Emma R. (2020). "Note From the Editor: Clade X, Coronavirus, and the Challenges of Global Health Security", *World Affairs,*-Sage Publications, *183*(2) June: 2020: 100-104. [https://journals.sagepub.com/doi/full/10.1177/0043820020922011, accessed 2 June, 2020].

Singhvi, Avishkar (2020). "The government slipped in not focusing on demand", *Hindustan Times,* Chandigarh/Punjab, May 20: 10.

The Economic Times (2020), April 08.[https://economictimes.indiatimes.com/news/economy/indicators/about-400-million-workers-in-India-may-sink-into-poverty-un-report/articlesshow/75041922.cms, accessed 8 April, 2020].

The Statesman (2020), April 5.

"Three Years of Peace and Development, Government of Punjab" (2020), *Hindustan Times,* Chandigarh/Punjab, March 16: 8-9.

Yechury, Sitaram (2020). "GS Writes to President with Suggestions on COVID-19", April 7.[www.cpim.org, accessed 10 April, 2020].

3
Aftermath of COVID-19
An Opportunity to the Indian Economy

Raj Kishor Pradhan and *Rahul Kumar*

Introduction

Indian economy is going through a challenging time. The dream period from 1991 to 2013 is now over. In between it has faced a lot of challenges like Global financial market crisis in 2008 and persistent slow down from 2017, which is aided by present COVID-19 pandemic. Indian economy is not a young economy, rather it is a matured economy. For last 75 years it has weathered a lot of up and down. Still its fundamental has been strong. Not long ago, the India's economic growth has termed as the "Hindu Rate of Growth" due to its steady undergrowth. But the watershed moment of the economy growth saga has been begun from 1991. That period was no hope for the economy as a whole still it has adopted path breaking LPG era or Liberalisation, Privatisation and Globalisation. Under the able leadership of the than PM, Mr. P.V. Narsimha Rao and the chief architect was Dr. Man Mohan Singh. After that India has scripted a dream growth story till two and half decades. In between them India has witnessed a lot of political turmoil and numerous prime ministers under different political parties and political alliances. Still the fundamental economy growth or the skeletal of the growth foundation has been intact. Notable leaders and architects besides P.V.N. Rao and Dr. M.M. Singh were P. Chidambaram. A.B. Vajpayee, Y. Sinha and Pranab Mukherjee etc. In the last three decades, India has able to move from abject poverty to the middle-income group. Still, it has a lot to do to feed the billion plus population and to provide the gainful employment and steady income it has to reform the economy more and more. But the unexpected global challenges like Sub-prime crisis of 2008 and COVID-19 pandemic in 2020, it has tested the resilience of our fundamentals of the economy.

Background

But in present the scale of pandemic is unprecedent in Global economy. The world has witnessed several epidemics such as the Spanish Flu of 1918, outbreak of HIV/AIDS, SARS (Severe Acute Respiratory Syndrome), MERS (Middle East Respiratory Syndrome) and Ebola. In the past, India has had to deal with diseases such as the smallpox, plague and polio. All of these individually have been pretty severe episodes. However, the COVID-19 which originated in China in December 2019 and over the next few months rapidly spread to almost all countries of the world can potentially turn out to be the biggest health crisis in our history. Many experts have already called this a Black Swan event for the global economy.

To check the severity of unknown but highly contagious disease, Government of India has taken unprecedent step by declaring total lockdown of the economy for 21 days and more. Although it could not fully prevent the pandemic to spread, but its severity has been curtailed. Initial four and five months, the COVID-19 has created havoc in the country. The unprecedented lockdown has had a significant adverse effect on the economy. Millions of jobs and livelihoods are now at stake. As activity around the country came to a halt, with no job or income, more than 50 million migrant workers either returned to their native villages or shifted to camps inside the cities because state borders were sealed. While there are reports of some of them returning back to the cities now in search of jobs and livelihoods majority have not yet come back thereby imposing a massive strain on labour supply in the urban areas. Transportation of raw materials and finished goods across states was also severely constrained. Countries have closed national borders bringing international trade and commerce to an abrupt halt. All these are severely disrupting supply mechanisms and distribution chains in almost all sectors. At the same time, there has been a complete collapse of consumption demand as millions of people stayed at home and postponed their non-essential expenditures.

But gradually due to the mass awareness and government's proactive action, the effect of pandemic has been controlled. Now the economy has been gradually opening up. But the main victim was the economy. The first quarter after the lockdown has witnessed about record negative growth.

Before drawing any conclusion about the pandemic effected economy, we have to understand the full impact of pandemic on the economy and its recovery. We have already known the background on which the unprecedent lockdown has been declared. Before that the economy has already been in downwards trend for the 36 consecutive quarters which is a record itself. Even the United Nation has predicted the downward trend of the economy. While the COVID-19 pandemic is constantly growing and showing little signs of containment as of 15 April, 2020, its adverse impact on economic growth of the country will probably be very serious. The UN warned that the coronavirus pandemic is expected to have a significant adverse impact on global economy, and most significantly, GDP growth of India for the present economy is projected to decline to 4.8 per cent (United Nations, 2020). Similarly, the UN 'Economic and Social Survey of Asia and the Pacific (ESCAP)' 2020 reported that COVID-19 would have extensive socio-economic consequences in the region with inundate activities across borders in the areas of tourism, trade and financial linkages (United Nations, 2020).

If we analyse the gain and loss of post-pandemic on the economy as a whole, it will be a gigantic exercise. Till date it is not declared or published anywhere about the **exact loss** of the economy. But one thing is cleared that lockdown has ravaged the economy in terms of both GDP growth rate as well as falling employment rate. It has both socio-economic as well financial pitfalls. As per official data released by the Ministry of Statistics and Programme Implementation, the Indian economy contracted by 23.9 per cent in the April-June quarter of this fiscal year. This is the worst decline ever recorded since India started compiling GDP statistics on a quarterly basis in 1996. For the Indian economy, private consumption and investment are the two biggest engines for growth. During the first quarter of 2020, private consumption—accounting for 59 per cent of India GDP—declined by 27 per cent, while investments by private businesses fell by 47 per cent. India's net exports turned positive due to sharp compression in imports. During the quarter, government spending increased by 16 per cent, but it was not adequate to compensate for the decline suffered by other engines of growth. Except for agriculture, all the major sectors of the economy were badly hit. Significantly, labour-intensive sectors such as construction, real estate, retail trade, transport and manufacturing contracted sharply during this quarter.

Recent Government Initiative: *Atmanirbhar Bharat*

Government of India has initiated self-reliant or *Atmanirbhar Bharat* to ease the import burden from the China and other countries. It is very difficult to achieve the import substitution, but not improbable. We can learn the valuable lesson from the success stories of Bangladesh and Vietnam. Now Bangladesh is the no. 1 exporter of readymade garments replacing India. Vietnam is also becoming the manufacturing hub of electronic equipment. In May 12, 2020, Prime Minister Narendra Modi announced in his address to the nation an economic package of Rs. 20 trillion to tide over the coronavirus crisis under the *Atmanirbhar Bharat Abhiyan*. He said the economic package would play an important role in making India 'self-reliant' and that it would benefit labourers, farmers, honest tax payers, MSMEs and the cottage industry. He said making the country self-reliant was the only way to make 21st century belong to India. According to the government, it is not protectionist in nature.

India's self-reliance will be based on five pillars:

1. Economy
2. Infrastructure
3. Technology driven system
4. Vibrant demography
5. Demand.

India's economy is largely supported by its large domestic consumption, not by export. So, we don't have to worry about external disturbance like China and other South East Asian nations. These economies are driven by export. Their growth engines are driven by export driven growth. Our economy is so broad and it has huge potential for further growth. Its young working population is its main source of growth capacity. Although we are able to feed our billion plus population. But the real definition of growth lies in full capacity utilisation and achievement of quality of life. India has a lot to do for its infrastructure, i.e. both physical and social infrastructure. Physical infrastructure includes road, railways, port and airport, telecommunication, power etc. and social infrastructure includes health, education etc. Present government has invested a lot in these infrastructure projects. The private sector has also invested a lot in these projects. These projects have a lot of potential to create millions of job opportunities. For example, our public healthcare system has not that capability to tackle the pandemic situation, the help of private healthcare system is also critical to fight the present situation. Therefore, both the public and private sector role is critical to revive the economy. This is important because there are widespread protests against government's recent step of privatisation. For example, the widespread protest against farm Bills and recent reforms are not welcome one. It has been widely accepted and supported by the large section of the people as well as among the experts. The agricultural reform was a long overdue and involvement of private sector is important step. So, it is right time to push for this long overdue of critical reform.

As we are aware that government is going for reform in banking sector, it is very critical for our sound financial system. Likewise, a reform in National Education Policy, Labour Law and increasing investment in healthcare system due to pandemic is also very welcome steps. We cannot revive our economy without reforming these critical infrastructures. Also, the recent spurt in self-reliant economy is also paving the way for revival of our manufacturing sector as a general and small and medium enterprise sectors in particular.

Here the role of technology is important one, particularly the use of information technology (IT). It has a lot potential to create the capacity built up. India is known as the IT super power so we can leverage our potential.

Our diverse demography is our main asset. As in next fifty years, the working young population will dominate our demography, we can use its full potentiality to revive our economy.

Last but not the least as our domestic demand is our main driver of our growth rate, we have to revive the rural demand. This can only be possible by reviving our agricultural sector. So, the reform in farm sector is also welcome one.

These are not day dreams; it is practical and realistic one. The recent revival of the economy as prompted by the different rating agencies as well as the World Bank and also the IMF and our own Economy Survey to estimate huge growth in next fiscal. The steep contraction in the current financial year will be followed by a bounce back to 10 per cent growth in FY22, putting India among the fastest-growing economies in 2021, said Andrew Wood, S&P director of sovereign and international public finance ratings. S&P has pegged India's combined Centre and state fiscal deficit at 14.5 per cent of GDP—which is expected to drop to 11.6 per cent in FY22 and further to below 10 per cent in FY23.

It is also historically proved that an disastrous year prompted healthy growth rate in coming years. We can take lesson from the growth story after disastrous year of 1991.

The growth rate of India has been shown in the following table.

Country: India, Year: 1991-1995, Indicator: GDP growth (annual %), Country Name India

Year	1991	1992	1993	1994	1995
Annual Growth rate	1.06	5.48	4.75	6.66	7.57

Fiscal position

Given the state of the economy and especially the state of the financial institutions, the policy levers available to the government to deal with the economic crisis are limited. When the effects of 2008 Global Financial Crisis (GFC) were felt in India, the domestic economy was in a better shape having experienced a credit boom and a high growth rate for the preceding years and the government was in a position to implement both monetary and fiscal stimulus measures. More importantly, the financial institutions were not so badly damaged. In contrast, the fiscal deficit of the government was already high in the pre-COVID-19 period and had breached the target as specified in the FRBM Act (Fiscal Responsibility and Budget Management Act). The fiscal deficit of the Central Government in 2019-20 was 4.6 per cent of GDP against the target of 3.5 per cent of GDP. This has been the highest fiscal deficit since 2012-13. The Finance Minister in her Budget Speech of February 1, 2020 had pegged the target for FY 2021 to 3.5 per cent (Table 3.1) which will be breached by a wide margin. The FM had already used the escape clause provided under the FRBM Act to allow the relaxation of target for 2019-20. The clause allows the government to relax the fiscal deficit target for up to 50 basis points or 0.5 per cent.

While presenting her Budget for 2021-2022, Finance Minister Nirmala Sitharaman had announced the government's intention to amend the Fiscal Responsibility and Budget Management (FRBM) Act. According to the finance minister, the Union Government's fiscal deficit should see a gradual reduction from 9.5 per cent of gross domestic product or GDP in 2020-2021 to 6.8 per cent in 2021-2022 and further down to 4.5 per cent by 2025-2026.

In its report, the 15th Finance Commission recognises the uncertainty in the economic outlook and revenue path of the Union government for a period of five years after 2021-2022. (Fig. 3.1)

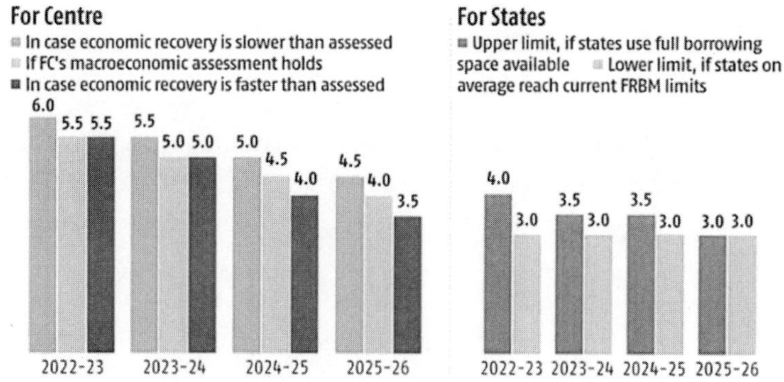

Source: 15th Finance Commission Report.
Note: All Figures in per cent of GDP, FC: Finance Commission.

Fig. 3.1: 15th Finance Commission's Fiscal Consolidation Road Map.

"The range of deficits reflects the uncertainty about the impact of the pandemic on the economy, its implications for the revenues of the Union and the resource requirements for fighting the pandemic and for stimulating the economy", the Commission has observed (please see charts).

Given this background, the finance ministry's decision to accept the deficit target of 4.5 per cent in 2025-2026 appears to have emanated from its endorsement of the Finance Commission's view that the Indian economy will continue to remain impacted by the pandemic, adversely undermining its growth potential.

The immediate objective of the policy responses to the economic impact of COVID-19 is to ameliorate the effect of the shock on economic agents in both the formal and the informal sectors and to help them tide over the crisis. Against the background of a weak economy, the twin shocks of COVID-19 and lockdown are operating at two levels: Creating supply-side disruptions, Triggering reduction in aggregate demand. The need of the hour are policy actions to deal with both supply- and demand-side problems. The supply-side has been reeling under three pre-existing shocks: (i) demonetisation of 2016, (ii) goods and services tax (GST) since 2017, and (iii) slowdown in credit growth.

Recovery of various sectors

Given this background and volatile scenario, it is now proved that economy is gradually opening up. A sharp rebound in construction and manufacturing helped the Indian economy move back into positive territory after two successive quarters of contraction. The Indian economy recorded a marginal 0.4 per cent growth in the October-December quarter, that also coincided with India's festival season, according to data released by the National Statistics Office (NSO). (Fig. 3.2)

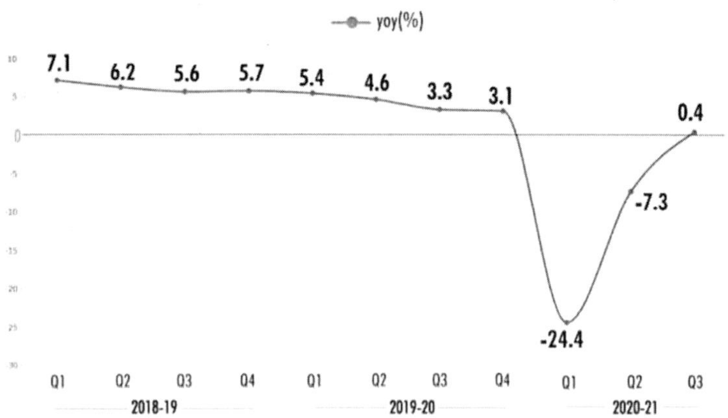

Source: MoSPI.

Fig. 3.2: After 2 successive quarters of contraction, India's GDP bounces back.

India's factory output, which is measured in IIP witnessed a growth of **1 per cent** on-year to 135.9 during the month of December 2020, separate data released by the MoSPI showed.

The IIP had grown 0.4 per cent in December 2019, the data showed.

Besides that the automobile sector has also shown sign of revival.

The table below shows the sales figure of automobiles for the month of December, 2020.

Segment	December Sales		
	2019	2020	%Change
Passenger Vehicles (PVs)	2,22,728	2,52,998	13.59
Three Wheelers	53,795	22,126	-58.87
Two Wheelers	10,50,038	11,27,917	7.42
Quadricycle	33	0	
Total	**13,26,594**	**14,03,041**	**5.76**

Source: Society of Indian Automobile Manufacturers.

SIAM figures showed that the contraction in sales during December was majorly for three-wheelers which saw a decline of 58.87 per cent to 22,126 units.

India's agricultural sector has shown its resilience amid the adversities of COVID-19 induced lockdowns. The Agriculture and Allied activities clocked a growth of 3.4 per cent at constant prices during 2020-21 (first advance estimate) says the Economic Survey.

The Economic Survey observes that as per the Provisional Estimates of National Income released by CSO on 29th May, 2020, the share of Agriculture and Allied Sectors in Gross Value Added (GVA) of the country at current prices is 17.8 per cent for the year 2019-20.

Record Foodgrain Production

According to the Economic Survey in the Agriculture year 2019-20 (as per Fourth Advance Estimates), total foodgrain production in the country is estimated at record 296.65 million tonnes which is higher by 11.44 million tonnes than the production of foodgrain of 285.21 million tonnes achieved during 2018-19.

Evidence from the experience of Spanish flu establishes that cities that intervened with lockdowns earlier and more aggressively experience stronger recovery in economic front in the long run. Learning from this experience, India implemented an early and stringent lockdown from late March to May to curb the pace of spread of COVID-19. With the economy brought to a standstill for two complete months, the inevitable effect was a 23.9 per cent contraction in GDP as compared to previous year's quarter. This contraction was consistent with the stringency of the lockdown.

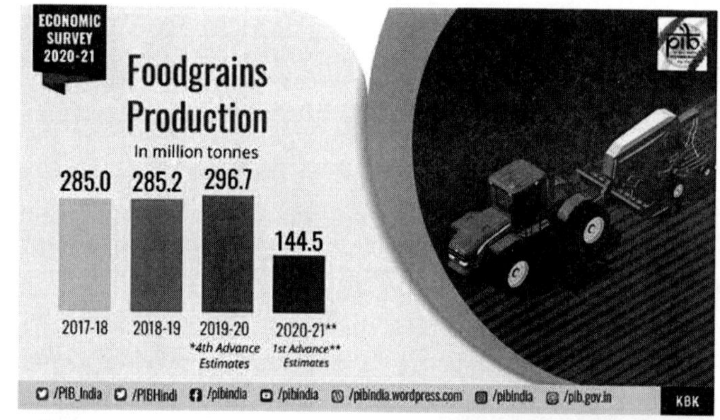

The Indian policymakers also recognized that the 'supply' shock induced by the lockdown would disrupt the productive capacity of the economy. This capacity would need to be strengthened to meet the pent-up demand once it resumes—any mismatch would lead to macro-economic instabilities. This was, in effect, an 'underheating' of the economy with lack of demand, disruption of supply chains and anticipated large scale corporate distress. A simple reflating of the economy through increased government expenditure would, under these circumstances, have led to runaway inflation especially given the inherent supply-side constraints in India's food economy. Therefore, India initiated a slew of multi-sectoral supply-side structural reforms to lend flexibility and resilience to supply chains as a part of the *Atmanirbhar Bharat Mission* (ANB). India is the only country to have undertaken structural reforms on the supply-side at the initial stages of the pandemic. This far-sighted policy response will generate productivity gains in the medium to long term.

The Challenges Ahead

At the time of writing this chapter India has been apparently witnessing the second wave of Pandemic. On 23rd March, 2021, the new cases added was 47,262 and among them more than 60 per cent active cases are coming from industrialised states like Maharashtra, Gujarat, Punjab, Kerala and Madhya Pradesh. So definitely it is a worrying factor. The exponential growth of infection rate or doubling rate has been more than the first wave. But in the first wave neither there was proper treatment for the COVID-19 nor any vaccine was there. After the first anniversary of lockdown, we are becoming wiser in terms of characteristics of virus and better treatment, vaccines and also in terms of better health infrastructure. Now India has two indigenously manufactured vaccines like Covishield and Covaxin. Now India has become importer of the PPE Kits to main exporters of it. Its "Vaccine Diplomacy" has won praise from all-over the world. Still, we have to be cautioned against this dangerous virus. We cannot afford to take it as granted. Although we have better treatment and vaccine still wearing the mask at crowded place and maintain hand hygiene with minimum social distancing is key to avoid the dreaded disease.

We have already opened up our economy after the stringent lockdown. So, we cannot afford another lockdown. There are various sectors in the economy like tourism industry, entertainment industry, hospitality industry, educational sector etc. which have not recovered at pre-pandemic level. A lot of employment has been lost. So, another round of lockdown will totally destroy the recovering economy. It is apparent that this virus may be live with us forever. But still, we can counter it by adopting appropriate behaviour and observing discipline. Therefore, community level awareness is required. Despite of this challenges, India is on the verge of recovery. This pandemic has taught a great lesson on fragile nature of the health system of the world. But the policymakers and all the stakeholders of the economy have determined to achieve the full growth potential. It have been proved in the past also. But we have to be extra cautious about the pandemic.

Conclusion

Therefore, from the above discussion we can conclude that the revival of pandemic ravaged economy is possible. It has been also historically proved. But the implementation is very tough one in present circumstances. Recent protest by farmers against the farm Bill is the best example. But if the government has will-power and determination to withstand these opposing factors than nobody can stop our economy to become another superpower. The V-shaped economic recovery while avoiding a second wave of infections make India a *sui generis* case in this unique, synchronized global recession. Despite the hard-hitting economic shock created by the global pandemic, India is witnessing a V-shaped recovery with a stable macroeconomic situation aided by a stable currency, comfortable current account, burgeoning forex reserves, and encouraging signs in the manufacturing sector output. India is reaping the "lockdown dividend" from the brave, preventive measures adopted at the onset of the pandemic.

References

A.K. Bhattacharya (March 23, 2021). "Covid will have long-term effect on economy", Rediff News.

"India to be among fastest-growing emerging markets in FY 22: S&P", (18th February 2021), *The Economics Times.*

Kanwaljit Singh (2020). "COVID-19 has Pushed the Indian Economy into a Tailspin. But There's a Way Out", *The Wire.*

Monika Chaudhary, P.R. Sodani, Shankar Das, (August 11, 2020), "Effect of COVID-19 on Economy in India: Some Reflections for Policy and Programme", *Journal of Health Management.*

Remya Nair (26 February, 2021), "India's 0.4% GDP growth good news, but January-March quarter likely to see contraction", *The Print.*

S. Mahendra Dev & Rajeswari Sengupta (2020). "COVID-19: Impact on the Indian economy", Indira Gandhi Institute of Development Research, Mumbai, Working Papers 2020-21, Mumbai, India.

The Economic Survey, (*2020-21*), PIB, India.

"What is Atmanirbhar Bharat Mission?" (2020), *Business Standard.*

4

Impact of COVID-19 Lockdown on the Human Rights of Vulnerable Groups and the Role of Judiciary

Tanvi Yadav and *Nagendra Ambedkar Sole*

Introduction

The COVID-19 (Coronavirus disease-2019) has affected the whole world, but the most affected sections are the vulnerable groups, including the women, minorities, marginalized, indigenous, and workers. COVID-19 is a transmissible respiratory infection caused by acute respiratory syndrome corona virus 2. The COVID-19 was first introduced to the WHO (World Health Organization) in December 2019 when health specialist found cases in China's Wuhan city. COVID-19 pandemic comes up with other parallel pandemics such as economic pandemic, gender base violence pandemic, equality pandemic, and resources pandemic. Where one section of society just faced COVID-19, others, especially the socio-economic marginalized faced other epidemics as well.

These vulnerable groups of all countries had a tough time physically, economically, and mentally during corona situations. Hence, it is vital to question why these people pay the price in such emergencies. To know the answer, we have to see the long history of political loopholes behind it, including prevalent inequality in all fields such as social, economic, cultural, gender, religion, race, and caste. Epidemics reveal the worst of the nation, and in India, the lockdown has exposed the pre-existing inequalities and discrimination among people. There is a need to understand whether there is a loophole in Constitution that equality among all sections could not progress properly or there is any political trick behind it. India's current political agenda is still in favour of overexploiting resources, workers, and labour-power, leading to a humanitarian crisis.

The lockdown was enforced in India to stop spreading pandemic corona, but its repercussions affected a vast population. Many people lost their sources of bread & butter and became homeless, mostly the vulnerable groups. Before discussing the tyrannies of the helpless people, there is a need to know how the government fails to understand the urgency of the matter. The chronology of the state's action shows how the government was taking a health emergency very lightly. WHO declared a health emergency about corona in December 2019. In India, the first case was noticed on January 30, 2020. However, the first-time Indian government reacted on March 5, 2020, when the Ministry of Health and Family Welfare advised to avoid mass gathering.[1]

Ministry of Road Transport and Highways took measures on March 17, 2020, to restrict citizens' travels in all states by transport departments.[2] The Home Affairs Ministry of India issued an order stated that "the National Disaster Management Authority (NDMA) is satisfied that the country is threatened with the spread of COVID-19 epidemic" on March 24, 2020.[3] In exercise of power under the Disaster Management Act, 2005, the government declared lockdown in the nation with effect from March 25, 2020.[4] The irony is, it took four months from December 2019 to March 2020, for the government to understand the health emergency.

After that, the government's actions were irresponsible and hasty without any preparation of healthcare services, shelters for the homeless, and food for daily wagers. Government decisions are made only for a class of people who could survive even without work. However, the Constitution of India starts with "We the people of India", where term "we" means all Indian citizens. Hence, the lives of poor, homeless, Minorities, Dalits, Tribals, migrant workers, daily wagers, and women have the same importance as the other resourceful and privileged people of the country. This chapter explores the plights of vulnerable people during corona, the violation of fundamental human rights, and the loopholes by the government's actions.

Vulnerable groups and their tyrannies

The rights of the women, Minorities, Marginalized workers, and Indigenous people are grossly violated when the lockdown was first suddenly announced. Some of the problems they confronted have been discussed, including the horrific incidents that occurred with them.

Women

Women are one of the vulnerable sections in society who have faced human rights violations related to sexual, emotional, and physical abuse in this corona time. Human rights violence women face daily, but the number of incidents and intensity has increased during lockdown. The number of domestic violence complaints that were registered during the first four phases of lockdown was similar to the number of complaints recorded in the last ten years (Radhakrishnan, Sen, & Singaravelu, 2020). Antonio Guterres—the United Nations Secretary-General—on April 6, 2020, asked for a "ceasefire" to deal with the "horrifying global surge in domestic violence." On April 7, 2020, the World Health Organization declared that "Violence against women during emergencies remains a significant risk to global public health and women's health" (WHO, 2020).

The women who experienced violence around 86 per cent of them, never asked or got help, and in 77 per cent cases women did not even talk about the incidents to any person (Radhakrishnan *et al.*, 2020). According to National Commission for Women

(NCW) India, there is 100 per cent increase in domestic violence complaints against women after the imposement of lockdown, in the beginning of April 2020. NCW issued a Whatsapp number to be more reachable to women after easily getting complaints. However, with approximately 57 per cent of India's women do not have access to phones, thus, during lockdown their rights to file complaint is limited there (Engage, 2020). The slogan "stay safe and stay home" could not become synonyms for women as they are not safe in the home either.

Migrant women workers faced numerous assaults during their way back home. In an incident, pregnant women gave birth on the road, walking to one of Madhya Pradesh village from Maharashtra. Just past her birth delivery, she stopped for 2 hours to take rest and then started her walk for another 150 kilometres (*India Today*, 2020). There are many covered violence that women cope with during lockdown. Due to a lack of information, police access, and fear of corona, several women remained silent during the lockdown.

Minorities

Once Prime Minister Narendra Modi echoed a statement that "COVID-19 does not see race, religion, color, caste, creed, language or borders before striking." It is right; coronavirus doesn't do discrimination; unfortunately, the governments do, media do, and political leaders do. The politics of blaming and stigmatizing also began in this crisis with suspicion of outsiders, leading to vigilante violence. One set of political ideologies initiated to blame minorities, especially Muslims, for COVID-19. It was an excellent opportunity to end communal biases and other governance discrimination by targeting the crisis and unity against it, but the government uses it otherwise in spreading hatred.

The United States emissary for "International Religious Freedom", Sam Brownback, called out COVID-19-related oratory and aggravation in India, particularly against Muslims (Lakshman, 2020). During the lockdown, allowing vegetables and fruit was necessary service proving to be a momentous assistance for the people. The daily wagers, whose income stopped due to lockdown started selling vegetables and fruits. Though, name, religion, and aadhaar cards are being asked from vendors at many places in Delhi (Mehra, 2020) and outside. A vegetable seller has been beaten up after questioning his faith (Jain, 2020). A BJP-MLA from Deoria district of Uttar Pradesh suggested the people for not buying vegetables from Muslim vendors to evade constricting the coronavirus infection in his constituency (*HT* Correspondent, 2020).

Fake news reports and unabashed provocation by an obnoxiously Islam phobic media on COVID-19, made life of minorities difficult. There has been setting up of diverse wards based on devotion and belief in hospitals in Gujarat. Recently, Punjab's Muslim Gujjars needed police security just to transport milk (Kannabiran, 2020) from one place to another.

Marginalized Workers

Workers in all fields suffered due to lockdown, but the most affected were the marginalized, migrant workers, and daily wagers. The sudden lockdown announcement left the migrant labourers and daily wagers bare hands without food, money, and home. Most of them tried to return to their native place, so they started to walk due to transports' non-availability. Several died in-between; police and robbers exploited many. The more horrible incident occurred on railway tracks leading to Aurangabad, where 16 migrant workers died due to running over running trains; after walking for 36 km, they were resting on track (BBC, 2020). The Indian government should seem worried about its letdown to sustain citizens' requirements and treat them by means of dignity by seeing hundreds of thousands of workers trudging home (Ganguly, 2020). Caste questions and atrocities also have been seen in villages. When migrant *Dalit* workers reached their home in some villages, they were restrained by the upper caste people from entering their villages.

Health workers faced different types of exploitation, such as discrimination by the public and government. Health workers were deprived of entrance in house by neighbours; a doctor could not get a noble burial (Ganguly, 2020). The people who buried the bodies of corona people were not given health kits. They are doing cremation without safety kits. Sanitation staff faced the same problem, doing their duty without kits and even faces humiliation by other people. It is inevitable to think whether economic-social backwardness makes these real frontline workers immune to corona.

Indigenous people

Indigenous people who do not have adequate resources to stock the essentials for days together are bound to step out of their houses. The governments' reasoning did not reach the most helpless lot of the disadvantaged until the Central Government announced the 1.7 lakh crore package for such people. Tribal families working in brick kilns near Mumbai, Maharashtra, in the event of their closure and the suspension of transport systems, had to walk several kilometers back to their villages with their kids crying for water and food (Guru, 2020). Due to the remote location, indigenous people suffered in education, health, and nutrition. The help from NGOs or other organizations could not reach them. The toxic combination of rage, panic, horror, propaganda, and governmental arbitrariness became poison for people at this time.

Violation of Human Rights

The preamble of UDHR[5] declares, "Recognition of the inherent dignity and the equal and inalienable rights of all human family members is the foundation of freedom, justice and peace in the world." For around 40 years, a considerable setback has been seen in women, workers, and indigenous people's collective human rights. A section of society has not enjoyed Social, Economic, and Cultural rights due to rapidly increasing inequality. COVID-19 has exposed that the root cause of vulnerability of a section of society is the existing inequality, which hinders the enjoyment of their fundamental rights.

Human rights violence in this pandemic has been noticed in the whole world. Antonio Guterres, the Secretary-General of the United Nations, highlighted that due to the public health emergency human rights crisis is taking place and warned that by suppressing the free flow of information, the individual's human rights are violating. The lockdown was adopted by the Indian Government to defeat the corona in the country. Unfortunately, before taking a hasty decision, the government could not account for that violation of fundamental human rights of a large portion of citizens, can occur due to unplanned decisions.

Free Movement Rights

After the lockdown, migrant labourers' stories on their troubles overwhelmed the web. After shutting down all business, all transports, and all income possibilities, labourers had just a single alternative to walking many kilometers back to their homes. They had to endure the lockdown and virus both. Many have died in both battles, either by hunger or accident or disease. Even though some organizations provided food, shelter, and other facilities, it is still doubtful whether they fulfilled the norms "inherent dignity," as envisioned by the human rights Covenants.

Police brutality became the outcome of stringent restrictions during the lockdown, which was unanimously seen on labourers and other citizens. Ordinary people were assaulted by Police legally and illegally from both forms; even the death of a man was reported when he went to buy milk. The ICCPR[6] provides the "right to liberty of movement" within a State's territory. Article 19 of the Constitution discusses "the right to carry on any occupation, trade, or business and reside in any part of India's territory".

The decisions related to lockdown were taking under the Epidemic Diseases (ED) Act of 1897 and the Disaster Management (DM) Act of 2005. The DM Act delivers that "the measures to be taken in the affected areas only, where the disaster has spread or likely to spread" and ED Act provides "powers to the Central Government to take measures and prescribe regulations, when India or any part thereof is threatened with an outbreak of any dangerous epidemic disease". By reading outline of both Acts, it is apparent that no provision talks about the restrain the movement of the people, excluding in the containment areas, in both the Acts. However, Government ignored the difficulties of workers, daily wagers and ordinary people, moreover imposed complete lockdown.

Livelihood Rights

The Indian Constitution laid down fundamental rights that include the right to life under Article 21. Living includes physical existence and dignified life, counting personal liberty with right to work & livelihood. No provisions of DM Act authorize Government to suspend right to movement, shelter, employment and economic activities. It only provides to prepare a National Plan under Section 11 by NEC (National Executive Committee) in consultation with the State Governments to prevent disasters. However, people were forced to discontinue their work and stop their livelihood by the state.

Several news from a thwart nation address starvation and hunger as more significant fear to life for widespread part of populace than the virus, particularly resulting the lockdown (Kannabiran, 2020). As per Industrial Disputes Act, 1948 (ID Act), if an employer is not capable to provide work for an employee for the reason of natural disaster or any other similar cause, then it will be call Lay off and in case of Lay off the payment of compensation must be applied.

In Olga Tellis *v.* Bombay Municipal Corporation[7] (Pavement Dwellers Case), it was held that right to livelihood is the part of right to life. A person cannot live without resources of living, i.e., ways of Livelihood. In this case, Constitutional court expanded the ambit and scope right to life. Thus, the State's directions could be considered as advisory and not mandatory. Lockdown outrightly denied the relationship of employer & worker, such as having the possibility of collective bargaining, earning a decent wage, having access to social security, freedom of association and access of workers to other human rights.

Information Rights

The right to look for and get Article 19 ICCPR secures data. The ICESCR[8] considers it an essential aspect of the right to health. India successfully imparted knowledge concerning the nature of the disease, the precautions, and the degree of the danger it can force. However, people also have to get information about the potential measures to be taken up by the authorities, early alerts of possible results, and data on the progressing reaction endeavours. The purpose is to guarantee that each one can get information and accordingly take health-related decisions considering precise information. Sudden lockdown, just with a four-hour notice, left the people confused and ill-equipped to deal with themselves for the coming days.

In the State of UP *v.* Raj Narain[9], the Court held that "the people of this country shall have a right to know every public act, everything, that is done in a public way, by their functionaries". In a writ petition[10], Supreme Court laid down that "we have noticed there is no proper adherence to the guidelines and the hospitals are not giving due care as concerned to the dead bodies. The media is reporting the deaths of patients; however, patients' relatives are not even informed about death. Dr. Tedros Adhanom Ghebreyesus, WHO Director General, stated that "We are not just fighting an epidemic; we are fighting an infodemic. Fake news spreads faster and more easily than this virus, and is just as dangerous and the disease of hate and mob violence has spread much further".

After lockdown, so many fake stories were invented, including hate against doctor, religion, caste or even workers. Any person who circulates or make false warning regarding disaster or its magnitude or severity which leads to panic can be charged under Disaster Management Act, 2005 and punished with imprisonment of one year or more along with fine. Sadly no action has been drowning against such people who spread such fake news. Even during the national lockdown, the government is obliged to protect its people under international human rights law. ICCPR states that derogation is not permitted under Article 4 as it is against the Right to life provided under Article 6. Instead of getting correct information, people got busy to believing on fake news which creates chaos in society and affected vulnerable groups immensely.

Health Rights

ICESCR recognizes "the right of everyone to the enjoyment of the highest attainable standard of physical and mental health"[11] for which India is also a Party. However, the Right to Health is not a straight right.[12] The right to health has been considered the part of the right to life narrated by Supreme Court in Bandhua Mukti Morcha *vs.* Union of India & Others.[13] Jan Swasthya Abhiyan in 2014 policy succinct on the understanding of Healthcare rights, critically stated that equitable assessment to safe water, adequate food and nutrition, secure livelihoods, housing, and sanitation are keys to enjoy the right to health. Presently, such determinants have been tossed on the name of emergency, unexpectedly, adapting procedures for the pandemic rely upon unequivocally such accessibility (Kannabiran, 2020).

As per section 12 guidelines of DM Act, for maintaining least values of aid pertaining to shelter, the NDMA could not issue food, drinking water, medical cover and sanitation for those infected by the virus and those whose life has become despondent due to lockdown. Health of health workers highly affected during lockdown. Health workers are the frontlines of corona battle, in India they were not provided even proper armor at many places. The health workers are required to be given relevant health information and appropriate protective clothing and equipment. The Government did modest to ascertain health workers' protection with their low obtainment policies and deferral in surrounding rules for PPE production. With the regulations coming in with the inconvenience of the lockdown, assembling and transportation of PPE has become a multiple assignment.

Appalling public health spending, insufficient staff, low interest in training, deficient health infrastructure, along with non-existence of state assurance to construct strong public health system are the hurdles to public health primary concern of state. In a writ petition, Supreme Court raps that the State on whom the obligation depends to deal with health issues of the country cannot renounce its duty of guaranteeing that every medical clinic, together with Government hospitals, watch the COVID-19 patients (Rajagopa, 2020). Profound vulnerabilities of healthcare system has exposed through COVID-19 in India. It is unfortunate that only 1.29 per cent of GDP (2019-20) spend on public health which is lowest from many other countries. The other aspect is also recognized why right to health must be a fundamental right under Constitution.

Privacy Rights

Right to privacy is provided by ICCPR's Article 17 and perceived as a fundamental Right under Indian Constitution in Article 21. As Virus taking in, the privacy is taking off in country through lockdown primarily. Passenger's sensitive information who travelled to Delhi was shared through facebook and whatsapp and the government had no answer to this except blaming oppositions. The leak of information became the threat to passengers' lives and their family, which led to ostracization of passengers' family members.

Aarogya Setu app is also indicated as breach of privacy as there are chances that the same can be misused. Government has made it mandatory indirectly by making it e-pass to visit public places. Thus, it will *ipso facto* make application mandatory that need to leave their homes. Even though government claimed that the data is encrypted, its location tracking and direct report to government can be regarded as mass surveillance. The right to privacy faced a critical setback in COVID-19 which need to be fix.

Role of Judiciary

When all the ways are closed, only judiciary can be a hope. As often, courts played in significant role in surviving the human rights of suffered people. The most vulnerable groups could not be able to approach the courts for safeguarding their human rights for two reasons. Firstly, due to lack of sources, resources and information, secondly most of the State Institutions are captured by the socially-economically well off people. Supreme Court of India took suo motu actions on some COVID-19 issues by exercising power under Article 142 read with Article 141.

Such as in its one suo motu action Court shows its concern about Mid-Day Meal Scheme[14] during corona. Court laid down that in rural and tribal areas nutritious food for children and nursing or pregnant women is essential to keep them healthy. Court ordered that state should form uniform policy for distribution of mid-day meal as non-supply can cause large scale malnutrition population. In another suo motu action[15], Supreme Court discuses problems and miseries of migrant labourers directed the government to provide Shramik trains to make possible the return journey to labourers. In one suo motu[16] petition Supreme Court discussed about "the proper treatment of COVID-19 patients and dignified handling of dead bodies in the hospitals etc". The court took cognizance on media report about covid dedicated hospital point out the feeble circumstances of admitted patients and unpleasant state of wards. Court issued the monitoring, supervision and management directions to be followed.

Along with courts' suo motu action many PIL activists filed petitions to get relief on different issues. As in Alakh Alok Srivastava *v.* Union of India[17], the petitioners highlighted the plight of thousands of migrant labourers and demanded "a direction to the authorities to shift the migrant labourers to government shelter homes/accommodations and provide them with basic amenities like food, clean drinking water, medicines, etc". Petitioner also demanded that the humanistic approach must be applied in dealing with migrant workers and stranded tourists by police administration and other authorities. Court laid down that "we trust and expect that all concerned Governments, Public Authorities and Citizens of this country will faithfully comply with the directives, advisories and orders issued by the Union of India in letter and spirit in the interest of public safety. Direct the media refer to and publish the official version about the developments. The police and other authorities should understand the anxiety and fear of the migrants."

In petition Dr. Arushi Jain *v.* Union of India & Anr.[18], the problem of doctors and health workers were raised primarily related to their safety, PPT kit for them, salary, quarantine accommodation etc. Petitioner submitted that all the doctors and healthcare workers are exposed to the high risk and should be given the benefit of lodging since if they go back to their family, it is more risky and opens the entire family to risk difficulty. Further submitted that a direction is necessary to the State Governments, Central Government, and all other concerned authorities to ensure that doctors' and health workers' salaries and emoluments are timely paid, who are frontline warriors. However, court was satisfied by the assurance from the government and no further directions were laid down.

Where in some petitions court took positive steps, in other petitions court shows different colours. Such as in Harsh Mander *v.* Union of India[19] was a petition filed by Advocate Prashant Bhushan and heard by three bench CJI Bobde, Justices S.K. Kaul and Deepak Gupta, this Petition was filed by the petitioners seeking the guarantee payments of wages to all the migrant workers. Court dismissed petition without relief. In fact, CJI asked the petitioners "why wages are required when the government provides meals".

The Supreme Court also rejected a petition which asked to nationalize all hospitals during pandemic by taking over all private hospitals by state for patients of COVID-19, by invoking Article 21 and Directive Principles of State Policy of Constitution. Through this case, Court got an opportunity to apply different path of inclusive justice by state accountability regarding access to healthcare services. However, unfortunately court rejected the petition. In another petition taking over the all hotels by the State was asked to make available practical lodging for dispossessed migrant workers to easily access shelter with basic facilities such as electricity, water, security, and hygiene. The petition was dismissed, thereafter, the Supreme Court observed that several people will approach with plenty of suggestions; state cannot pay attention to each and every one.

The pandemic and lockdown have been forced on deprived people when Court decline to investigate a special idea of justice that is deeply provided by Constitution of India, even after briefed about suffering and harms of marginalized (Kannabiran, 2020). There is a awfully flimsy, vague eminence to the response of Court to the misery of this country's poor workers on whom the state is outrightly reliant. Ironically, Court failed to be aware of that workers do not rely on the country in fact country depends on workers (Mahajan, 2020).

Conclusion

While announcing the lockdown, the government assumes that every person has equal access to food, shelter, drinking water, and other basic amenities. Equality economic, social prevailed in our county in the government's mind, so they need not do anything about it. The policies of government reflect that like lockdown as a clear example of thoughts. The COVID-19 scenario shows that the issues of labour protection socially and economically, reformation of healthcare, addressing food security, and eradicating social, economic, cultural. Gender inequality needs specific attention of the State. However, most government measures are taken to strengthen the economic elites through tax relaxation, which causes socio-economic loss to vulnerable groups. It is generally acknowledged that socio-economic factors are prevalent in our country, diminishing access to quality healthcare and other services. Surprisingly, the government do not have data of dead workers and doctors due to COVID-19.

Constitutionally, a state must diminish persistent inequality in facilities, opportunities, status, and income, among gender, caste, religion, and race. Equality can be brought into existence by incalcating directive principles in state policies as by securing justice under Articles 39A, 41, 43 and 47.

The lockdown would have been properly executed, had it been done in a staged way to permit people to plan, get ready, and take proper decisions. The state or judicial must act by considering empathy and dedication to constitutional morality, not on the claim of privilege and the distribution of charity. Surprisingly, the government do not have data of died workers and doctors due to COVID-19.

Upendra Baxi detects that merely novel forms of solidarity and human compassion can aid in conquering this deadly and impressively inauspicious challenge and aid in building a bright future for worldwide politics manifest by rights, justice, empathy and fraternity (Baxi, 1969). During public health emergency, government must be guided by proportions of constitutionalism, human rights and justice. The focus of State and Judiciary ought to be on health, ethical state practices, rights of women and minorities, and empathy for the daily wagers and poor labourers.

Notes

1. Query from States on Mass Gathering, Ministry of Health and Family Welfare, Government of India, https://cdnbbsr.s3waas.gov.in/s3850af92f8d9903e7a4e0559a98ecc857/uploads/2020/05/2020051168.pdf
2. Measures to restrict the travels by citizens due to Novel Coronavirus (COVID-I9), Ministry of Road Transport and Highways, Government of India, https://cdnbbsr.s3waas.gov.in/s3850af92f8d9903e7a4e0559a98ecc857/uploads/2020/05/2020050643.pdf
3. Order, Ministry of Home Affairs, Government of India, https://cdnbbsr.s3waas.gov.in/s3850af92f8d9903e7a4e0559a98ecc857/uploads/2020/05/2020051363.pdf
4. *Ibid.*
5. Universal Declaration of Human Rights, 1948.
6. The United Nations International Covenant of Civil and Political Rights.
7. 1985 SCC (3) 545.
8. The International Committee on Economic, Social and Cultural Rights.

9. AIR 1975 SC 865.
10. In Re: The Proper Treatment of COVID-19 Patients and Dignified Handling of Dead Bodies in The Hospitals etc. Suo Motu Writ Petition (Civil) No.(s). 7/2020, Supreme Court of India 12-06-2020
11. Article 12.1 ICESCR.
12. As shown under Article 4 of ICESCR.
13. 1984 AIR 802 SC.
14. In Re: Regarding Closure of Mid-Day Meal Scheme, Suo Motu Writ Petition (C) No.(s). 2/2020, 18-03-2020.
15. In Re: Problems and Miseries of Migrant Labourers, The Supreme Court of India, Civil Original Jurisdiction, Suo Motu Writ Petition (Civil) No.(s). 6/2020.
16. In Re: The Proper Treatment of COVID-19 Patients and Dignified Handling of Dead Bodies in The Hospitals etc. Suo Motu Writ Petition (Civil) No.(s). 7/2020, Supreme Court of India, 12-06-2020.
17. Civil Writ Petition-Diary No.(s)-468/2020.
18. Civil Writ Petition-Diary No.(s)-10852/2020.
19. Civil Writ Petition-Diary No.(s)-10801/2020.

References

Baxi, U. (1969). Directive Principles and Sociology of Indian Law—A Reply to Dr. Jagat Narain. *Journal of the Indian Law Institute, 11*(3), 245-272. Retrieved from https://www.jstor.org/stable/43950028

BBC (2020). Indian migrant deaths: 16 sleeping workers run over by train.

Engage (2020). COVID-19, Domestic Abuse and Violence: Where Do Indian Women Stand? Retrieved from EPW website: https://www.epw.in/engage/article/COVID-19-domestic-abuse-and-violence-where-do

Ganguly, M. (2020). India Cannot Expect to Beat COVID-19 Without Tackling Hate and Corruption. Retrieved August 1, 2020, from Scroll.in website: https://www.hrw.org/news/2020/05/26/india-cannot-expect-beat-COVID-19-without-tackling-hate-and-corruption

Guru, G. (2020). "Reason of the State and COVID-19". *Economic and Political Weekly, 55*(13). Retrieved from https://www.epw.in/journal/2020/13/editors-desk/reason-state-and-COVID-19.html

HT Correspondent (2020, April 28). BJP MLA says stop buying vegetables from Muslim sellers, defends remark. *Hindustan Times*. Retrieved from https://www.hindustantimes.com/india-news/bjp-mla-says-stop-buying-vegetables-from-muslim-sellers-defends-remark/story-X0SQ9kLEmmk4LCpbyUTYGM.html

India Today (2020, May 13). Pregnant migrant labourer delivers baby while walking home, walks another 150 km after delivery. *India Today*. Retrieved from https://www.indiatoday.in/india/story/pregnant-migrant-labourer-delivers-baby-while-walking-home-1677374-2020-05-13

Jain, H. (2020, April 14). Police arrested man who beats vegetable vendor after asking religion. *News Track*. Retrieved from https://english.newstracklive.com/news/delhi-police-arrests-man-who-was-beating-vegetable-vendors-asking-their-religion-sc103-nu612-ta612-ta294-1084794-1.html

Kannabiran, K. (2020, May). "Justice and Rights" in Viral Contexts in India. *The India Forum*. Retrieved from https://www.theindiaforum.in/article/justice-and-rights-viral-contexts-india

Lakshman, S. (2020, May 15). U.S. envoy calls out COVID-19 related harassment of minorities in India. *The Hindu*. Retrieved from https://www.thehindu.com/ news/ international/us-envoy-calls-out-harassment-of-minorities-in-india-over-COVID-19/article31591566.ece

Mahajan, S. (2020). Migrant Workers' plight during Coronavirus Lockdown: Will not interfere in government decision for few days, CJI SA Bobde. Retrieved September 27, 2020, from Bar And Bench website: https://global.oup.com/academic/product/the-global-model-of-constitutional-rights-9780199664603?cc=in&lang=en&

Mehra, S. (2020, April 19). Delhi: Daily wagers forced to sell vegetables, being asked to show Aadhaar before entering colonies. *India Today*. Retrieved from https://www.indiatoday.in/india/story/delhi-daily-wagers-forced-to-sell-vegetables-being-asked-to-show-aadhaar-before-entering-colonies-1668727-2020-04-19

Radhakrishnan, V., Sen, S., & Singaravelu, N. (2020, June 22). Data | Domestic violence complaints at a 10-year high during COVID-19 lockdown. *The Hindu*. Retrieved from https://www.thehindu.com/data/data-domestic-violence-complaints-at-a-10-year-high-during-COVID-19-lockdown/article31885001.ece

Rajagopa, K. (2020, June 17). Coronavirus | Supreme Court raps Delhi government on state of COVID-19 hospitals. *The Hindu*. Retrieved from https://www.thehindu.com/ news/ national/coronavirus-supreme-court-raps-delhi-government-on-state-of-COVID-19-hospitals/article31850187.ece

WHO (2020). COVID-19 and violence against women What the health sector/system can do. Retrieved from https://apps.who.int/iris/bitstream/handle/10665/331699/WHO-SRH-20.04-eng.pdf?sequence=1&isAllowed=y

5
Management of COVID-19
Lessons from Kerala

Nithya N.R.

Introduction

The COVID-19 is a human, economic and social crisis. The COVID-19 has its impact on all sections of the population and is mainly detrimental to members of those social groups in the most vulnerable situations. Until the preparation of this abstract (18 February, 2021), more than 11,04,29,984 cases of COVID-19 have been reported in more than two hundred nineteen territories, resulting in over 10,91,989 deaths but more than 2,88,60,879 people have recovered from this deadly virus (Worldometer, 2021). Globally, 8 of the 15 countries are most affected by COVID-19—the United States of America, India, Brazil, the Russian Federation, Cambodia, Argentina, Spain, and Peru—were among the 7 countries from which the highest amounts of remittances were sent in 2018. (UN DESA, 2019; WHO, 2021). The pandemic is deepening pre-existing inequalities, exposing vulnerabilities in social, political and economic systems which are in turn amplifying the impacts of the pandemic. Every sphere of life, the impacts of COVID-19 aggravated for females because of their sex (UN, 2020). If not appropriately addressed through proper plan, the crisis created by the COVID-19 pandemic may also increase inequality, exclusion, discrimination and global unemployment in the short and long term. The UN Sustainable Development Goals call for making sure no one is left behind, including migrants. Different age groups face varying vulnerabilities as both migrants and being part of a certain period in life (UN, 2020). In order to end pandemic, a large share of the world needs to be immune to the virus. Several research teams rose to the challenge and developed vaccines that protect from SARS-CoV-2, the virus that causes COVID-19.

Table 5.1: Statistics on COVID-19

Countries infected	**No. of Countries—Zero cases**	**Total cases**	**Total deaths**
219	6	11,04,29,984	24,40,928
Continents Infected	Continents Not Infected	Cases in India	Deaths
Asia, Africa, Europe, North and South America, Australia	Antarctica	1,09,49,546	1,56,038

Source: Worldometer, February 18, 2021.

As of 21 May, 2020, the Ministry of Health and Family Welfare have confirmed a total of 1,09,49,546 cases, 1,06,54,706 recoveries and 1,56,038 deaths in the country. India currently has the first largest number of confirmed cases in Asia with number of cases breaching the 1,00,000 mark on 19 February, 2021. Maharashtra, Andhra Pradesh and Karnataka were reported the highest number of cases. However, infections are rising rapidly in states like Tamil Nadu, Uttar Pradesh and West Bengal (Union Ministry of Health and Family Welfare, 2021). The outbreak has been declared an epidemic in more than a dozen states and Union territories, where provisions of the Epidemic Diseases Act, 1897 have been invoked, and educational institutions and many industrial firms have been shut down. India has suspended all tourist visas, as a majority of the confirmed cases were linked to other countries.

According to Michael Ryan (chief executive director of the World Health Organisation's health emergencies programme), India had "tremendous capacity" to deal with the coronavirus outbreak and, as the second most populous country, will have enormous impact on the world's ability to deal with it. The Indian Government has responded more stringently than other countries in tackling the pandemic. It is noted government's swift action, emergency policy making emergency investment in healthcare, fiscal measures, investment in vaccine research and active response to the situation, and scored India with a "100" for its strictness (GoI, 2020). The Government of India stated that the vaccination coverage in the country has crossed 9.06 million doses ranking India at the third position after USA (55.2 million doses) and the UK (16.12 million doses). It is reported that nine States/UTs have recorded a coverage of more than 75 per cent of first dose of HCW. These include Bihar (84.7%), Tripura (82.3%), Odisha (81.5%), Lakshadweep (81%), Gujarat (80.2%), Chhattisgarh (78.8%), Madhya Pradesh (76.7%), Uttarakhand (76.6%) and Himachal Pradesh (75.1%). As of February, 17, 2021, more than 85 lakh Beneficiaries Vaccinated against COVID-19 (GoI, 2021).

Profile of Kerala

Kerala is one of the smallest states in the Indian union. It occupies 1 per cent of the total land area of India with a population of 3.33 crore, which is 3 per cent of the total population of India at the 2011 Census. The state of Kerala consists of the slight coastal strip compounded by the Western Ghats in the east and the Arabian Sea on the west. Kerala has had a vibrant history starting from the ancient times to the present era. Modern Kerala came into being on 1st November, 1956, by merging the states of Travancore-Cochin and Malabar on the basis of the State Re-organization Act. While Travancore, Cochin were princely states, Malabar district was a part of erstwhile Madras Presidency under British-India. Due to historical reasons, the three regions witnessed uneven development. Particularly, Malabar was a 'neglected outpost of Madras Presidency' whereas Travancore was one of the most socially progressive states that joined Indian Union soon after Independence. With the general elections of 1957, the Communist Party of India came to power with E.M.S. Nambudiripad as Chief Minister. Bi-polar coalition politics became the prominent theme of Kerala's political framework since 1970 (Gopa, 2012). The population distribution of Kerala according to religion is about 56.20 per cent Hindu, 24.7 per cent Muslim and 19 per cent Christian. At present the state is administratively divided into 14 districts, which in turn are divided into 77 Taluks, 152 Blocks, 1670 Villages, 941 Grama (Village) Panchayats, 87 Municipalities and 5 Corporations (Economic Review, 2020).

Significance of the 'Kerala Model of Development'

Since 1970s, a number of international intellectuals have held up the South Indian State of Kerala as a "Model of Development" (Ratcliffe, 1978; Amin, 1991; Frank and Chasin, 1994). It is defined as Kerala's high standard of living (comparable to US or Europe) at very low per capita income which is only 1/80th of US citizens per capita income. According to Frank and Chasin (1994) this model is "a set of economic practices developed in the state of Kerala, resulted in attaining a high level of standards in human development, despite having a very low industrial development" (Frank and Chasin, 2000). The basic characteristic of the Kerala Model is the high level of social development and physical social quality of life disproportionate to its level of economic development.

Contemporary economic theory suggests that this amalgamation of underdevelopment and high standard of living is impractical. How has Kerala done it?. There were a number of reasons facilitating the evolution of the 'Kerala model'. The notable activities of the Christian missionaries, social reform movements, well structured peasants' and workers' movements and Left political movements and initiatives increased the desire of people for education and better healthcare (Kannan *et al.*, 1991; Asokan, 2005; Kabir and Krishnan, 1992). Social equality is one of the hallmarks of

Kerala Model over the past sixty years or more, Kerala has been transforming itself from an extremely poor state, ridden with caste and class conflicts and loaded by high birth rate, infant mortality and population growth rates, into a social democratic state with low birth, infant mortality and low population growth rates and a high level of literacy (Govindan, 2000). What we call 'development experience' or the 'Kerala model' is a unique pattern of social and economic changes that have been taking place in Kerala as a result of initiatives, both governmental and non-governmental, based on public action. Most importantly, the change has begun to take place peacefully even during the era of monarchy. It strengthened further with democratic framework by enfranchising most of the formerly dispossessed groups and communities in Kerala society. However K.P. Kannan argues that Kerala's development record should not be perceived, analysis as merely the achievement of high quality of social life, despite low income growth. Robin Jeffrey, a noted scholar on Kerala, holds the view that a set of ingredients that evolved over a period of time actually produced the conditions for the Kerala model. The major ingredients are politicization, maritime and commercial connections, the presence of a plural society, social reform groups and their leaders, Christianity and Christian missionaries, Communism and communist activists, reform-minded Indian princess and the position of women (Robin, 1976).

According to Ramachandran, the factors responsible for Kerala's achievements can be attributed to: meaningful land reforms; 'food for all' schemes through fair-price shops and feeding programmes for school children, infants and mothers; providing easy access to primary and precautionary healthcare; encouraging high literacy, through free and universal primary and secondary education; high mandated agricultural and farm wages; cost-effective transportation facilities; full electrification; engaging the poor and working people in decision making process, cultivating public discourse on environmental related issues; and developing socio-cultural movements through vibrant civil society to promote environmental conservation and other grassroots projects. Various analysts attribute either one or a combination of the following factors for Kerala's 'success': Kerala's ability to carry out public action through the enlistment of agriculturalists, tenants and industrial workers by leftist political parties (Ramachandran, 1982); the spread of literacy, particularly among women; maintaining women's rights (though these rights were mostly a result of historically contingent factors) (Sen, 1992); reducing social inequality and decreasing inequalities in income and consumption (Ratcliffe, 1991); and indigenous evolution and popularization of social movements concerned with environment and development issues. According to Franke & Chasin, the best description that can be ascribed to Kerala's experience is a 'social justice model of development'.

Kerala Model of Health

Health is considered as a fundamental human right and a worldwide social goal. According to WHO, health is "a complete state of physical, mental and social well-being and not merely the absence of illness or disease". Kerala has made remarkable achievements in health almost comparable to that of even developed countries. Kerala model of health is the legacy of the erstwhile princely states in Kerala. The healthcare paradigm followed by the rulers of the princely states of Travancore, Cochin and Malabar has been adopted more or less in the same way by Kerala. Kerala's achievement in health despite of its economic backwardness has encouraged many scholars to discuss on a unique "Kerala Model of Health"—'Good health at low cost', 'good health with social justice', worth emulating by other developing parts of the world. There are many positive conditions exceptional to Kerala, which have been contributed to this health model possible. Kerala has a highly literate sate compared to other Indian states. This especially the high female literacy, has to be given due recognition when we look for illustrative factors. Kerala's highly praised developments in healthcare sector were to a great extent largely based on its wide network of public healthcare institutions with the sub-centre and Primary Health Centres, Community Health Centres, Taluk/

District Hospitals and Medical College Hospitals at the primary, secondary and tertiary levels, the hallmark of which was universal accessibility and availability of medical care to the marginalised sections of society. Apart from Modern Medicine, *Ayurveda*, Homeopathy, and other alternative systems are also very popular and are accepted in Kerala. According to National Family Health Survey of 2007, the incidence of anemia among females is the least in Kerala among the states in the country. In spite of the remarkable developments in basic health indicators, it is also noticeable by the absence of any bias against the girl child and women (K.P. Kannan, 2012). There are many positive conditions unique to Kerala, which have contributed to this health model possible one. One reason for the better health status of Kerala is its healthier living conditions. The state has been able to reduce the infant mortality, child mortality, peri-natal and neonatal mortality and maternity mortality substantially (Nithya, 2013).

Census 2011 put Kerala's population at 3,33,87,677 persons, with a sex-ratio (females per 1000 males) of 1084, is the only state in India with a positive figure. In the human development and related indices, Kerala occupies prime position among Indian states in lower level of birth rate, death rate and infant mortality rate and highest life expectancy (Table 5.2) (Pillai, 1994). One of the reasons for the better health status of Kerala is its better living conditions. The sustained efforts of the government, both before and after independence, along with high literacy rate, especially female literacy rate, were the major correlates of this achievement (George and Ajith, 1997).

Table 5.2: Vital health statistics of Kerala and India: 1951-2011

Year	Birth Rate		Death Rate		Infant mortality		Sex Ratio	
	Kerala	India	Kerala	India	Kerala	India	Kerala	India
1951	44	40	18	22.8	128	146	1028	946
1961	39	41	16.11	17.6	94	129	1022	941
1971	32	37	11	15.4	61	114	1016	930
1981	26	34	6.6	13	34	110	1034	935

(Contd.)

Year	Birth Rate		Death Rate		Infant mortality		Sex Ratio	
	Kerala	India	Kerala	India	Kerala	India	Kerala	India
1991	18	30	6.0	10	16.5	92	1040	928
2001	17.3	26	6.6	9	11	70	1058	933
2011	14.8	20.9	7	6.6	13	48	1084	940

Source: Census of India, Various Years.

Kerala's Experiences and Achievements in COVID-19 Pandemic

Kerala was the first Indian state to be affected by COVID-19 with the highest number of cases at one point in time, but today it has a flat infection curve and one of the highest recovery rates in India. When the first positive case of corona virus in India was reported in Thrissur on January 30, 2020, the entire attention of the country was focused on Kerala to know how the infection was going to be regulated. The number of infected patients started to rise in Kerala until the end of March, as a section of international migrants started to return to the state. The quick action programmes of the Kerala government in identifying the potential social contacts and consequently tracing them started to show results by early April, 2020. This extraordinary achievement of Kerala has nowadays attracted worldwide attention much like the renowned 'Kerala Model' of development. This has also received approval from the medical profession, social activists, academics, international bodies, media attention and people at large. Many developed nations are in wonder of the achievements of Kerala in its fight against COVID-19 pandemic (*The Hindu*, April 28, 2020). This is the speciality of Kerala model. Hence, it is essential to analyse Kerala's experience.

Highest political and administrative commitment and proactive timely interventions were evident in the state as far as COVID-19 management was concerned. Kerala has initiated stringent action in preparing for the Covid attack even before the first case was reported. Kerala has survived two consecutive devastating floods which formed enormous health allied challenges and still remains alert against Nipah Virus attack, Kyasanur Forest Disease (KFD) and bird flu (avian influenza) learning lessons from these attacks, the Health Department got its act together quickly this time and alerted the officials from top to bottom. As soon as the first case was detected, elaborate contact map tracing was done. In a short span of time, the Health Department of Kerala developed the skills for contact tracing, often in partnership with different agencies and individuals. The ward-level committees, set up by the government for the anti-corona virus fight, was collecting information of those under home isolation, elderly persons and those at the risk of the disease using a questionnaire in this regard and upload it on the server of the private agency (Gok, 2020). According to Health Minister of Kerala, "We are fighting COVID-19 in the same way we handled Nipah. That time we were poorly equipped and lack of previous exposure remained a major handicap. But now we are well-resourced with better experiences."

On March, 2020, the state government arranged special isolation wards across the state and shut down all colleges and schools and offices. The government also imposed restrictions on pilgrim centres, weddings celebrations, public gatherings and cinema shows. The government also launched a mobile application called GoK Direct for users to get information and updates concerning the COVID-19 disease. An initiative 'Break the Chain' was introduced by Government of Kerala. The campaign aims to educate people the importance of public and personal cleanliness. Under this campaign, the present government has installed water taps at public spots such as at the entry and exit gates of the railway stations with hand wash bottles. The Health Minister of Kerala, Smt. K.K. Shailaja strongly warned the people to follow the instructions from Health Department of Kerala. On 23 March, Chief Minister Pinarayi Vijayan announced a state wide lockdown till 31 March and later it was extended to May 31 to prevent further spread of Corona virus. This was before the Central Government declared a nationwide lockdown. Public transports were shut down. Kerala is the only state in India that mandates 28 days of home quarantine for those returning from countries affected by corona virus or red/high risk zones, while the national guidelines for India is

14 days. People who are advised home quarantine are advised to stay at their homes during the 28-day period, and report to healthcare authorities if they show symptoms of corona virus infection. Kerala government has classified Green, Orange and Red zone areas based on COVID-19 threat, number of cases (GoK, 2020).

Table 5.3: COVID-19 pandemic in Kerala by districts

District	Active cases	Recoveries	Deaths	Total cases
Ernakulam	9574	49045	196	58826
Thrissur	7950	44612	188	52755
Alappuzha	7826	34752	131	42726
Kozhikode	7242	53592	164	61005
Malappuram	6619	55861	195	62684
Thiruvananthapuram	5795	61186	507	67536
Palakkad	5322	27846	73	33243
Kollam	4692	38131	147	42977
Kottayam	3833	26883	77	30795
Kannur	3657	26014	143	29819
Idukki	2010	7665	11	9688
Pathanamthitta	1958	16154	16	18129
Kasaragod	1786	18805	74	20669
Wayanad	1132	7914	21	9067
Total (all 14 districts)	**69,396**	**4,68,460**	**1,943**	**5,39,919**

Source: GoK, February 18, 2021.

The surveillance system has been well functioned. Right from the beginning, health staffs were deployed in the airports to screen patients coming from abroad. This process became systematically elaborate and energetic. The Health Department led observation system initiated on a community-based character with the energetic participation of elected representatives of local governments, members of the self-help groups (SHGs) and 'Kudumbashree' workers. The state government invited religious leaders, private partners, local bodies and civil society organizations to participate in policy design and implementation, considering its specific socio-economic conditions. It has communicated successfully in different languages to educate all, including migrants, and to check stigmatization of those infected, even opposing the term 'social distancing', which has caste connotations, with 'physical distancing and social solidarity'. The Police department actively got involved in this process. The level of coordination seen in this exercise is very difficult to achieve in a governmental set-up and that too in the face of real personal risk (Vijayanand, 2020).

From the beginning, the state resorted to energetic planning anticipating an extreme scenario. At the same time, local R&D (research and development) efforts were made to build up vaccines, improve testing systems and facilities, and even attempt advanced technological interventions such as plasma therapy. Kerala was the first state to come up with a separate law to handle the COVID-19 pandemic. The state also resorted to a lockdown to reduce the spread of Virus. The lockdown was implemented fruitfully as the public cooperated. Directions for reaching out to the public were frequently issued and the police was sensitised to make it as humane as possible. Chief Minister and Minister for Health are conducting press conferences on a daily basis to keep people aware of the gravity of the issue and the steps taken by the government each press meet provides plenty of practical information to the ordinary people about the pandemic that sweeps the world (Health Department, GoK, 2020).

Since March itself, the state came up with a Rs. 200 billion relief package. Social security pensions were dispersed, support from the welfare funds was released and interest free loans to the members of the SHGs were provided. The public distribution system (PDS) was activated and free kit and rice provided to every card holder irrespective of the type. In addition, kits having essential condiments are also being provided through the PDS outlets (*The Times of India*, May 15, 2020). For the beneficiaries of *Anganwadis* (childcare centres), their quota of food is provided at their doorstep once a week. Since Kerala has a large number of in-migrants estimated at around 2.5 million, special arrangements were made to provide them with cooked food or food materials, as per their choice. Free cooked food is being provided by local governments to all those who need it, with the support of *Kudumbashree* members. Further, help lines are available to elderly people who can access their medicine or food materials through volunteers. Thus, the policy of 'no one left behind' has been operationalised. Kerala launched a campaign mode to mobilise people for a variety of activities ranging from 'break the chain' campaign to setting up community kitchens (Vijayanand, 2020).

In fighting COVID-19, Kerala followed a community-based approach under the leadership of local self-governments, especially village panchayats, municipalities, and municipal corporations. The local governments mobilised the support of *Kudumbashree* and other units. Under the leadership of the elected ward members, squads were formed for outreach and feedback. This has succeeded to a large extent in reducing the anxiety, particularly of those quarantined and citizens confined to their homes. Government hospitals at all levels, from the primary health centres to the medical colleges, were given clear responsibilities. The field-level staff including ASHA (Accredited Social Health Activists) workers functioned as teams with clear protocols and regular instructions. Capacity-building manuals and electronic classes has been arranged for the elected representatives and the *Kudumbashree* members. Coordination has also done by the District Collectors working closely with the District Medical Officers and the district-level heads of the police. The most visible and applauded initiative of the government has been the CM's daily communication with the people followed by a press conference. The communication focuses on facts, hides nothing, states all problems, stresses the dangerous situation, and comforts the people with specific assurances. Every major issue that arose during the day is highlighted in these communications, along with the measures the government has taken or intends to take. Good deeds are published and bad behaviour is mildly rebuked. This has complimented the grassroots initiatives perfectly. The Kerala Health Department has prepared an action plan to expand the COVID-19 vaccination to commence the next phase of the drive meticulously. Around 10,786 Covid frontline workers and 802 health workers were vaccinated (GoK, 2021).

Conclusion

The world is being profoundly affected by the global virus pandemic. In addition to the threat to public health, the economic and social disruption threatens the long-term livelihoods and well-being of millions. WHOs landmark resolution underlines the role in promoting access to safe, effective health technologies to fight the pandemic. Government of India is taking all necessary steps to ensure that we are prepared well to face the challenge and threat posed by the growing pandemic of COVID-19—the Corona Virus. Kerala has tackled not only the current health disaster that is ravaging the world, but also earlier catastrophes including containment of the spread of Nipah virus and natural disasters with deft. Kerala has done a wonderful job in COVID-19 control so far, keeping the numbers at a very low level. This remarkable achievement of Kerala has now attracted international attention much like the famous 'Kerala Model' of development. All the aspects of Kerala's strategy to manage COVID-19 could be adapted in an emergency situation by any state of India or the world. For that we need a sustainable environment, the nature of the State needs to be changed with much focus on care and welfare. The biggest learning that needs to be replicated is the strengthening of the primary healthcare system, local democracy and local self-government institutions.

References

Ashokan, A. (2009). *Perspectives of Health Economics*, New Delhi: Serials Publications.

Commonwealth Local Government Forum. India: key facts, 2020. Retrieved from: http://www.clgf.org.uk/default/assets/File/Country_ profiles/India.pdf

Cros, Jaques (1950). *Le néo-libéralisme et la révision du libéralisme*, Thèse Droit, Toulouse: Imprimerie Moderne.

Datt, Ruddar and Sundharam, K.P.M. (2008). *Indian Economy*, New Delhi: S. Chand and Co.

Directorate of Health Services, Government of Kerala, 2021. Retrieved from: https://dhs.kerala.gov.in

Eapen, K.V. (1985). *Church Missionary Society and Education in Kerala*, Kottayam: Kollet Publication.

Friedman, Milton (1970). "The Social Responsibility of Business is to Increase its Profits", *The New York Times Magazine*, 13th September.

George, K.K. and Ajith Kumar, N. (2009). "Kerala's Education System: From Inclusion to Exclusion?", *Economic and Political Weekly*, October 10, Vol. XLIV, No. 41, pp. 55-61.

Ghosh, B.N. and Namboodiri, Padmaja, D., (Eds.), (2009). *The Economy of Kerala—Yesterday, Today and Tomorrow*, New Delhi: Serials Publications.

Government of Kerala (2020). *Economic Review 2020,* State Planning Board, Thiruvananthapuram, Kerala.

Government of Kerala, *Economic Review*, *Various Years*, Kerala State Planning Board, Trivandrum.

Govindan, Parayil (1996). "The 'Kerala model' of Development: Development and Sustainability in the Third World", *Third World Quarterly*, Vol. 17, No. 5: 941-957.

Harvey, David, (2005): *A Brief History of Neo-liberalism.* Oxford: Oxford University Press. Retrieved from https://www.business-standard.com/article/news-ani/kerala-launches-break-the-chain-mass-campaign-to-combat-coronavirus-120031700580_1.html Retrieved https://www.ideasforindia.in/profile/sm.html

https://www.theguardian.com/world/2020/may/14/the-coronavirus-slayer-how-keralas-rock-star-health-minister-helped-save-it-from-COVID-19

https://www.washingtonpost.com/world/aggressive-testing-contact-tracing-cooked-meals-how-the-indian-state-of-kerala-flattened-its-coronavirus-curve/2020/04/10/3352e470-783e-11ea-a311-adb1344719a9_story.html (Last accessed on June 9th 2020).

Huang, C., Wang, Y., Li, X., *et al.* (2020). "Clinical features of patients infected with 2019 novel coronavirus in Wuhan", China. *Lancet*, 395: 497.

Jin, Y.H., Cai, L., Cheng, Z.S., Cheng, H., Deng, T., Fan, Y.P., *et al.* (February 2020). "A rapid advice guideline for the diagnosis and treatment of 2019 novel coronavirus (2019-nCoV) infected pneumonia (standard version)". *Military Medical Research*, *7*(1): 4. doi:10.1186/s40779- 020-0233-6. PMC 7003341. PMID 32029004

Kumar, Gopa, G. (2012). *Civil Society-Politics Interface: The Kerala Experience*, New Delhi: Manak Publications Pvt. Ltd.

Nicola, M., Alsafi, Z., Sohrabi, C., Kerwan, A., Al-Jabir, A,, Iosifidis, C., Agha, M., Agha, R. (2020). "The Socio-Economic Implications of the Coronavirus and COVID-19 Pandemic: A Review", *International Journal of Surgery, 67*(4).

Nithya, N.R. (2013). "Impact of Globalization on 'Twin Pillars' of the Kerala Model: Readings from the Post Globalization Studies", *International Journal of Advanced Research in Management and Social Sciences,* Vol. 2, No. 12: 258-276.

Policy Brief: The Impact of COVID-19 on Women by UN (2020), Retrieved from https://www.unwomen.org/en/digital-library/publications/2020/04/policy-brief-the-impact-of-COVID-19-on-women

Rajan, Irudaya S. & Zachariah, K.C. (2019). "Emigration and remittances: New evidences from the Kerala migration Survey, 2018", *CDS Working Paper*, 483.

Rene Veron (2001). "The New Kerala Model: Lessons from Sustainable Development", *World Development*, Vol. 29, No. 4: 601-617.

Retrieved from http://documents.worldbank.org/curated/en/428451587390154689/pdf/Potential-Responses-to-the-COVID-19-Outbreak-in-Support-of-Migrant-Workers-April-21-2020.pdf

Retrieved from http://niti.gov.in/content/infant-mortality-rate-imr1000-live-births National Health Mission, 2020. Retrieved from: https://nhm.gov.in/images/ pdf/monitoring/crm/4thcrm/report/kerala.pdf#page11

Retrieved from https://ec.europa.eu/migrant-integration/news/COVID-19s-impact-on-migrant-communities?lang=de

Retrieved from https://www. thehindubusinessline.com/news/national/COVID-19-kerala-seesnew-cases-recoveries-at-new-single-day-highs/article31755071.

Retrieved from https://www.ilo.org/global/about-the-ilo/newsroom/news/WCMS_738742/lang--en/index.htm

Retrieved from https://www.ilo.org/wcmsp5/groups/public/@asia/@ro-bangkok/@sro-new_delhi/documents/publication/wcms_124657.pdf

Retrieved from https://www.ohchr.org/Documents/Publications/MigrationHR_and_Governance_HR_PUB_15_3_EN.pdf

Retrieved from https://www.social-protection.org/gimi/RessourcePDF.action?id=55654

Retrieved from https://www.theweek.in/wire-updates/national/2020/05/05/mds14-kl-expatriates-airport.html

Retrieved from https://www.un.org/en/un-coronavirus-communications-team/above-all-human-crisis-calls-solidarity

State Poverty Eradication Mission, Government of Kerala, 2020. Retrieved from: http://www.kudumbashree.org

The Hindu, May 6, (2020).

WHO (2020), Shared Responsibility, Global Solidarity: Responding to the socio-economic impacts of COVID-19.

World Health Organization Director-General's opening remarks at the media briefing on COVID-19—24 February 2020 Available at:https://www.who.int/dg/speeches/detail/who-directo r-general-s-opening-remarks-at-the-media-briefing-on-COVID-19—24-April-2020 (Accessed on February 26, 2020).

Worldometer, (2020). COVID-19 Coronavirus Pandemic, 2020 Available at: https://www.worldometers.info/coronavirus/ (Accessed on 2020, April 29).

Wu, Z., McGoogan, J.M. (2020). Characteristics of and Important Lessons from the Coronavirus Disease 2019 (COVID-19) Outbreak in China: Summary of a Report of 72,314 Cases from the Chinese Center for Disease Control and Prevention. JAMA 2020.

6
COVID-19 and Food Security Challenges in South Asia

Santhosh Mathew

Introduction

Food is one of the basic need and after this pandemic period, world is going to suffer food shortage according to the scholars. The novel coronavirus disease (COVID-19) is having an unprecedented impact around the world, both in health and socio-economic terms. By 11 April, 1.6 million cases and nearly 1,00,000 deaths had occurred globally (WHO, 11 April, 2020).

South Asia consists of eight countries and each country has its agricultural background that also has huge impact on the region's economy. Before modernisation, the main source of economy was agriculture and food production. The region was also known as most densely populated region in the world. Emerging economically developed countries of the region could be considered India and Bangladesh. But again these countries have their history of continuous struggle against poverty and unemployment.

During and after the COVID-19 lead pandemic, which is believed to be spread from China to the rest of the world, is a new threat in health sector and taking lives around the world. Economically high profile countries along with underdeveloped and poor nations around the globe are facing security threat from this virus and they are following the lockdown strategies to avoid coronavirus. South Asia is not different and also following the lockdown strategy, but the problem here is people who live by hand and mouth fearing that they would die out of hunger as this lockdown hampering their means of livelihood. Government is trying its best to support these people in need but corruption, mismanagement and lack of resources misleading the supportive activities. This chapter aims to find out the challenging facts on food security in South Asian region focusing on Bangladesh and India, during and after the pandemic.

Food Security and the Pandemic

Food insecurity refers to the lack of secure access to sufficient amounts of safe and nutritious food for normal human growth and development and an active and healthy life. For people to be food secure, food must be both consistently available and accessible in sufficient quantities and diversity and households must be able to utilize (store, cook, prepare and share) the food in a way that has a positive nutritional impact. [The fourth annual Global Report on Food Crises (GRFC 2020), 2020]

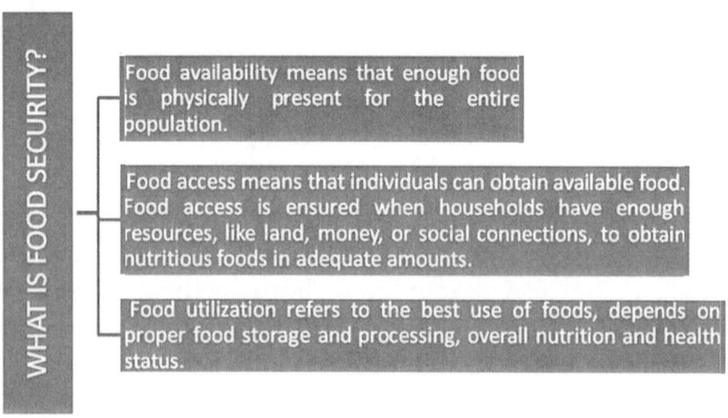

The influenza pandemic of 1918 killed more than 50 million people and caused more than 500 million infections worldwide.

This time coronavirus lead pandemic has already taken more than two and a half lakh people's lives around the world. In South Asian region, the number is not so high till now, comparative to the western developed countries and the African countries. But during this pandemic lockdown and quarantine period people are starving. The food system's dependence on the transportation system creates a major vulnerability. The transportation system has already shut down because of the pandemic, causing the movement of vital cargo to halt. The food system has become increasingly dependent on transportation to deliver its products over long distances. (How resilient is the United States' food system to pandemics? Andrew G. Huff & Walter E. Beyeler & Nicholas S. Kelley & Joseph A. McNitt, 2015).

Experts saying that, these countries may face an excruciating trade-off between saving lives or livelihoods or, in a worst-case scenario, saving people from the corona virus to have them die from hunger. To prevent these millions of people already facing food crises from succumbing to the virus or to its economic consequences, all actors need to mobilize and coordinate along a set of operational and strategic priorities.

The impact on health and nutrition: Supply of food and the availability of food disrupted by the lockdown that leads its impact on health and nutrition of the citizens. In South Asian region if we take example of Bangladesh, people who are living by hand and mouth always struggling to fulfil their basic health and nutrition needs. So the picture is more complex during the pandemic and if these people survive the pandemic, the survival will not be easy after pandemic as experts are indicating probable economic crisis and food shortage around the globe that will also affect the country like Bangladesh.

The impact on food availability: Due to pandemic, food production facing hindrance, in the peak period off cutting the ripen crops labour shortage causing problems. That is directly impacting on food availability. Peasants are facing economical loss as they are not able to sell the crops and vegetables in the market properly, at the same time vegetables and agro products are selling at a high price at towns and people are suffering, some aren't able to buy necessary foods. People of the low and middle income are suffering and passing their days with starvation.

The impact on displaced populations: This part of the region in the world, with a vast population is also facing displacement problems. People are migrating because of environmental, economic problems. During this COVID-19 pandemic period its adverse effect also seen in this kind of communities. People who are living in slums are at high risk. They are facing food availability as well as food accessibility problems. Along that they have to share washrooms and toilets with so many families, which may help the virus to spread through the entire slum community. Besides these health risk factors, the displaced people are facing economic problems as well. Their only means of income rely on housemaid work, driving work, day labour etc. hand to mouth jobs. Because of coronavirus now they are out of their work. Many do not even know they have their jobs or not.

Social tensions and conflict: Coronavirus lead insecurity enhances the social tensions that may lead social conflicts. Food shortage and starvation might cause security threats as the rate of smuggling, extortion may increase. Middle income people are facing physiological conflicts as they cannot go for taking rations and cannot ask for financial help as well. After this corona lead pandemic people are expected to facing job losses and it has already started in the western world. Around 1 lakh people in the USA only lost their jobs due to COVID-19. The rate will be high in the region like South Asia, especially in Bangladesh as it is estimated that only from Saudi Arabia around 2 lakh people will be returning after losing the jobs. So the social tension and conflict rate is quite high here.

Impacts on humanitarian assistance: This part of the globe humanitarian assistance and economic aid is essential for its overall development. Due to COVID-19 whole world will be facing economic challenges so there is definite possibilities that the region will be facing financial and humanitarian aids as well as assistances cut-off from the donor countries. Already USA cut-off its financial help for Afghanistan.

COVID-19 is marked as the pandemic of this century which is taking lives every day around the globe. Humankind will be winning over the fight against Coronavirus but the scars left by the virus will be taking long time to heal. International political economy will most probably be changed due to the aftermath. Food security of the countries completely rely on the steps and measures taken during and after pandemic. Countries like Bangladesh and India needs to be prepared as it is not too late yet.

Bangladesh

Bangladesh is a small country with huge population where most of the people living below the poverty line. Although world is going to experience food scarcity, Bangladesh has its positive vibe in this situation if the country take measures to focus on its agricultural sector as agriculture and food production has its huge contribution to country's gross domestic products. So it is high time to focus on agriculture with country's huge number of unemployed youths with government and private supervision. Agriculture is a sector that is strategically favourable to Bangladesh in regards its geographic location.

Due to COVID-19 people has to stay at home and it is affecting the country's economy. The largest contributing sector, readymade garments and industries are having trouble as importing countries are cancelling their orders due to pandemic. So this sector is facing challenge that could last for a long time as the after-effects of the pandemic would take long time to recover and restore the world situation. There is a possibility that the Political power and blame game will lead another world crisis like proxy war, limited war and in worst scenario, the actual war among the nations. So in the coming days, the economy of the world will face a downstream as expert's opinion. As a developing nation and most populated delta, Bangladesh needs to plan and organize its manpower to prepare itself for the after-effects of the pandemic.

Before the pandemic International development agencies have projected that Bangladesh will stand out by growing at record 8 per cent in 2019 and 2020, making it the fastest growing economy in Asia-Pacific as Bangladesh is seen as a model for growth even in this difficult global economic outlook. But the pandemic changes everything and the coming days are even more challenging where the country has to survive with its huge population and fight to minimize the hunger. Some steps government can take to minimize the starvation as primitive agro economy based country:

1. Encourage self-quarantined peoples to engage backyard and roof gardening. In this regard creative advertisements and effective techniques of gardening may help.
2. Government needs to take initiatives to ensure safe labour at the crop fields as well as ensure social distance during farming.
3. To tackle food scarcity after the pandemic, government can buy crops and vegetables from the primary producers and store.
4. Ensuring the engagement of youths to tackle the food insecurity

India and Food Security Challenges

The first confirmed case of coronavirus was detected on January 30, 2020, in the state of Kerala. As the pandemic was leaving deep scars around the globe, India was able to foresee the depth of the socio-economic hit that could be caused shortly by the pandemic. Fortunately, the government has handled the aftermath of the outbreak with the utmost presence of mind so far. The ordinary lives of every Indian took a turn when a nationwide lockdown was declared on 21 March, 2020, for 21 days. Even though, the Indian government has taken some measures to protect the lives of 1.3 billion people, the COVID-19 cases were increasing day by day. By 20 April, 2020, India had 15,712 confirmed cases and 507 deaths. After the 21 days of lockdown, the government has extended the lockdown until 3 May 2020, and restrictions of the least affected areas will be reviewed after 20 April, 2020. However, these draconian measures have a drastic effect on the lives of the ordinary people and local food systems.

With nearly 195 million undernourished people, India shares a quarter of the global hunger burden. Nearly 47 million or 4 out of 10 children in India are not meeting their full human potential because of chronic undernutrition or stunting. Stunting has consequences such as diminished learning capacity, poor school performance, reduced earnings and increased risks of chronic diseases. The impacts are multi-generational as malnourished girls and women often give birth to low birth-weight infants. There has also been an increase in the prevalence of overweight and obesity in children and adolescents in India, which has life-long consequences of non-communicable diseases in adulthood.

The government has large food security and anti-poverty programmes but there are critical gaps in terms of inclusion and exclusion errors. Women and girls are particularly disadvantaged. Despite the achievement of national food self-sufficiency, new challenges have emerged: Slowing agriculture growth, climate change, land degradation and shrinking bio-diversity. Large tracts of farmlands in India have become barren due to imbalanced fertiliser use and excessive use of a single fertiliser, urea. Along with these challenges, the most recent challenge faced by India due to COVID-19. The whole country is facing lockdown and trade is visibly interrupted, same happened to the farming and agriculture. The worst part of the countrywide lockdown was that it coincided with the country's peak harvesting time of a variety of crops of the season. Summer vegetables and fruits were ripened and ready to pick; wheat, paddy and barley crops were ready for harvest but all the farmers' hard work went to waste due to the sudden halt of the country.

As an agro-based country, India has its opportunity to tackle upcoming food shortage around the world. With a huge population and land area that is fertile, India can lead in the upcoming post-COVID-19 food security scheme. Food will be probable means of economic tool in upcoming days and India can play a vital role by taking necessary measures to ensure safe agricultural production during COVID-19 period. The government and supportive actors has taken measures to keep the agriculture and food sectors alive includes:

As the agricultural activities were at stake, the Indian Council of Agricultural Research (ICAR) became the focal point for managing activities in the country under the umbrella of the Ministry of Agriculture and Farmers Welfare and implemented the following actions. ICAR started to assess the possible impact on agriculture and allied sectors and provided measures to lower its negative effect on the local food system.

Crop-specific safety measures regarding harvesting, post-harvest operations were advised to the farmers by ICAR experts. Special attention was given to rabi season crops like wheat and barley as their harvesting time is around the corner. Experts also advised farmers to postpone wheat harvest which was about to give record harvest after the great monsoon.

Responsibilities were given to local field agencies to ensure hassle-free movement of agricultural produce and related machinery to reinstate farming activities.

Nevertheless, the government has guaranteed India's food security by the buffer stock which is overflowing in the warehouses of Food Corporation of India. Other measures by the Central Government includes: Official memorandum was released to support the poultry farmers who went into loss due to false connotation of poultry and the source of the virus. They were given monetary support of Rs.100 (USD 1.3) per bird as compensation for zero business. Food safety inspectors at local levels were instructed to inspect fresh goods such as vegetables, meat and fish products to prevent tarnishing on a daily basis. Many big multinational corporations also have stepped in along with the government to feed the daily wagers. Private-public-partnerships aided the government to raise money to tackle the situation which has invested in many strategies for mass testing, medical research and hand-washing campaigns. These collective and practical approach has proved positive so far to contain the virus.

Still there is challenges in front of the countries like Bangladesh and India. People are more emotional than rational or realistic. Religiously blind countries in the region is having trouble to tackle the contamination and maintaining social distances, as people are not ready to leave religious gatherings. Although government is trying its best to keep them safe and stay at home during the lockdown. The country like Bangladesh cannot stay at a state of lockdown for so long and recently the idea of herd immunity being told to apply, which will be more harmful in my opinion. Developing immune system is necessary, that needs nutritious food as well as availability and access of food. So food security is an important challenge in front of the countries like India and Bangladesh.

7

Accomplishing *Atma Nirbhar Bharat* amidst COVID-19 Pandemic

Prospects of Government Policies and Social Entrepreneurship

Iftekhar Alam

Introduction

Atmanirbhar Bharat or Self-Reliant India is a noble attempt to realise the past glory of our country which existed ever since ancient India till the colonization of the country. Once an economic power house of the world contributing to staggering 27 per cent of global GDP in 1700 to 23 per cent global GDP in 1800, dwindled to mere 3 per cent share in global GDP when Britishers invaded India owing to loot, deprivation and drain of wealth. Socio-cultural and psycho-social dimensions should be reviewed and revamped to start valuing the dignity of labour, significance of work by hand and shared gender roles in the society, and reinventing the culture of innovation and analytical mind to tap the vibrant energy and enthusiasm of youth in India which constitutes the highest in the world. India has the largest number of MSME, i.e., more than 6.5 crores can be used as a foundation for realising the dream of self-reliance. Another strength of our country is that it is agro-based economy, agriculture has always been the economic backbone of our country where more than fifty per cent of the workforce engaged in agriculture, and the brighter part is that they are least affected by the current pandemic and economic crisis. *Atmanirbhar Bharat* or Self-Reliant India is an umbrella term that encompasses empowerment, self-dependent, enablement and development. The term has wider implications on all development parameters of the country. India has shown unprecedented ability, strength and unrelenting spirit of self-reliance in COVID-19 pandemic. The Government of India has executed direct benefit transfers during the pandemic lockdown period amounted to approximately USD 4 billion (MoF, 2020). From witnessing high level of resilience among the people during the lock down to producing masks and Personal Protective Equipment (PPE) from miniscule to millions per day, every Indian stood in unison with the government to fight against this menace.

The Government of India has also announced pro-poor package of USD 23 billion to offer direct cash transfer, goods for basic consumption and cooking gas cylinders for free to the needy, especially to women, socially disadvantaged groups and the elderly (PMO, 2020). This stimulus is posed to bolster Indian economy through a well-organized reform under that flagship movement known as *Atmanirbhar Bharat Abhiyan,* i.e., Self-reliant India. This programme has a two-pronged approach, the first is to transfer direct cash to the poor in crisis and second to boost the manufacturing sectors to make it more competitive. The COVID-19 pandemic has triggered the need of required stimulus across the country.

This pandemic has created a huge burden on the already burdened healthcare infrastructure of the country, which is going to linger for a year or more. In order to ensure accessible, sustainable and good quality services, well designed strategies and required investments need to be made to tackle future pressures on healthcare systems in India. The diminishing GDP, 3.5 per cent in 2017 to 1.18 per cent in 2016 (MoHFW, 2019), India's spending in health sector stands the lowest compared to other countries, which calls for robust investment in this sector. Though

Ayushman Bharat scheme aims to provide free health coverage comprising of testing and treatment facilities to the 40 per cent of poor and vulnerable segment population, the remaining 60 per cent of the population has to bear all healthcare expenditure themselves (OECD, 2019). At the juncture, a judicious spending of resources and funds should be pushed in greenfield infrastructure that will accelerate the productivity and enhance purchasing power of the most distressed section of population namely the daily wage labourers and migrants. Sector need to be re-looked and reviewed for suitable reforms to make a holistic development. Consequently, these measures will restore the growth of economic parameters and create opportunities in the sectors like agro-business, micro, small and medium enterprises (MSMEs), defence, trade, commerce, industry etc. The five phases of *Atmanirbhar Bharat* formulated by the government are as follows (NPOI, 2020):

Phase-I: Businesses including MSMEs: India has the largest number of MSMEs in the world, which has a lot of potential to grow, provided it gets financial support. The financial stimulus initiated by the government will have a great impact on the sustainability and growth of this sector.

Phase-II: Poor, including migrants and farmers: This is the much-needed sector in terms of financial support. Skill Development and Youth Development Programme already initiated for rural youth training in vocational courses or job-oriented courses bear a huge impact in promoting livelihood. The vocational training to develop job-oriented skills are highly productive in promoting livelihood. Moreover, further fiscal support will be very useful in this sector, as it has a potential to alleviate poverty and deprivation.

Phase-III: Agriculture: This sector has always been the backbone of our economy, having the highest arable land in the world, agriculture has huge potential to grow in terms of productivity and variety if more areas through this financial stimulus come under irrigation. Half of the workforce livelihood is associated with agriculture, and it is one of the prominent contributors to country's GDP.

Phase-IV: New Horizons of Growth: New Horizon of growth inspires us to work harder in this so-called global village, where competition is high. Technological advancement is taking place in leaps and bounds, and India having respect in the software technology globally has huge potential to grow. Growth is an unending process and sky is the limit when it comes to technological advancement of our country.

Phase-V: Government Reforms and Enablers: At the backdrop of pandemic, the realisation of *Atmanirbhar Bharat* is a herculean task which will be possible only through bringing some reforms in the necessary sector. In an attempt to bring reforms in the governance of ease of doing business, labour reforms due to crisis and health sector reforms owing pandemic.

The current stimulus package has favourable impact on the broad sectors of economy:

(a) **Primary Sector:** The measures announced for the agricultural and allied sectors are highly productive. These reforms are designed to achieve the objective of "One Nation One Market" and assist India become the hub of "food factory of the world". Farmers through FPO can be engaged in the process of value addition of their produce. Also, through funding MGNREGA to the tune of Rs. 40,000 crore may assist in alleviating the repercussions of reverse migration. Fifty per cent of our workforce are engaged in Agriculture, which is an advantage as they are least affected by the pandemic.

(b) **Secondary Sector:** India has 6.5 crore MSMEs which is the largest number in the world. Utilising this huge opportunity, the Government offers Rs. 3 lakh crore collateral-free loan facility for MSMEs to boost the cash flow to the finance-starved sector and trigger the growth rate of economy. This measure will help sustain the labour-intensive industries and build manufacturing ecosystem in India which generates the second largest employment in India.

(c) **Tertiary Sector:** The government had initiated a wonderful teaching-learning resources through MOOC, Swayam etc. which is becoming more relevant during the pandemic:

(i) PM e-Vidya programme, national Digital Library and many more have built a uniform learning platform with farther and quick reach in the entire country. The online platform is not only supporting the learning processes of students but teachers as well, also the Faculty Development Programme, Webinars etc. are conducted online in Universities and Colleges, without further loss of teaching hours.

(ii) Digital India Campaign has also started yielding results as the use of rupee notes are mostly restricted by people due to coronavirus infection. Money transfer is just a click away from your mobile or laptop/PC etc.

(iii) Public expenditure on health especially in grassroot healthcare institutions such as Community Healthcare (CHC) and Primary Health Care (PHC) as well as other government hospitals in rural and urban areas have catered to community health needs. The Government of India has launched health sector programme, spending USD 2 billion to expand health infrastructure and COVID-19 testing capability (PMO, 2020).

Objectives for accomplishing the goal of *Atmanirbhar Bharat*

(a) Innovation should address the problem of a country, and find solution to address the grassroot need of the community in the remotest part of the country.

(b) Development model of India should provide service for all. No regional variation should be entertained, equal consideration should be given for both rural and urban areas.

(c) Valuing the dignity of labour.

(d) Boosting suitable technologies in sectors and industries where use of technology is unavoidable, it should not disrupt labour intensive industries.

(e) Giving preference to local finished goods for consumption over foreign goods to boost the local enterprise and local economy.

Government Policies

The government has formulated plethora of development policies and programmes that can propel the accomplishment of *Atmanirbhar Bharat Abhiyan* and to boost various sectors as well. Few schemes and programmes launched by the Government of India, are highlighted below:

(a) Digital India Mission (2 July, 2015): Making all government services electronically accessible and available to the people.
(b) Start-up India (16 January, 2016): To Promote entrepreneurial ecosystem in the country and especially in Higher Education Institutions (HEIs) through recent National Innovation and Start-up Policy in 2019.
(c) Stand Up India (5 April, 2016): Disbursement of Loans up to Rs. 10 lacs to 1 crore for establishing new companies for SCs/STs and Women Entrepreneurs as well.
(d) Jan Dhan Yojana (28 August, 2014): Enabling more people to access to financial services or banking services for financial empowerment.
(e) Skill India Mission (28 August, 2014): Developing skills among vibrant youth of the country.
(f) Make in India (28 September, 2014): Promoting manufacturing ecosystem in the country.
(g) Swachchh Bharat Mission (2 October, 2014): Striving for cleanliness and hygienic environment in the country.
(h) Sansad Adarsh Gram Yojana (11 October, 2014): Attaining socio-cultural development in the villages.
(i) Beti Bachao Beti Padhao (22 January, 2015): Empowering the girl child through education and protection and make them self-reliant.
(j) PM Mudra Yojana (8 April, 2015): Micro loan from Rs. 50 thousand to Rs. 10 lakh for small enterprises.

(k) Ujala yojana (1 May, 2015): Distribution of lost price LED bulbs to reduce electricity consumption.

(l) Smart city scheme (25 June, 2015): Developing 100 smart cities in the country from 2015 to 2020.

Economic Patriotism and Techno-nationalism

(a) **Fiscal stimulus:** Though the government policy has taken a conducive measure to provide financial support or fiscal stimulus to all the sectors, special attention should be given to those industries, which are dependent on China or other countries for the imports of necessary parts. Instead of importing those parts from China, the local industries should be encouraged by the government through special fiscal stimulus and all other technical and non-technical support.

(b) **Develop manufacturing ecosystem:** Government should have ownership on Industry, Commerce, Trade and Agriculture so that manufacturing ecosystem can be developed in the country.

(c) **Boost economic patriotism or Swadeshi:** It is high time we encourage economic patriotism by opting only local products over foreign products even at a little higher price to boost the national economy and local industrialists and entrepreneurs.

(d) **Techno-nationalism:** Our country should invent local technologies which are tailored to our local needs and demands, that assists our farmers and workers in remote areas as well. We should not be consuming foreign technologies without any urgent need or actual demand.

(e) **More funding for R&D:** Our country should increase more funding on R&D to satisfy the future prospects, compared to China (2.2%) and Israel (6%), India shells out 0.9 per cent of its GDP for its funding.

Not only Made in India but Made by India

Self-Reliant India Mission aims at checking import syndrome and managing fiscal deficits by exploring an alternative measure, by becoming "vocal for the local products and make them global", a clarion call by the Government of India to give preference to products made by India and not made in India only, and also make the product globally competitive in terms of quality and assurance. "The Self-Reliance neither signifies any exclusionary or isolationist strategies but involves creation of a helping hand to the whole world." Due consideration is given to the local products and local enterprise, in two phases, in the first phase, it will include sectors like medical, electronics, textiles, plastics and toys where local manufacturing and exports can be promoted and in second phase it will include products like gems and jewellery, pharma and steel, etc. These two phases have logically listed the sectors based on the necessity in the given circumstances and conditions. As you can see that due to pandemic medical field has taken precedence over other sectors followed by textiles and the like.

The Movement is braced on five pillars viz. Economy, Infrastructure, System, Vibrant Demography and Demand. This mission will concomitantly propel 'Make in India Initiative' that strives to accelerate manufacturing eco-system in the country.

Social, Culture, Education and Technology

(a) Socio-cultural aspects are the fundamentals to make a society self-reliant. To make India *Atmanirbhar*, socio-cultural scenario needs to be revamped. The idea of self-employment has been looked down upon in the society, the dignity of labour has not been respected due to myth circulating that work by hand is not dignified. Time has come to break these misconceptions, and encourage people who are self-employed. There should be culture of innovation, skill building and start-ups to enable livelihood promotion among the needy. The skill development programme and youth development schemes initiated by the government will further accelerate the process of *Atmanirbhar Bharat.* To develop a strong socio-cultural dimension, true nurturing should start in the formative years of childhood. The cognitive and psycho-social upbringing should be done through good schooling, good education in Universities and Colleges. The educational institutions should become the hub of building a good character and conduct.

(b) Education imparted by the Universities and Colleges should impart knowledge for creating scope and opportunities. The knowledge and skills should be career oriented, that makes the professional saleable in the market. Lack of proper education and mismatch between industry needs and educational institutes preferences will lead to lack of opportunities in the market. As we have seen that most of the Universities and Colleges give prime focus to education and less preference to research and innovation. This is completely obverse to the needs and expectations of industries. The Industries which are going to absorb the trained personnel give more focus to innovation, followed by research and education. Classroom teaching should not be confined to four walls, the students should be exposed to field practice, lab research etc. The outcome shall be directly applied to the field, and translational research should be given due importance by the educational institutes.

(c) Technology should be need-based and user friendly, it should be tailored that cater to the needs of both rural and urban areas. Technological inputs should be employed only in the critical sectors, which are in much need of it. Labour intensive industries should be preferred over technological intensive industries, there should be a balance in deciding the limits of technological inputs in the industry. It has been observed that more investments are made in high tech inputs covering the higher echelons of the society, and poor in remote areas are mostly neglected. One example shared by our resource person Shri Kamaljeet Ji who is a mentor based in New Delhi for start-up said that why there is no remote technology developed for farmer for the grass cutting machine who are vulnerable to many accidents or remote run water pumps etc. When remote run machines are so common these days or even mobiles used as remote for running home appliances being in the far away office. We need to look inwards before developing a technology, we should not become dumping grounds for multi-national companies as gullible consumer.

(d) The National Innovation and Start-up Policy 2019: The Government of India is giving a due importance and significance to the role played by students as well as teachers in the higher educational institutes in promoting the culture of innovation, incubation and start-ups, has formulated a well acclaimed policy. The National Innovation and Start-up Policy 2019 for students and faculty of Higher Education Institutions (HEIs) is a guiding framework to enable the institutes to actively engage students, faculties and staff in innovation and entrepreneurship related activities.

Social Entrepreneurship & Start-up

Social entrepreneurshiphas gained more prominence in recent decades in addressing social needs (Peredo and Chrisman, 2006). Social Entrepreneurship is a process which involves innovation and risk along with other factors of production engaged by an entrepreneur in launching a start-up by finding the solution of problem and by engaging innovation and technology to create economic, social and environmental value. Start-ups should adopt need oriented innovation, solution-based technology and problem-solving approach to generate economic value (Schuler and Cording 2006). The truth is many social entrepreneurs face many hurdles and failures before succeeding in the venture, owing to lack of financial support, marketing decisions, or shortage of demand among the consumers. Social Entrepreneurs showcase their skills and competence in converting challenges into opportunities, see a solution in problem, think out of box in realizing their dreams.

This unprecedented crisis has taken a heavy toll on the entrepreneurial business models and approaches creating a dent in the opportunities available in this sector. While huge number of start-ups have endured during the pandemic, COVID-19 has also showed some silver lining, by increasing entrepreneurial activities into new ventures. Globally, organizations and people have responded to the crisis responsibly. Individuals and start-ups producing masks, sanitizers, PPE kits etc. promoting local producers and strengthening local economies have eventually made them adapt to new-normal (De Cuyper, Kucukkeles & Reuben, 2020).

(a) **Steer Economic Growth and Social Development:** The role of social entrepreneurship and start-ups has been evolving ever since, it gained attention in the discourse of business studies, particularly on the approach of self-sufficiency and self-reliance. It became a significant tool of generating business opportunities and employment through innovation and technology. It became the forefront in the growth of economies and brought about a paradigm shift in creation of innovative products and services that solve the problems of consumers, thereby enhancing their quality of living. Social Entrepreneurs attract funding from various sources viz. through crowd funding to the loans from the bank to establish their venture and engage in value creation at the local economy. It has a potential to accelerate the national economy and industrial ecosystem of the country.

(b) **Bolster Local Economy and Infrastructure:** Social Entrepreneurship helps in eradicating economic and regional disparities by establishing value addition centres in the remote areas or at the production areas and create income opportunities for the local communities. This will boost local economy and local infrastructure development such as roads, public transportation, health facilities, educational institutions etc. resulting into vibrant economy.

(c) **Create and Redistribute Wealth Equally:** Social Entrepreneurs are engaged in business with the people at the Bottom of Pyramid (Prahalad, 2002) earning 1$ per day according to renowned social scientist Prahalad (2002) which constitutes around 4 billion people globally, and stimulate fair redistribution of wealth and incomes for the interest of the country through a large population covering a larger geographical area and thus offering benefits to larger sections of society. An enterprise contributes to increasing the Gross Domestic Product (GDP) and income per resident, which results in economic growth.

(d) **Explore the Unexplored Areas:** While seeking new business opportunities by finding a solution of people in need, Social Entrepreneurs explore and exploit various possibilities encouraging the active mobilization of resources, networks, funds and skills. They contribute to new products and services and develop new markets which grow an economy, most often neglected by capitalists.

(e) **Enhance quality of life:** Improving the quality of life of a population is a characteristic of a country's economic development. Social Entrepreneurs play a vital role in improving the quality of our communities and individuals' lifestyles; they adopt innovations in the production of vast and various goods and services on a large-scale to reduce the cost. The goal is to offer a better product or service at a irrationalized cost with an aim to achieve social needs.

(f) **Encourage Innovation:** A social entrepreneur is person who takes the risk of applying innovative ideas in finding a product that acts as solution to the targeted consumers' problem. An entrepreneur is flexible to the change and tries to maximize profits through innovation and suitable technology. When company business approaches are driven by the evolution of suitable technology, supporting entrepreneurship in a motivating, innovating and stimulating environment will result in socio-economic development. The decision-makers should prioritize the responsibility to lead and channelize entrepreneurship projects through sectors that are part of the development strategy.

(g) **Check Migration:** The opportunity available in local market due to local enterprise and start-up, will stimulate local job demands will be fulfilled and people will not be forced to migrate to big cities, a dream come true for *Atmanirbhar Bharat*, that wishes no forced migration of unskilled and semi-skilled labourers shall take place in the country. As most of the social entrepreneurship and start-ups prefer to establish their plant in outskirts of the city or remote area.

(h) **Enhance Local Economy:** Social entrepreneurship and start-ups in the local area will create value added service centres in the local area itself. For example, instead of supplying milk to dairies, the farmers engaged in livestock rearing can form their own cooperative which can start their own collected centres and chilling centres, this value addition of milk will lead to wealth creation and more flow of money in the local economy.

Challenges in the way of accomplishing *Atmanirbhar Bharat*

(a) During COVID-19, more than 30 million or 3 crores have experienced reverse migration, 1.5 crore were unemployed people. Total 4.5 crore in remote areas are unemployed.

(b) Bringing more land under irrigation, currently only 7 crore hectares out of 16 crore hectares arable land are under irrigation, this can be achieved through channelizing river water resources.

(c) Making the livelihood of farmers, by engaging them in value addition, through rural enterprise, FPO etc.

(d) Cash flow hurdles: The package of Rs. 20 lakh crore comprises both fiscal and monetary measures, the latter being in the nature of credit guarantees and liquidity infusions into banks and other financial sector institutions rather than the economy *per se*.

(e) Majority of the packages are liquidity measures that are supposed to be transmitted by RBI to Banks and Banks to Citizens. This transmission may not be smooth.

(f) Dwindling Demand: The lockdown has led to reduction in aggregate demand, which are craving for fiscal stimulus is needed. However, the current package, is relying overwhelmingly on credit infusion to boost the economy, has to acknowledge that investment will be boosted only when people across income segments have affordability and propensity to spend.

(g) Disruption of Backward and Forward Linkages: The MSME sector which rely heavily on domestic economy may face a shortage of demand, and its production may soon dwindle down.

(h) Increasing Fiscal Deficit: As it is mentioned that the stimulus package is around 10 per cent of India's GDP, its financing would be difficult as the government is concerned about checking the fiscal deficit.

(i) Difficulty in Mobilising Finances: "The government seeks a disinvestment to mobilise the finances for the plan" (Drishti, 2020).

Conclusion

The idea of *Atmanirbhar Bharat* was very much part and parcel of Indian society since time immemorial. It is high time we realise this wonderful dream of self-reliance through self-empowerment and dignity. The unprecedented economic stimulus impregnated in Indian economy by the Government of India will start showing its results sooner or later. The clarion call of *Atmanirbhar Bharat* by the Government of India will never be fulfilled unless we become economic patriots or *Swadeshi*, and give preference to local products over foreign products, this will strengthen the backbone of our economy. Such culture has been very common in other countries, where the citizens never prefer foreign product. We have to be very transparent and firm in following these words with full determination and honesty. The phase-wise development of this *Atmanirbhar Bharat* Movement is orderly and logical. The culture of innovation should be rejuvenated and Universities and Colleges should become the hub of incubation centres and builders of entrepreneurial ecosystem. Translational research to bring lab discoveries to field and commercialization of ideas should be encouraged. All the educational institutions should become the citadel of *Atmanirbhar Bharat*, and discharge its socially conscious responsibility of innovation, research and knowledge generation.

References

De Cuyper, L., Kucukkeles, B. & Reuben, R. (2020). Discovering the real impact of COVID-19 on entrepreneurship. *World Economic Forum*, 19th June, 2020. https:// www.weforum.org/agenda/2020/06/how-COVID-19-will-change-entrepreneurial-business/

Drishti (2020). Atma Nirbhar Bharat Abhiyan: Challenges https://www.drishtiias.com/daily-updates/daily-news-editorials/atma-nirbhar-bharat-abhiyan-challenges accessed on 27-06-2020.

Drishti, (2020). Atma Nirbhar Bharat and Economic Stimulus https://www.drishtiias.com/daily-updates/daily-news-analysis/atmanirbhar-bharat-and-economic-stimulus accessed on 27-06-2020.

MoF (2020). https://pib.gov.in/PressReleasePage.aspx?PRID=1616022

MoHFW (Ministry of Health and Family Welfare) (2019). *Public Health Expenditure*, New Delhi: MoHFW, Government of India, URL: https://pib.gov.in/Pressreleaseshare.aspx?PRID=1580410

NPOI (2020). National Portal of Indiahttps://www.india.gov.in/spotlight/building-atmanirbhar-bharat-overcoming-COVID-19 accessed on 27-06-2020.

OECD (Organisation for Economic Co-operation and Development) (2019), *OECD Health Statistics 2019*, France: OECD, URL: https://stats.oecd.org/Index.aspx?DataSetCode=SHA

Peredo. A.M., Chrisman, J.J. (2006). "Towards a theory of community-based enterprise". *Acad Manag Rev, 31*(2): 309-328.

PMO (2020). https://pib.gov.in/PressReleasePage.aspx?PRID=1618955

Prahalad, C. & Hart, S. (2002). "The fortune at the bottom of the pyramid". *Strategy and Business*, (48): 1-23.

Schuler, D.A., Cording, M. (2006). "A corporate social performance—corporate financial performance behavioural model for consumers". *Acad Manag Rev., 31*(3): 540-558.

8
CSR Practices of Companies to Tackle the Coronavirus Pandemic
A Descriptive Study

D. Divyaprabha

Introduction

Historically, corporations took a step back during crises. However, as the role of business in society continues to evolve and stakeholder capitalism becomes mainstream, businesses are rising to the challenge. As the coronavirus pandemic has now spread to nearly every country in the world and has claimed thousands of lives, companies were among the first to step up, pledging more than 80 per cent of early funds to coronavirus response efforts. Multinational Companies, Entrepreneurs, businesses and multimillionaire philanthropists are pledging their support, in various ways. From manufacturing sanitizers to financial contributions, from working along with public bodies to supporting their employees and customers during this crisis, companies are undertaking a host of activities to handle this critical situation.

A great many large companies talk about having a social purpose and set of values, or about how much they care for their employees and other stakeholders. Now is the time for them to make good on that commitment. Research suggests that people only truly believe that their company has a purpose and clear values when they see management making a decision that sacrifices short-term profitability for the sake of adhering to those values. It is clear that the Coronavirus pandemic is putting Corporate Social Responsibility of companies to an acid test. The way companies respond to this test is a defining moment that will define their legacy for decades.

Objective of the Study

To identify the corporate contributions (Financial and Non-financial) around the world to combat the coronavirus pandemic.

Research Methodology

This descriptive research study was done using the secondary data collected.

Here is a round-up of some of the activities and initiatives undertaken by private-sector organizations that are helping to combat the coronavirus pandemic.

The various MNCs' activities undertaken by MNCs include:

- Microsoft announced that they will keep paying the hourly workers who support their campus. Also, Microsoft's Bing team has launched a web portal to track its progress worldwide. The website provides up to date infection statistics for each country and the interactive map developed allows users to click on the specific country to see the specific number of cases and related articles from a variety of publishers. Apart from this, Microsoft is making an initial $1 million anchor donation to COVID-19 Response Fund (CRF) to help launch this effort immediately.
- Google established a COVID-19 fund that enables all temporary staff and vendors, globally, to take paid sick leave if they have potential symptoms of COVID-19, or can't come into work because they're quarantined. They have also made their video conferencing service, Hangouts Meet, available for all G-suite customers until July 1, 2020.

- Loom, a video recording and sharing service has made Loom Pro free for teachers and students at K-12 schools, universities, and educational institutions. They have also removed the recording limit on free plans and have cut the price for Loom Pro in half.
- Shine Distillery in Portland started making and giving away hand sanitizer in an acute shortage.
- The Barbara Bush Foundation for Family Literacy's in-house team of literacy and education experts has created a toolkit of high-quality online resources that can be used anytime, anywhere, helping parents navigate the vast amount of available options.
- LinkedIn is opening up 16 of its learning courses for free. Courses that provide tips on how to stay productive, build relationships when you're not face-to-face, use virtual meeting tools and balance family and work dynamics in a healthy way.
- Adobe is giving higher education and K-12 institutional customers of their Creative Cloud apps the ability to request temporary "at-home" access for their students and educators. This is being granted through May 31, 2020 at no additional cost and is available globally.
- One Dine, a restaurant payment technology solutions provider is offering a free Tap & Pay Touchless Payment system to restaurants during the COVID-19 crisis.
- Amazon, the commerce giant is hiring 1,00,000 more workers and giving raises to current staff to deal with coronavirus demands.
- Sweetgreen, an American fast casual restaurant chain that serves salads has announced it will start dedicating Outpost operations and teams to support "those on the front lines" (meaning hospital workers and medical personnel) by delivering free salads and bowls to hospitals in the cities it serves.

- & Pizza's, an American fast casual pizza restaurant chain has notified its employees last week that the company is offering free, unlimited pizzas to them and their immediate families, as well as to hospital workers who show identification. The company is also raising hourly pay by $1 and 14 days of "health and safety pay" to employees who have tested positive or who have come in contact with someone with coronavirus.
- Everytable, a Los Angeles-based café launched a helpline to ensure that everyone in its market has access to healthy meals during this time.
- Starbucks has extended its mental health benefits. In partnership with Lyra Health, Starbucks is offering its partners personalized, confidential mental healthcare, 20 free in-person or video sessions every year for partners and each of their eligible family members, online scheduling with most providers available within two weeks, and access to a provider network of mental health therapists and coaches.
- UberEats and DoorDash have waived commission fees for independent restaurant partners, while Postmates has launched a pilot programme for small businesses that temporarily waives commission fees for businesses in the SF Bay Area.
- Dolce & Gabbana announced that it has partnered with Humanitas University to fund a coronavirus research project.
- Giorgio Armani has donated $1.43 million dollars to four hospitals in Rome and Milan, as well as to the Civil Protection Agency.
- French luxury group Kering, which owns brands like Gucci and Bottega Veneta, has donated 2 million euros to help the fight against the coronavirus outbreak.
- Alphabet (Google's parent company) created a COVID-19 fund to provide sick leave to affected workers globally, including all temporary staff, contractors, and vendors. Alphabet Inc has donated more than $800 million (645

million pounds) in funds towards producing medical supplies used to fight COVID-19, and in ad credits to government and health organizations and businesses. The company is also working with Magid Glove and Safety to produce 2 million to 3 million face masks, and will financially support efforts to boost the production capacity for lifesaving medical devices and personal protective equipment.

- Amazon through its Amazon Web Service is providing assistance to WHO and its Epidemic Intelligence from Open Source initiative in tracking trends in epidemiology through artificial intelligence from around the world. Amazon has also created a $25M fund to help its delivery drivers and seasonal workers cope with coronavirus, and a $5M dollar fund to help affected small businesses in Seattle.
- Apple has donated in excess of $15 million to help support treatment of the sick and mitigate the economic impact of the crisis. This has included substantial donations in Italy. The company also supports two-to-one corporate matching for any employee donations that relate to coronavirus. The company is presently sourcing and donating millions of masks to health professionals in the U.S. and Europe. Apple has also closed all of its stores outside of Greater China, and will re-open in several weeks after an extensive deep cleaning. All employees will be paid for the duration of the closure.
- McDonald's has stated that it will cover sick leave for any employees at corporate-owned locations who are asked to quarantine for two weeks. As the country faces a task ensuring people stay indoor and avoid social contact, quick service restaurant chain McDonald's launched its global social media campaign in India, splitting the letter M in its logo.
- Walmart has deployed an Emergency Leave programme, which provides time-off for employees depending on various coronavirus threat levels. On March 26, the Walmart Foundation announced $10 million to nine

organizations that support food banks, schools and senior meal programmes. The organizations, though different, share an overarching goal: providing access to food for underserved populations —a mission taking on even greater urgency in response to the novel coronavirus.

- Uber announced they will provide 14 days of sick pay for drivers or delivery workers—technically considered independent contractors who have not previously qualified for paid leave or benefits —who are sick with the coronavirus or are required to be isolated.
- Bank of America, Goldman Sachs, Bank of New York Mellon, Citigroup, JP Morgan Chase, Morgan Stanley, State Street, and Wells Fargo have stopped all stock buybacks for the 2nd quarter in order to maintain their solvency and liquidity for customers during the outbreak.
- Comcast, Charter, Verizon, Google, T-Mobile and Sprint have signed a pledge to keep Americans internet-connected for the next 60 days, even if people cannot afford to pay.
- Delta, a major airline of the United States has taken proactive and voluntary steps to help customers have a healthy flying experience. This includes a high-grade, EPA registered disinfectant used on all flights, a new fogging process often used by the food industry, state-of-the-art air circulation systems, more hand sanitizer, more gloves for our flight attendants, and additional sanitation procedures for inbound catering equipment at international gateways. Delta's CEO is forgoing his salary for the year to try and diminish layoffs.
- Disney has closed its parks and cruises in response to coronavirus. They have promised to continue paying their employees during the closure, and will give refunds to all those who had planned on visiting. In order to offer better pay to its employees, Disney has decided to reduce the salaries of its vice presidents by 20 per cent, senior vice presidents by 25 per cent, and executive vice presidents and above by 30 per cent effective from 5 April, 2020 till there is a substantial recovery in business.

- Hilton is waiving cancellation fees to their hotels for people in coronavirus infected countries. Hilton is also assisting local and national governments to provide housing for first responders and healthcare workers and also have been donating excess food to local pantries.
- Salesforce, an American cloud-based software company offering enterprise applications focused on customer service, marketing automation, analytics, and application development has created a $1.5 million dollar coronavirus fund for affected citizens in San Francisco.
- U-Haul, an American moving equipment and storage rental company, has announced 30 days of free self-storage to all college students who have been impacted by schedule changes at their universities.
- LVMH, the parent company of Christian Dior, Guerlain and Givenchy, is helping French health authorities by manufacturing hand sanitizers and providing it to them for free. LVMH said it will use all the production facilities of its perfumes and cosmetics brands to produce large quantities of hydroalcoholic gel, or hand sanitizer.
- NBC Universal, the leading American media and entertainment company is now offering its newest movies including. "The Hunt" and "The Invisible Man" for affordable rates on demand. NBC Universal is also making MSNBC and CNBC available, in partnership with its distribution partners, to all their video customers, regardless of the packages to which they subscribe.
- Restaurants like Ideal Bite Community Kitchen are donating food to organizations like Cass Community Social Services (CCSS), a non-profit organization working with at-risk communities in Detroit.
- Esri, the world's biggest location intelligence company, which is always at the forefront in disaster mapping and helping agencies with data gathering, has designed a special COVID-19 ArcGIS Hub to gather and share relevant

information from all across the globe. Esri is involved in attempting to help with the COVID-19 planning and response efforts by sharing its dashboards, apps, information and data for free.

- Alibaba, the Chinese multinational has provided $340 million in Google ad credits to small and medium businesses active on its platform and $250 million in ad grants. So far, African countries have recorded low rates of coronavirus infection. But Jack Ma, the billionaire founder of Chinese e-commerce giant Alibaba, is taking no chances; through his foundation, he is donating 1.1 million testing kits, 6 million masks, and 60,000 protective suits and face shields. They are all being sent to Ethiopia first, from where they will be sent out to every other country on the African continent.
- Swiss pharmaceutical giant Roche has started shipping coronavirus tests to the US and plans to get at least 4,00,000 out every week. Its fully automated tests are capable of delivering up to 960 sets of results every eight hours using one of its powerful analysis machines. The test kits are destined for around 30 labs that have a broad geographic reach and high patient impact.
- Facebook has said it will donate $20 million to support coronavirus relief efforts. The new COVID-19 Community Help hub of Facebook will allow people to request or offer help to those impacted by the coronavirus outbreak, as well as donate to non-profit fundraisers.

Companies in India across sectors are pitching in to help the government and citizens fight the COVID-19 pandemic

- From making masks and sanitisers to contributing funds, many Indian companies have united to help citizens and government fight the virus, which is gradually spreading across the country.
- For instance, Diageo India has pledged to produce around 3,00,000 litres of bulk hand sanitiser across 15 of its

manufacturing units in the country to help cope with the demand for the product. It also plans to donate 5,00,000 litres of Extra Neutral Alcohol (ENA) to the sanitiser manufacturing industry to enable the production of more than two million units of 250 ml bottle sanitisers. Diageo India is also planning to support the hospitality sector with Rs. 3 crore as health insurance cover for bartenders. Apart from that, it also plans to donate 1,50,000 masks to five state public departments.

- Metals and mining giant Vedanta Ltd. on Sunday announced setting up of a Rs. 100 crore fund to combat the coronavirus outbreak. The fund will be utilised to provide preventive healthcare to daily wage workers, company employees and contract workers in and around various plants of the company.
- Mukesh Ambani's Reliance Industries Limited (RIL) has also pledged to support the people and government in fighting the novel coronavirus crisis. It announced via a press release that Sir HN Reliance Foundation Hospital in collaboration with the BMC has set up a dedicated 100-bedded centre at Seven Hills Hospital in Mumbai, Maharashtra. The HN Reliance Foundation Hospital has also offered to set up medical facilities to quarantine travellers from other countries. It has also offered initial support of Rs. 5 crore to the Maharashtra Chief Minister's Relief Fund.

In addition, Reliance Foundation will provide free meals to people across various cities in partnership with NGOs during the crisis situation. The company announced that it is enhancing production capacities to produce 1,00,000 face masks a day along with a large number of other protective equipments to help health workers and medical professionals. It will also help in providing a communication hub for all lessons in a school year, with free storage available for individuals and teams. Apart from that, Reliance also announced free fuel for all emergency service vehicles in the country. Reliance Retail has also announced longer hours from 7 am to 11 pm at its outlets for customers.

- India-based online payment company Paytm has announced to contribute Rs. 500 crore to Prime Minister's Citizen Assistance and Relief in Emergency Situations Fund (PM CARES Fund) to fight against coronavirus. The company is also contributing up to Rs. 10 for every payment transaction using the Paytm app and instruments. The money would be directly transferred to the PM CARES Fund.
- Hero Cycles has announced that the company is setting aside Rs. 100 crore as a contingency fund to address and mitigate the impact of the COVID-19 outbreak on the company's partners and the community at large. According to a statement by Hero Cycles, the contingency fund will be put to use as and when required to mitigate the impact of COVID-19 situation on employees, suppliers, customers and communities across India. Hero Cycles has also reached out to the governments in states where it has major facilities (Punjab, Bihar and Uttar Pradesh) to extend any help required by authorities in addressing the crisis.
- Another major firm Mahindra and Mahindra has started working on making ventilators for COVID-19 patients. Anand Mahindra, the chairman of the group, also announced that "Mahindra Holidays resorts will be offered to government as temporary care facilities. The Mahindra Foundation has created a fund to assist the hardest hit in our value chain small businesses and the self-employed" Mahindra added. He said he would contribute 100 per cent of his salary and gradually increase collections in the fund to assist small-scale businesses.
- The Godrej Group and other FMCG players like Hindustan Unilever and Patanjali are reducing prices of soaps and hygiene products. They are also ramping up production of such items to fulfil demand.
- Chinese tech giant Xiaomi also said on Monday that it will deliver imported N-95 masks and hazmat suits, which it will donate to hospitals across the country to help medical professionals.

- Leading software company Icertis, in partnership with the Pune Municipal Corporation (PMC), has decided to contribute Rs. 25 lakh to tackle COVID-19.
- DCB Bank, which is a private scheduled commercial lender, has committed Rs. 1 crore as part of CSR for intervention and measures to manage the outbreak of COVID-19 in India."The bank will engage with various agencies and partners to manage the response to COVID-19 in India. "It aims to deploy this fund within the next 3 months", the bank said in a statement.
- In a bid to keep its staff motivated amid the coronavirus outbreak, the country's biggest lender State Bank of India (SBI) has set up a quick response team (QRT) to ensure the safety of its employees. The bank has set up a helpline number manned by doctors and psychologists to assist its staff and employees to deal with the coronavirus outbreak as well as stress and anxiety related to this.
- India's Biggest industrial group, The Tata's have contributed Rs. 500 crore for manufacturing Personal Protective Equipment (PPE) for the medical personnel on the frontlines, Respiratory systems for treating increasing cases, Testing kits to increase per capita testing, Setting up modular treatment facilities for infected patients, Knowledge management and training of health workers and the general public.

Conclusion

As society struggles with the profound implications of coronavirus, corporations have a responsibility to step up and help support the government in taking action. As the function within companies which has direct relationships with non-profit partners and the communities they are part of, Corporate Social Responsibility (CSR) professionals should be on the frontlines helping urgently with funding and solutions in kind.

References

https://www.crn.com/news/cloud/microsoft-giving-priority-on-azure-capacity-to-coronavirus-response-effort

https://corporate.walmart.com/newsroom/2020/03/26/where-its-going-walmarts-25-million-COVID-19-commitment https://www.livemint.com/companies/news/coronavirus-mcdonald-s-splits-logo-to-promote-social-distancing-11585028681401.html

https://www.computerworld.com/article/3533361/17-ways-apple-is-responding-to-coronavirus.html

https://www.firstpost.com/health/coronavirus-outbreak-amazon-ceo-jeff-bezos-to-help-who-in-providing-coronavirus-test-kits-8197571.html

https://in.reuters.com/article/uk-health-coronavirus-alphabet/google-parent-alphabet-to-donate-800-million-in-response-to-coronavirus-crisis-idINKBN21F05J

https://www.uber.com/in/en/coronavirus/

https://news.delta.com/coronavirus-deltas-vigilance-safety-customers-and-employees-continues-who-declares-pandemic https://www.firstpost.com/health/coronavirus-outbreak-disneys-bob-iger-to-forego-salary-new-ceo-bob-chapek-will-take-pay-cut-8209191.html

https://www.usatoday.com/story/money/2020/03/26/coronavirus-furloughs-job-cuts-hilton-ceo-forgoing-salary/2922894001/

https://www.salesforce.com/blog/2020/03/letter-to-our-customers.html

https://edition.cnn.com/2020/03/13/us/uhaul-college-students-coronavirus-trnd/index.html

https://corporate.comcast.com/press/releases/nbcuniversal-news-networks-vital-programming-coronavirus-pandemic

https://www.geospatialworld.net/blogs/initiatives-by-geospatial-companies-to-curb-coronavirus/

https://techcrunch.com/2020/03/31/facebook-launches-a-global-version-of-its-community-help-feature-in-response-to-the-COVID-19-pandemic/

https://energy.economictimes.indiatimes.com/news/oil-and-gas/coronavirus-vedanta-ltd-announces-rs-100-cr-fund-to-fight-pandemic/74793557

https://techgraph.co/inside/coronavirus-update-paytm-to-contribute-rs-500-crore-to-pm-cares-fund/

https://auto.ndtv.com/news/coronavirus-pandemic-hero-cycles-allocates-rs-100-crore-contingency-fund-2199803

https://www.indiatoday.in/india/story/coronavirus-india-tata-trusts-five-hundred-crore-covid19-pandemic-1660732-2020-03-28

9
Impact of COVID-19 on Consumer Behaviour in Automobile Industry

Lijo Mon L.

Introduction

Consumer behaviour has assumed paramount importance in the automobile industry in general. It has opened several challenges to the automobile manufacturers and dealers in formulating effective and competitive promotional strategies for growth and acceptance in the market. The term consumer behaviour is defined as the behaviours that the consumers display in looking for, purchasing, using, evaluating and eliminating products and services that they expect will satisfy their needs. Thus, consumer behaviour focuses on how individuals make decisions to spend their available resources like time, money and effort on consumption related items. This includes the 5 W's; what they buy, why they buy it, when they buy it, where they buy it from, and how often they buy it.

The Indian automobile industry started off by assembling vehicles in the pre-independence era. It encompasses commercial vehicles (CV), multi-utility vehicles (MUV), passenger cars, two-wheelers (2W), three-wheelers (3W), tractors and auto components. Automobile industry in India continues to be in its infancy but growing rapidly. The opportunities within the automobile industry in India are attracting the big names with big purses and they are investing rapidly in infrastructure, design and development, and marketing. Indian automobile industry is home for the biggest motorcycle manufacturer, the second largest two-wheeler manufacturer, and fifth largest commercial vehicle manufacturer within the world. The Customer Relationship Management (CRM) is a well-defined series of functions, skills, processes and technologies which together allow organizations to manage customers more profitably. The automobile industry is the fastest growing sector of India. The increase in demand of automobiles in this date of time is due to the safety measures adopted by the public. The Indian auto industry through its various forms of transport facilities, provides the scope for optimum utilization of resources which are scattered throughout the country and also to disseminate the benefits of development in the far-flung areas.

However, the automobile industry in India is still tormented by a number of weaknesses in contrast to the firms in other Asian countries such as China, Thailand etc. Even now in India passenger cars are viewed as luxury products subject to high taxations. Though the present passenger car industry offers a large variety of modern world class vehicles and depicts dramatic changes in safety measures and emission levels. Even though all these are there, the automobile industry has conquered great heights in Indian markets.

The recent growth proliferation of the consumer durable sector in India has extended its outreach not only to urban but rural areas also. The high elasticity of demand for durable goods is mainly attributable to the fact that consumer durables are high priced and can be used for a long term period. So it is imperative to conduct a study to explore, understand and evaluate motives and purchase motives which affect consumer buying behaviour for durables in the present scenario.

In today's world, the bottom line of a firm's marketing strategies and tactics is to make profits and contribute to the growth of the company. Consumer satisfaction, quality and retention are global issues that affect organizations. It is not possible to anticipate and react to consumer's needs and desires without a complete understanding of consumer behaviour. Discovering consumer's current needs is a complex process but it can generally be accomplished by direct consumer research. It is not easy to win new automobile users, and it is becoming accepted that there is a strong link between automobile user's satisfaction, consumer's retention and profitability.

These are the various reasons for the changes in perception of consumers of automobiles and levels of satisfaction. To be a successful marketer, it is absolutely essential to study the perceptions of the prospective buyers and track their interests.

Objectives of the Study

- To comprehend the buying behaviour of consumers who are interested in automobiles.
- To determine various factors that significantly influence consumer behaviour which further impact purchasing process and decisions.
- To investigate the change in buying behaviour due to the effect of COVID-19 on automobiles.
- To compare the behaviours of rural and urban consumers on automobiles during COVID-19 using critical ratio.

Review of Literature

Valarmathi, A. (2015), This study was used to identify the factors that influenced the buying behaviour of two-wheeler bikes among students in Tripura. To empirically prove that there are students' influence in a purchase decision for two wheelers; simple percentage and factor analysis had been used in this study. And factor analysis yielded two factors which had empirically proved that there was an influence on students' purchase decision of two-wheelers. Their two-wheeler purchases were driven by different factors such as after sales service, price and new models, etc. It was found that regions had strong influence on better look & style, good mileage, pick-up and speed, easy maintenance, after sales service, price and new models of students buying behaviours.

Priyanka Jain (2015), This research analysed the satisfaction of the customer towards two wheelers. The study was restricted only to New Delhi. A total of 100 consumers of online, surveyed with structured questionnaires. Statistical analysis was done such as percentage analysis. India is one of the largest manufacturers and producers of two-wheelers in the world. The preference of the consumers clearly signifies that their importance of family and friends influenced their purchase, the additional facilities expected, and many.

Shanthi and Sakthivel Murugan (2014), The focus of this research was to study the women consumer awareness, preferences and purchase decision of two-wheelers in metro cities like Chennai, Mumbai, Delhi and Kolkata. Also, the study aims to examine the influence of regions on women consumers upon their preference, attitude, decision making and satisfaction. A survey was conducted and 400 completed questionnaires were used in data analysis, i.e., 100 in each four metro cities. The findings revealed that the perception of women consumers towards the two-wheeler purchase decision differed widely.

Keshav. Y. Shinde and Samadhan K. Khamkar (2014), It had been found from their survey that most of the young individuals preferred bikes that are aesthetically appealing and cost-effective. At the same time those who preferred geared bikes, had majorly two reasons, mainly better control and better aesthetics, while those who preferred non-geared bikes were of the opinion that it was easy to ride non-geared bikes. At the same time projecting a bike for a particular user group would not be a feasible idea for a company as it may induce other users to turn away from buying that particular bike.

Bagodi V. and Mahanty B. (2011), The sale of two-wheelers in India has shown a remarkable growth in the last decade. This unprecedented growth had also necessitated for the manufacturers to offer better services to sustain the growth, achieve customer loyalty and enhance user's reliance on the vehicles. There is a remarkable change in the phrasing of the questions and the structure of the questionnaire after the pre-test. This was done to enhance the readability as well as to make the questionnaire more focused to its target group.

Ramarao B.S.V. (2009), says that in the present marketing scenario, competition plays a vital role. There is a need for improvements of new products to face various challenges in the world market. Because of this, companies are working on innovative ideas to bring improvements in their product design, efficiency, look and better workability and so on. Now-a-days, motor vehicles have become the middle-class people's comfortable mode of transport.

Weinert, J., Ogden, J., Sperling, D. & Burke, A. (2008), The method of force field analysis was used to examine the future technological and market evolution of electric two-wheelers (E2W) in China. The authors identified key forces of driving and resisting future E2W market growth, root causes behind these forces, and important insights about the likelihood of a wide shift to larger three and four-wheel electric vehicles (EV).

Subbu D. Subramanian, (2008), In his article "India can be a Big Player—Third Generation Automobile Industry", automobiles are moving from a mechanical to an electronic platform with more intelligence and communicative features powered by IT. The world is now in the era of third generation automobiles 'The Software Cars'. With technology and innovation, India was unequally placed to exploit this opportunity. The third-generation cars would be high-tech cars and green cars, to find solutions to the escalating fuel prices and environmental problems. From hybrids to hydrogen cells, the world's leading auto markets are working furiously to increase the production of green cars. BMW, GM, Honda, and Toyota have already produced such green cars. Also observed that, the direct employment in the industry was 2 lakhs in vehicle manufacturing and 2.8 lakhs in component companies. The production of various categories of automobiles in the Tenth Five Year Plan period grew at a compound annual growth rate (CAGR) of 16 per cent crossing the 10 million mark in 2006-07.

Jagdish Khatav (2006), In his article "Positive Growth Indications" highlights the global forum in the car industry. According to him, there are four major growth drivers: (1) economic growth, (2) falling interest rates and availability of finance, (3) reduction in taxes, and (4) development of road infrastructure. He states that all these growth drivers are present in India also. He also says that faster upgradation of automobiles and the expansion of finance with declined interest rates simultaneously have helped in the booming of business.

Rayport and Jaworski (2003), This study revealed that most of the consumer research will be based on seven stages and how different elements affect consumers' decisions in different terms and consolidation of stages. The new kind of non-shop retailing format has begun replacing catalogue and TV shopping and its development is rapid and found in comparison with existing non-shop retailing models.

Keshav Sharma (2002), found that rural customers believed in joint buying decision making in consultation with the elders and the ladies of the house for their personal use according to their own independent buying decisions. The respondents were aware of the availability of products and they preferred quality to price.

Methodology

Data from the respondents were collected by using a structured questionnaire. The questionnaire was prepared with utmost care and incorporating all necessary information by using closed-end questions. The questionnaire was sent using google form. Google form is survey administration software for collecting information from users through surveys. In order to fulfil the objectives, set forth for the study, the researchers collected both primary and secondary data from different sources.

The study adopted a convenient sampling method for selection of samples to represent the population of Thiruvananthapuram district. In order to study the impact of COVID-19 on the consumer behaviour of automobiles, 200 respondents—100 urban and 100 rural, have been selected from various areas of Thiruvananthapuram district.

Result and Discussion

The process of data analysis uses analytical & logical reasoning to gain information from the data. The main purpose of data analysis is to find out the meanings in the data so that knowledge derived can be used to make informed decisions. Data integrity can be ensured by the accurate and appropriate analysis of research findings. In today's business world, data analysis plays a significant role in making decisions which are more scientific and thereby helping business to operate more effectively.

Data collection for our study is done through the distribution of google forms. Our data is analysed and concluded on the basis of area, i.e., urban & rural areas. The total number of samples collected for data analysis is 200, out of which 100 is from urban areas and 100 is from rural areas. Various factors are also being analysed with the help of the data collected.

Classification based on the purpose of possessing an automobile

The purpose of possessing an automobile differs from an individual to individual. Consumers living in the same district may have different purposes to purchase an automobile. Here in our project, the main four classification given based on the purpose of possessing an automobile are multi-purpose, official purpose, personal purpose and commercial purpose.

Table 9.1: Classification based on the purpose of possessing an automobile

Purpose of possessing an automobile	No. of respondents	Percentage
Multi-purpose	72	36
Official purpose	15	7.5
Personal purpose	61	30.5
Commercial purpose	52	26
Total	**200**	**100**

From the Table 9.1, data can be interpreted as out of 200 consumers in total 72 (36%) use automobile for multi-purpose, 15 (7.5%) use automobile for official purpose, 61 (30.5%) use automobile for personal purpose and 52 (26%) use automobile for commercial purpose. The highest percentage of preference is for multi-purpose usage (36%).

Classification on Vehicle Type

Vehicle type is an important classification in purchase of automobiles. There are mainly two types of automobiles: first-hand ownership and second-hand ownership. There will be change in buying behaviour with respect to change in area and financial status of an individual. Here the two basis for classification are first-hand ownership and second-hand ownership.

Table 9.2: Classification based on vehicle type

Vehicle type	No. of respondents	Percentage
First-hand ownership	138	69
Second-hand ownership	62	31
Total	**200**	**100**

From Table 9.2, it is clear that out of all the 200 respondents, 138 (69%) likes to own first-hand ownership vehicles whereas 62 (31%) of respondents prefer second-hand ownership vehicles. The highest percentage is 69 per cent for first-hand ownership vehicles.

Customers' Attitude Towards Brand Image

Brand image is the current view of the customers about a brand. It can be defined as a unique bundle of associations within the minds of the target customers. It signifies what the brand stands for at the present. The customer's attitude towards a brand image is done to find the fondness of each individual. The attitude scale has been divided into extremely important, important, indifferent, not important and not at all important.

Table 9.3: Customers' attitude towards brand image of a vehicle

Attitude towards brand image	No. of respondents	Percentage
Extremely important	67	33.5
Important	80	40.0
Indifferent	23	11.5
Not important	25	12.5
Not at all important	5	2.5
Total	**200**	**100**

In Table 9.3, data is taken from 200 people out of which, 67 people (33.5%) feels that brand image is extremely important, 80 people (40%) feels that brand image is important, 23 people (11.5%) feel indifferent towards a brand image, 25 people (12.5%) feels that brand image is not important and 5 people (2.5%) feels that brand image is not at all important. The highest percentage of respondents are the people who feel that the brand image is important.

Customers' Attitude Towards Fuel Efficiency

The capacity of an engine, especially that of a vehicle, to obtain energy from a fuel is known as fuel efficiency. The customers' attitude towards fuel efficiency of a vehicle is done to find the liking of each individual to work out the objectives of the study. The attitude scale is divided into extremely important, important, indifferent, not important and not at all important.

Table 9.4: Customers' attitude towards fuel efficiency of a vehicle

Attitude towards fuel efficiency	No. of respondents	Percentage
Extremely important	87	43.5
Important	84	42.0
Indifferent	18	9.0
Not important	7	3.5
Not at all important	4	2.0
Total	**200**	**100**

In the Table 9.4, data of 200 people shows us that, 87 people (43.5%) feels that fuel efficiency is extremely important, 84 people (42%) feels that fuel efficiency is important, 18 people (9%) feel indifferent towards fuel efficiency, 7 people (3.5%) feels that fuel efficiency is not important and 4 people (2%) feels that fuel efficiency is not at all important. The highest percentage of respondents are the people who feel that fuel efficiency is extremely important.

Customers' Attitude Towards Fuel Types of a Vehicle

In the recent years, consumers have started to divert their vehicle preferences from conventional vehicles to those fueled by alternative energy sources, considering the issues that have arisen in recent years, such as environmental deterioration, increasing oil prices etc. Under such an existing scenario, it is important to determine the consumer's attitude towards fuel type and the attitude scale of importance act as an aid to the same.

Table 9.5: Customers' attitude towards fuel types of a vehicle

Attitude towards fuel types	No. of respondents	Percentage
Extremely important	51	25.5
Important	68	34.0
Indifferent	22	11.0
Not important	55	27.5
Not at all important	4	2.0
Total	**200**	**100**

In the Table 9.5, data can be interpreted as from 200 people out of which, 51 people (25.5%) feels that fuel type is extremely important, 68 people (34%) feels that fuel type is important, 22 people (11%) feel indifferent towards a particular fuel type, 55 people (27.5%) feels that fuel type is not important and 4 people (2%) feels that fuel type is not at all important. The highest percentage of respondents are the people who feel that fuel type is important.

Customers' Attitude Towards Resale Value

Resale is the act of selling again, usually to a new party. The price which something can achieve, when sold in the future is known as the resale value of that item. The customers' attitude towards the resale value of a vehicle is used to find the preferences of each individual. The attitude scale is divided into extremely important, important, indifferent, not important and not at all important.

Table 9.6: Customers' attitude towards resale value of a vehicle

Attitude towards resale value	No. of respondents	Percentage
Extremely important	42	21
Important	102	51
Indifferent	28	14
Not important	20	10
Not at all important	8	4
Total	**200**	**100**

In the Table 9.6, data can be interpreted as from 200 people out of which, 42 people (21%) feels that resale value is extremely important, 102 people (51%) feels that resale value is important, 28 people (14%) feel indifferent towards the resale value, 20 people (10%) feels that resale value is not important and 8 people (4%) feels that resale value is not at all important. The highest percentage of respondents are the people who feel that the resale value is important.

Various Statistical Calculations of Consumer Behaviour in Urban Area

Various statistical calculations that are carried out of scores obtained from rating scale to measure the consumer behaviour in urban areas are given in Table 9.7.

Table 9.7 shows that the value of arithmetic mean of consumer behaviour in urban areas is 31.28 and standard deviation is 4.045, this shows that there is a small variation from mean score. The median is 32, mode is 35, and range is 20. The maximum score and minimum score are 40 and 20 respectively.

Table 9.7: Various statistical calculations of consumer behaviour in urban area

Statistical calculation	Consumer behaviour
Mean	31.28
Median	32
Mode	35
Maximum score	40
Minimum score	20
Range	20
Standard deviation	4.045
Total number of samples	**100**

Various Statistical Calculations of Consumer Behaviour in Rural Area

Various statistical calculations that are carried out of scores obtained from rating scale to measure the consumer behaviour in rural areas are shown in Table 9.8.

Table 9.8: Various statistical calculations of consumer behaviour in rural area

Statistical calculation	Consumer behaviour
Mean	32.48
Median	33
Mode	34
Maximum score	40
Minimum score	23
Range	17
Standard deviation	4.134
Total number of samples	**100**

From Table 9.8, it is clear that the value of arithmetic mean of consumer behaviour in rural areas is 32.48 and standard deviation is 4.134, this shows that there is a small variation from mean score. The median is 33, mode is 34 and range is 17. The maximum and minimum score are 40 and 23 respectively.

Comparison of Consumer Behaviour in Rural and Urban Areas

This section shows the comparison of consumer behaviour in rural and urban areas which are carried out statistically and the results of the test significance obtained are given in Table 9.9.

Table 9.9: Comparison of consumer behaviour in rural & urban areas

Sample	Size	Mean	SD	Critical ratio	Significant difference
Rural	100	32.48	4.045	2.075	
Urban	100	31.28	4.134		

Table 9.9 shows that the mean of consumer behaviour in rural areas is 32.48 and that of urban areas is 31.28. It is clear that the mean of rural areas is higher than urban areas. It also shows that the obtained critical ratio 2.075 is greater than standard t-value 1.96. Hence, it can be concluded that there is a significant difference between rural & urban areas in their consumer behaviour.

Summary and Conclusion

After going through various chapters, explaining many theories, analysis and findings now it is the time to conclude by giving a summary to the entire study. As explained in our first chapter, this study was carried out to find the impact of COVID-19 on consumer behaviour in the automobile industry with special reference to Thiruvananthapuram district.

As the study was limited to Trivandrum district, samples were derived from a population, which consists of persons from different age groups mainly scattered over rural and urban areas. Conceptual framework was designed for analyzing the stated problem statement in this study.

Through the phase of data collection, analysis and interpretation, it revealed that consumers are giving more preference to the safety systems in the vehicle due to the outbreak of the COVID-19 pandemic. Also 66.5 per cent of the people prefer four-wheelers over two-wheelers. Hence, it is clear that people are giving more importance to health in this phase.

The study also shows that there is a tremendous increase in purchase of vehicles on credit basis rather than cash basis and this is due to the availability of flexible finance schemes in the market. A heavy competition is also experienced for the same. It was also found that apart from the recognized financial institutions there is a big market of private lenders who are also providing funds at lower interest rate to the consumers for the purpose of purchase of a vehicle. The important steps taken by the Reserve Bank of India to waive the interest or to provide long term loans during the pandemic phase have also impacted the automobile industry.

The analysis also reveals a very distinctive picture in case of preference to the price of vehicles. It shows that nowadays and after that the pandemic, price is considered as an important factor and not as an extremely important factor and thereby giving more importance to comforts. This proves the change in need of cars being a necessity rather than luxury.

It is also suggestive that the findings of the study may be used by the manufacturing companies to have a better understanding of the buying behaviour of domestic customers and their new needs and expectations. It will also help them to analyze how to formulate their marketing strategies in the pandemic situation and to convert uncertainties into opportunities.

The entire study provides a pathway for market researchers and philosophers for the future studies in the area of consumer behaviour in the automobile industry.

The study reveals that maximum of respondents made their self-decision before making a purchase. It was extracted from the responses that when a buyer enters a showroom to purchase a product, then most of the time he is with the frame of mind for the product he is going for, the buyer does his homework and comes down with a frame of mind to go for the product. Hence, it can be concluded that an intensive study is done beforehand by the buyer before going for a particular vehicle.

References

Al Karim, R. (2013). "Customer Satisfaction: a study into the reasons for motivations and inhibitions." *IOSR Journal of Business and Management, 11*(6), 13-20.

Amalendu Ganguly, J. Roy and others (1960). *Studies on Consumer Behaviour.* Asian Publishing House, Bombay.

Anita Ghatak (1985). *Consumer Behaviour in India.* D.K. Agencies Pvt. Ltd., New Delhi.

Belk, Russell.W. (1975). "Situational Variables and Consumer Behaviour." *Journal of Consumer Research, 2*(3):157-64.

Bhattacharya, C. B., & Sen, S. (2003). "Consumer-company identification: A framework for understanding consumers' relationships with companies." *Journal of Marketing, 67*(2), 76-88.

Blythe, Jim & Martin, Jane (1998). *Essentials of Marketing* (7th edition). Published by Pearson.

Capon, N., & Burke, M. (1980). "Individual, product class and task-related factors in consumer information processing." *Journal of Consumer Research, 7*(3), 314-326.

Douglas Lamont (1996). *Global Marketing.* Blackwell Business Publications.

Gary Armstrong and Philip Kotler (1980). *Principles of Marketing.* Published by Pearson Education, 2008.

Graeme P. Maxton, John Wormald (2004). *Time for a Model Change: Re-engineering the Global Automotive Industry* by Cambridge University Press.

Gupta, S.P. & Gupta, M.P. (2010). *Business Statistics.* Published by Sultan Chand & Sons, 2019.

Hemanth, K.P. & Shruthi, V.K. (2013). "Determinants of Consumer Buying Behaviour: A Theoretical Framework of Rural India." *Journal of Exclusive Management Science, 2*(3). pp. 1-16.

Kothari, C.R. (1985). *Research Methodology: Methods and Techniques* (4th edition), New Age International, 2004.

Mangal, S.K (2004). *Statistics in Psychology and Education* (2nd edition). Published by PHI Hearing Pvt. Ltd., 2002.

Naik, Krishna C.N. & Reddy, Venugopal, L. (1999). *Consumer Behaviour* by Discovery Publication House, New Delhi.

Nair, Suja (2014). *Consumer Behaviour including Skill Development,* Himalaya Publishing House.

Oliver, Richard C. (1997). *Satisfaction: A Behavioural Perspective on the Consumer* (2nd edition). Published by ME Sharpe Inc.

Sherlekar, S. (2010). *Marketing Management.* Published by Himalayan Publishing House.

Warren Keegan (1989). *Global Marketing Management* (8th edition). Published by Pearson.

10

Changing Gender Perspectives in Managing COVID-19

Case Studies on Revamped Role of Women PRI and SHG Leaders in Odisha

Smita Nayak

Introduction

The current pandemic was a catastrophic factor in disrupting the lifeline in rural and urban pockets of Odisha but the timely action of state government could befittingly combat the global menace with persistent zeal and combined endeavours of all the stakeholders. Odisha created a glaring example in the national scenario by putting equal thrust on COVID management in rural areas as compared to the urban counterparts. The government in Panchayati Raj and Drinking Water Department kept no stone unturned to equip the rural Odisha in combating the pandemic with new vigour and zeal. Panchayats were declared as the pivot on which the wheel of strategic initiatives revolved. Gram Panchayats were not only declared as the nodal points for putting a check on the spread of Corona virus but also the Sarpanch of GPs were entrusted with special roles for disseminating pertinent awareness, making people careful about the prevailing regional and national norms and managing Temporary Medical Camps. Gram Panchayats in Odisha being the frontline institutions under the aegis of PR & DW Department strived incessantly to propel the government's strategies in right direction. From facilitating preparation and dissemination of IEC messages to strengthening the capacity of community members and other key stakeholders, the women Panchayat leaders could make their presence visible down the line at the functional stages. Some of the landmark achievements of women Panchayat leaders are depicted in the form of case studies collected by the researcher from sample districts of Odisha.

Research Questions

The researcher has built up the questions that can contribute to construct the evidence base on functioning of women Panchayat in response to the pandemic. Accumulated information on state's perspective, response of PRIs and the strength of women's leadership is essential to suggest stipulated directions for subsequent research. The researcher has identified the following research questions to guide the agenda around COVID-19 and women Panchayat leaders:

(a) What is our learning on women's leadership in decentralized governance while combating the crises of pandemics? How can it substantiate variations across contexts?

(b) How does the convergence between women Panchayat leaders and Self Help Groups for managing COVID-19 crisis? What are the promoting and impeding factors in the context of women's leadership in Gram Panchayats?

(c) Does contribution by women leaders moderate the adverse impact of COVID-19 and consequent socio-economic trauma in the rural context?

Objectives of the Study

The study has identified three objectives in which the efficacy of Corona combating measures has been impacted by the team building, leadership and motivation styles of women Panchayat leaders as furnished below:

- To assess the role of women Panchayat leaders in augmenting preventive measures like lockdown, quarantine, social distancing etc.
- To analyze the steps furthered by elected women representatives especially Sarpanch in safeguarding rural communities from socio-economic shock caused by the pandemic.
- To acknowledge the perceived impact of women PRI leadership in partnership with Community Based Organizations like SHGs in promoting income generation for the community.

Review of Literature

Gender as a differentiator of leadership effectiveness has spawned polemic in the past five decades (Megargee, 1969). Several journals have devoted special issues to gender and leadership effectiveness—for example, *The Leadership Quarterly* (Eagly & Heilman, 2016), *American Psychologist* (Chin, 2010), and *Education Sciences* (O'Connor, 2018); hence, our review is brief.

Research on gender and leadership effectiveness typically adheres to either a micro or a macro level of analysis. Micro research studies individual-level variables—for example, leader behaviours—whereas macro research investigates "the shaking and moving" of a firm to face the future, cope with change, and achieve organizational-level results (Nicholls, 1988, p. 16). The present study bridges the micro-macro divide by relating a micro predictor (governors' sex) to a macro outcome (state death count). This cross-level research answers a call by Hoobler *et al.* (2018).

Garikipati and Kumbhampati[1] argue that explanation of gender differences in response to the pandemic is to be found in the leadership styles of men and women. Studies suggest that men are likely to lead in a "task-oriented" style and women in an "interpersonally-oriented" manner. Women therefore tend to adopt a more democratic and participative style and tend to have better communications skills.

An IWWAGE[2] research study suggests that women leaders at the grassroots have emerged as frontline workers and the last mile connect between governments and the people during this crisis. Women leaders are playing a pivotal role in responding to COVID-19; they are making masks, hand sanitizers, PPE kits, distributing take home ration, disseminating COVID-19 related information and running community kitchens to feed the vulnerable. The role of PRIs has never been more important than now and can prove to be a rare silver lining in the distress that PRIs are dealing with. Women can come forward and take leadership and development roles in their villages. It is an opportunity that the PRI movement must capitalize on.

A recently conducted World Bank Study[3] suggests that now, more than ever, these women many of whom escaped poverty through the SHG route and know what it is like to be destitute and poor are living up to their motto of self-help and solidarity. Groups across the country are working furiously to make up the shortfall of masks and personal protective equipment (PPE). In Odisha, for instance, poor rural women who were once engaged in stitching school uniforms are sewing masks instead. Over the past couple of weeks, these women have produced more than 1 million cotton masks, helping equip police personnel and health workers, while earning something for themselves. All told, more than 19 million masks have been produced by some 20,000 SHGs across 27 Indian states, in addition to over 1,00,000 liters of sanitizer and nearly 50,000 liters of hand wash. Since production is decentralized, these items have reached widely-dispersed populations without the need for complex logistics and transportation.

An article published by Pallikkutam[4] says that the motivated, enthusiastic and committed approximately 690 lakh women members of around 63 lakh Self Help Groups (SHGs) across the country formed under the Deendayal Antyodaya Yojana-National Rural Livelihoods Mission (DAY-NRLM), Ministry of Rural Development, have always contributed in addressing economic and social needs that have emerged at the community level. These women are engaged in livelihoods activities, bringing social change through awareness generation, leading movements and responding during natural calamities. During the on-going crisis also, SHG members have emerged as community warriors by contributing in every possible way to contain the spread of COVID-19. The SHG network across the country was made aware of the various aspects of the disease including the need to maintain personal hygiene, social distancing etc. through Audio Visual (AV) IEC material and advisories developed by Health Ministry which were circulated to all State Rural Livelihoods Missions (SRLMs). All such information, along with material developed by the state governments, is being used by the SRLMs to ensure that the correct message is communicated to the community about all required precautions. The SRLM staff and SHGs members are creating awareness in the local communities by various means like telephone calls, wall writings, pamphlets/fliers etc. Social media is also being used extensively. SHG volunteers are playing their role in ensuring that people maintain social distancing in markets, PDS shops etc.

An article published in the HT[5] says that in several states, SHGs have taken up the task of production, packaging and distribution of take-home ration (THR) as *Anganwadi* centres across the country are shut due to the lockdown. In Odisha and Chhattisgarh, the SHG women also distribute eggs along with THR. This ensures that the State reaches every child under five, pregnant women, lactating mothers, and vulnerable target groups. In many states, SHG members engaged as BC Sakhi (banking correspondent agents) help home-deliver the Centre's financial relief packages for the rural community facing socio-economic distress, pensioners, and those who are dependent on the Mahatma Gandhi National Rural Employment Guarantee Act.

Methodology

The research based on exploratory case studies doesn't entail to have hypotheses. The findings of this research are informed by case studies of 'good practices' in the area of women PRI and SHG leadership. The state overviews cover the changes in the perspectives of gender analysis in the context of decentralized governance and women's empowerment concerning PRIs and SHGs. Based on this perspective, cases have been collected based on stratified sampling methods covering key Gram Panchayats those have taken decisive actions in management of COVID-19.

Corona Combating Measures: Case Study of Lilima Pradhan, Sarpanch, Nandika GP [6]

In the present time, when the entire world is struggling hard to combat Corona pandemic, India is totally geared up from villages to national capital to respond to the dire needs of the situation. The rural population of Odisha has been showing great resilience and steadfastness in collaborating with the local administration to fight with Corona. The villagers of Nandika Gram Panchayat coming under Hinjilicut Block of Ganjam District adhering to the norms have taken a vow to fight against the disease in a unified manner. The Gram Panchayat has a population of around 3812 villagers. The moment the threat of Corona pandemic started spreading, the Sarpanch Mrs. Lilima Pradhan along with the villagers were smart enough to take proactive measures to stop the COVID-19. They moved in groups throughout the villages maintaining social distance to make people aware about the symptoms and solutions for staying safe. IEC materials like leaflet and wall paintings were used with adequate information for the people conveying from outside of the state to get immediately registered by dialing 104.

Abiding by the direction of the State Government advance ration under PDS has been provided to 845 beneficiaries. Similarly, 185 persons have been given Old Age Pension while 86 have received Widow Pension on 4 months advance basis. In the process of PDS and Pension distribution, the social distance norms have been strictly followed throughout the Gram Panchayat. Two Temporary Medical Centres have been set up in the Gram Panchayat with provision of 136 beds where 116 persons coming from outside of the state have been quarantined. For the benefit of the inmates of the Temporary Medical Centre, 12 toilets have been set up besides adequate provisions of drinking water, soaps and sanitizers. The Gram Panchayat has been managing the food distribution in a proper manner by following the menu on principles and sticking to the quality and hygiene parameters.

Government functionaries including school teacher, *Anganwadi* Worker, ANM, Panchayat Executive Officer, *Gram Rojagar Sevak* and Sarpanch have taken responsibility for managing TMC as a regular basis. As on date 426 persons have registered to avail quarantine facility after returning to Odisha. For providing recreation facilities to the inmates several programmes like Folk music, *Bhajan, Sankirtan* and other cultural programmes are being arranged with the participation of artistic talents found in the group. The quarantine centre has been creatively wall painted with the inherent talent of some inmates for which the surrounding has been recharged with a new vibrance. The commitment, zeal and endeavour demonstrated by the Sarpanch and the villagers of Nandika Gram Panchayat is being landed by the block and district administration. This evidently signals the appropriateness of the State Government's decision in empowering the Gram Panchayats as the frontline.

Case Study of Woman Sarpanch Mani Majhi from Kalahandi District[7]

Women have been reckoned as apostles of change in every walk of our existence and endeavours. Their will-power, vision and creative genius have resulted in bringing turn around changes in the course of human civilisation. To talk of India, especially in progressive states like Odisha, women's active participation in Panchayati Raj Institutions have revolutionised the whole process of decentralised governance itself. Women leading the PRIs have staged a paradigm shift from dole to dignity, from paternalistic generosity to reinforced community action. A woman Sarpanch from tribally populated district of Kalahandi has demonstrated her steadfastness in affirming our firm conviction regarding the strength of woman power in establishing the significance of local governments.

Thuamul Rampur is a remote community development Block situated at a distance of 45 kilometres from Kalahandi's district headquarters Bhawanipatna. Padepadar is a small GP under Thuamul Rampur Panchayat Samiti, where most of the villagers are migrant labours working in states like Andhra Pradesh, Telengana, Tamil Nadu and Gujarat. As soon the returning of migrant labours to their native places were permitted under the constitutional provisions, Government of Odisha in Revenue and Disaster Management Department and Panchayati Raj and Drinking Water Department issued joint guidelines invoking the PRIs for mandatory registration of incoming migrants, compulsory quarantine for them and stringent measures against offenders violating the basic norms of the guidelines issued by the government.

Special power at par with Collectors was conferred on the Sarpanches for implementing the guidelines and taking disciplinary action against the perpetrators of abusive actions. Woman Sarpanch Mani Majhi of Padepadar GP understood this power by taking the onus of responsibility for smooth management of TMC. She not only ensured measures for cleaning the TMC area situated in the GP headquarters but also put strong barricades around the TMC building so that no outsiders can intrude into the quarantine centres and no inmates can move away from the campus . Provision for 100 beds was ensured in the TMC. In the first phase, fifteen incoming migrants were mandatorily registered and quarantined in the TMC under direct supervision of the Sarpanch Ms. Mani Majhi. She also remained present to oversee distribution of fresh and hygienically cooked meals to inmates thrice a day such as breakfast, lunch and dinner prepared by the members of the SHGs.

The women SHG members under the guidance of the Sarpanch also went a step forward in tailoring masks for all the villagers. The masks were made available for the villagers at a nominal cost of five rupees only. The aim of the SHGs was focused on encouraging the village folk to be sensitised on wearing the mask rather than generating resources out of this process.

The efforts of the woman Sarpanch was widely appreciated among the villagers as they not only became aware on the issue of wearing mask but also made it a healthy practice by necessitating changes in their lifestyles. She ensured organising special *Yoga* sessions for the quarantined persons and also made it appoint to regularly participate in these sessions. The personal presence of Sarpanch in such sessions could strike a phenomenal difference in the quarantine process adopted in the TMC. Furthering the welfare measures and humanitarian steps adopted by the Panchayati Raj and Drinking Water Department, the Sarpanch Ms. Majhi ensured doorstep distribution of social welfare assistance like various pensions to enlisted beneficiaries. She also personally monitored distribution of food security assistance of Rs. 1000 to ration card holders and special assistance of Rs. 1500 to Mahatma Gandhi NREGS job card holders. As a mark of humanitarian pursuit as directed by the government, destitute and needy differently abled persons were served with fresh cooked free meals prepared by the women SHG members. Sarpanch Ms. Mani Majhi has expressed her satisfaction for being able to serve the people during such a massive crisis of rarest severity. Her contentment in this regard signals a bright future for the elected PRI members in strengthening a resilient mechanism to cope up with disasters having such massive implications.

Case Study of Sarpanch Alaka Pradhan in securing Livelihoods during the Pandemic[8]

Boudh is a small tribal district situated in the centre of Odisha. Forming a part of the northernmost extremity of the Eastern Ghats and the river Mahanadi bordering it along with the industrially prominent district Angul, Boudh has carved out a special geographical significance for itself as the connecting link to many happening districts of Odisha. Its historical importance has been propagated through its Buddhist vestiges justifying the very name of the district itself. But in recent days as the world was combating the Corona pandemic, a tiny tribal Khamanmunda GP of Boudh district could come forward as a trendsetter in revamping livelihood initiatives for the tribal villagers.

Very alike the process of managing natural disasters, the Corona combating measures were chalked out traversing the paths of rescue, relief and rehabilitation. Immediately following the news regarding spread of the dreaded virus, 1329 villagers out of 4996 recorded population of the GP were provided with three months' advance PDS ration along with food security allowance of Rs. 1000. Around 150 destitute persons were provided with fresh cooked meals prepared by the SHG members for a period ranging from 27th March to last week of May 2020. Similarly, 605 widow and old age pension holders received three months' pension in advance.

The most phenomenal step taken by Khamanmunda GP has been focused on convergence of Mahatma Gandhi NREGA activities with those promoted through NRLM and other benevolent rural development programmes for strengthening productive rural infrastructure. These activities include pond renovation in the villages of Kharibahal and Digurimal, watershed reservoir construction at Gunjarmal and improvement of road connectivity from Chhapapati to Gunchitara. Along with improvement of rural infrastructure individual beneficiary oriented convergence activities like pond and cowshed renovation, land development etc. have been carried out through active involvement of the Sarpanch and Ward Members.

The management of two major Temporary Medical Camps set up in the campuses of ST & SC Residential School's Hostel, Nuapally and Kalyan Mandap at Digurimal has been appreciated by the inmates and block administration. The inmates of these two TMCs were quite happy with the fresh cooked meals and snacks provided by the SHG members four times a day. The inmates also practiced *Yoga* and took part in cultural activities like storytelling, *Bhajan* etc. Expressing satisfaction over the convergence activities, the delighted Sarpanch Ms. Alaka Pradhan of Khamanmunda GP has lauded the efforts of 13 SHGs and the villager's wholehearted cooperation for the overwhelming success of Covid management in the GP and has said that such cooperation has proved to be a trendsetter for other PRIs.

Case Study of Sanjukta Pujari, Woman Sarpanch of Tribally Populated Gajapati District[9]

Ramgiri Udaygiri is a small Gram Panchayat situated in the hilly terrain of R Udaygiri block in the tribally infested Gajapati District. Situated 60 km away from district headquarters of Gajapati Parlakhemundi, the GP consists of 9 villages and around 3900 inhabitants. The villagers of this GP have shown tremendous resilience and exemplary steadfastness in managing Corona pandemic when the leading nations of the globe have been shattered under the clutches of the rapidly spreading virus.

The Sarpanch and the Ward members kept no stone unturned to spread awareness about the pandemic as soon it reached the public domain. Around 20 awareness campaigns were organized involving the local leaders and intelligentsia for disseminating important information among the villagers like social distancing, isolation, quarantine, hand wash and use of mask etc. The elected PRI members received phenomenal support from the villagers and especially the tribal youth came forward to lend a supporting hand in pioneering the door to door campaign.

Out of the 3900 inhabitants, 1389 PDS beneficiaries were provided with three months' advance ration along with special food security allowance of Rs. 1000. Around 4400 destitute and differently abled beneficiaries were served with cooked meals by the SHG members of the GP under direct supervision of Ward Members and the Sarpanch Ms. Sanjukta Pujari herself. 648 beneficiaries were provided with old age and widow pensions for a period of three months in advance.

Gearing up benevolent steps, the women SHG members under the guidance of PRI representatives, sold hand stitched masks @ Rs. 20 and thereby earned some money for empowering the

SHGs along with spreading the message of compulsory use of masks. Because of the steps taken by the Sarpanch and Ward Members, 279 construction workers received Rs. 1500 as special assistance provided through dedicated initiatives by the Construction Worker Welfare Board of Government of Odisha.

The commendable cooperation extended by the villagers is evident from the qualitative management of TMC set up in the GP campus of R Udaygiri. Around 40 inmates were provided with four times meals and snacks under hygienic conditions. The toilets were cleaned thrice a day with facility for sanitization being provided for all the rooms and corridors. The inmates of the quarantine centre praised wholeheartedly the contribution of the PRI members and local youth organizations extended during the hardest days of initial fighting against the terrorizing disease. But what they applauded was the praiseworthy cooperation of all the villagers belonging to the GP during the tough times.

Case Study on Decisive Stand by Woman Sarpanch Swarnamayee Jena[10]

As the entire world strives hard to fight the threat of Corona pandemic, Odisha as a front ranking state of Eastern India emanates inspiration for others to imbibe. The ground breaking decision taken in this regard is empowering the Gram Panchayats as the field level coordination hub for smooth facilitation of COVID-19 combating measures. Odisha Government created history by first time empowering the Sarpanch of GPs to exercise the power of a Collector & District Magistrate in the context of identification of probable cases, management of Temporary Medical Camps (Quarantine Centres) and strict corrective measures for the deviants and habitual offenders in this regard. Such a power on principle was conferred on each and every Sarpanch but few of them could stand out in turning this principle to a practice as evident in the case of woman Sarpanch Ms. Swarnamayee Jena of Bhatapada GP coming under Tihidi Panchayat Samiti of Bhadrak district. As soon the news regarding the threat of pandemic reached Tihidi, the Panchayat Samiti revamped its awareness measures and utilised the platform of 'Tihidi Mahotsav', the block level annual event to educate the people on gravity of the situation and immediate steps available on maintaining social distance and adopting frequent hand washing practices at regular intervals. Sarpanch Ms. Jena convened an emergency meeting involving the elected PRI members like the Naib Sarpanch, all 23 Ward Members, the PS member and Key functionaries like PEO, GRS, AWW, ASHA and health workers like ANM etc. It was unanimously resolved to gear up sensitising measures for making people understand the needs and basic steps of sanitisation, personal hygiene and safe distance to avoid contamination. Campaign through public address system and door to door counselling by elected representatives and officials were carried out in the streets and corners of the GP on war footing to fight the menaces of spread of the disease.

The Sarpanch kept no stone unturned to expedite the vigilant measures meticulously to check the pace of such rocketing infection. All the offices, health centres and establishments including the lanes and by lanes were thoroughly sanitised. To avoid overcrowding, the Khanki vegetable and fish-meat market was immediately shifted to Kaali Padia under overall supervision of the Sarpanch. As an innovative step, the youth club members rendered support to the PEO and GRS in distributing three months' advance pension to the eligible beneficiaries at their doorsteps. Similarly, advance ration for three months along with food security assistance of Rs. 1000 was distributed to the ration card holders while ensuring social distancing through provision of barricades. As a humanitarian measure, under instruction of the government, arrangement of free meals was made by members of Shyamakaali and Subhadra Self Help Groups for around thirty to ninety destitute persons and migrant labours of outside Odisha stranded during the critical lockdown period. Two Temporary Medical Camps (Quarantine Centres) were set up by the Gram Panchayat inside the CRF High School and UGME School at Khanki Haat with provisions for 172 beds. Sarpanch Ms. Swarnamayee Jena and her team ensured all basic amenities like mattress, pillow, bed sheet, hand wash basin, water purifier and geyser along with usable items like liquid hand wash, bleaching powder etc. Round the clock electricity and proper lighting measures for the TMCs were also monitored from time to time. 154 migrants coming from states like West Bengal, Andhra Pradesh, Telengana, Kerala, Karnataka, Maharashtra and Jharkhand were quarantined for the stipulated period while cleanliness was strictly maintained by cleaning the toilets three times during a day and adhering to sanitisation norms. The GP also provided 10 Personal Protection equipment to the persons attending the inmates of TMCs.

Most importantly, the Sarpanch utilised the power conferred on her in true spirit. With identifications of three Corona positive cases in the GP area, Ms. Jena exercising the power of a Collector & DM declared immediate 48 hours 'shut down' in Ward No. 20 and 21. Similarly taking strict actions against seven inmates, whose 'tik tok' video shot at the TMC at CRF High School became viral, a case was lodged at Tihidi Police Station by the Sarpanch and the members were fined Rs. 5000 each by the GP for their erratic behaviour in violating the COVID-19 guidelines for management of TMC issued by Government of Odisha. The timely and bold steps taken up by the woman Sarpanch have been lauded by the conscious citizens and the block administration as well. This step goes a long way in justifying the prudence of the state government in empowering the Sarpanch as the frontline warrior in the battle against Corona pandemic.

Concluding Observation

Stories of women PRI and SHG leaders taking up pivotal roles to protect rural Odisha from succumbing to the COVID-19 crisis have been coming up since the beginning of the nationwide lockdown in March 2020. Guided by Block and District administrative bodies, these women leaders, with support from the Panchayat Extension Officers and key persons of their respective villages, are designing and implementing local solutions that are compatible with their socio-cultural contexts. From generating awareness on government guidelines for COVID-19 prevention in the community, to linking health workers with the households, from enrolling for livelihood opportunities, to activating food security programmes and active role in surveillance, the role of women elected representatives of PRIs and SHG leaders has been extremely critical.

Notes

1. Garikipati, S. and Kumbhampati, *Are women leaders really doing better on coronavirus*? Web source: https://voxeu.org/article, accessed on 27th November, 2020.
2. *Can COVID-19 provide opportunities to strengthen the SHG movement?*, Web source: https://iwwage.org accessed on 27th November, 2020.
3. *In India, women's self-help groups combat the COVID-19* (*Coronavirus*), websource pandemichttps://www.worldbank.org/en/news/feature/2020/04/11 accessed on 28th November, 2020.
4. *COVID-19: NRLM Self Help Group women emerge as community warriors*, web source https://www.pallikkutam.com/edu-news/covid19 accessed on 28th November, 2020.
5. *COVID-19: In times of crisis, women self-help groups lead the way* https://www.hindustantimes.com/analysis/COVID-19, accessed on 28th November, 2020.
6. *Reports and Documents, PR & DW Department, Govt. of Odisha* web source https://odishapanchayat.gov.in/accessed on 28th November, 2020.
7. *Ibid.*, web source, accessed on 28th November, 2020.
8. *Ibid.*
9. *Ibid.*
10. *Ibid.*

11

The Disproportionate Impact of COVID-19 on Indian Society

A Study

Imtiyaz Ahmad Wani and *Akumarthi Nageswara Rao*

Introduction

An outbreak of a typical pneumonia (Coronavirus Disease 2019, COVID-19) emerged in Wuhan, China, in late December 2019. The virus rapidly spread across China and the rest of the world, and India also has borne the brunt of the same. "The outbreak of a mysterious pneumonia characterized by fever, dry cough, and fatigue, and occasional gastrointestinal symptoms happened in a seafood wholesale wet market, the Huanan Seafood Wholesale Market, in Wuhan, Hubei, China. Initially, an outbreak involving a local market, the Huanan Seafood Market, with at least 41 people was reported. The local health authority issued an "epidemiologic alert" on December 31, 2019, and the market was shut down on January 1, 2020. A total of 59 suspected cases with fever and dry cough were referred to a designated hospital (the Jin Yin-tan Hospital). Of the 59 suspected cases, 41 patients were confirmed by next-generation sequencing or real-time reverse transcription-polymerase chain reaction (RT-PCR)."[1] The spread was so colossal that the World Health Organization (WHO) had to declare it as a pandemic on March 11, 2020. Coronavirus disease 2019 (COVID-19) is an emerging respiratory infection caused by a novel coronavirus called Severe Acute Respiratory Syndrome coronavirus 2 (SARS-CoV-2). COVID-19 has created a global health crisis where countless people are dying, human suffering is spreading, and people's lives are being upended. It is not only just a health crisis but also a social and economic crisis, both of which are fundamental to sustainable development. This pandemic has affected all segments of society. However, it is particularly damaging to vulnerable social groups, including people living in poverty, older persons, persons with disabilities, youths, indigenous people and ethnic minorities. "In terms of employment, youth are disproportionately unemployed, and those who are employed often work in the informal economy or gig economy, on precarious contracts or in the service sectors of the economy, that are likely to be severely affected by COVID-19. Many vulnerable youth such as migrants or homeless youth are in precarious situations. They are the ones who can easily be overlooked if governments do not pay specific attention, as they tend to be already in a situation without even their minimum requirements being met on health, education, employment and well-being."[2] In the current COVID-19 pandemic, inclusive social protection is even more vital to protect young people who are already, in normal times, at a higher economic and social risk. Because young people are disproportionately affected by unemployment, the COVID-19 pandemic will likely drastically increase unemployed youth, a population already overrepresented in the informal economy (around three quarters of young workers are in informal employment around the world. "The COVID-19 pandemic has unleashed suffering and economic crises of historic proportions, adding to the urgent existing need for accelerated transitions to low-carbon economies. Concerns were raised about how the economic fallout from COVID-19 would affect climate action."[3]

Since women in India spend more hours caring for children, the elderly and sick family members, and masks and other personal protective equipments are often designed and sized for men; women may be at risk of more exposure to the virus. "Over 30 million people have been infected by the coronavirus in India. COVID-19 can infect people of all gender and ages. However, some women and girls may be at higher risk because they are poorer and lack information and resources, or because they are at the frontline as caregivers and workers in the health and service sectors. In India, women make up a significant proportion of all healthcare workers and more than 80 per cent of nurses and midwives. Yet, when it comes to decision-making roles in the health sector, they are largely absent, and they are paid much less than their male counterparts. Only 13 per cent of the members of the national COVID-19 task force are women."[4] The second wave of COVID-19 in India brought unprecedented losses. The poorest and the most marginalized, including women and girls, face more risks without the means to absorb the economic shocks and mitigate the health crisis. They are caring for their families, sustaining livelihoods and leading efforts to fight the pandemic, amidst the threat of a third wave.

Psychological Effects of COVID-19

Pandemics have devastating effects on not only the psychology of people experiencing the pandemic during the process, but even the psychology of future people. Pandemics such as HIV/ AIDS, influenza, SARS, MERS, which have appeared in the past and threatened the health of people, have also led to negative consequences in people's psychology. Considering the effects of pandemics on the groups of people living in the community, it can be seen that it affects directly patients, and their relatives, healthcare staff, and all other people who are at risk of disease (Morganstein *et al.*, 2017). The psychological reaction of each person in the face of intense stress and fear caused by pandemics can be different. It has been observed that pandemics cause psychological effects such as depression, anxiety, fear of death, losing loved ones, post-traumatic stress disorder, psychotic symptoms and mourning in general (Taylor, 2019). However, some people can control the negative emotions of pandemics and continue their lives normally. But some people cannot cope with these feelings and need professional support. In this regard, the negative consequences for individuals and the society from the beginning of its spread to its control are regarded as unpredictable disaster. Physiologically and psychologically, the most affected people by the COVID-19 pandemic are those who suffer from this pandemic. Quarantine and home isolation are one of the most important issues in the investigation of the psychological impact of the COVID-19 epidemic. During the period when COVID-19 began to emerge and spread, the education process of the youth continued. Because of the rapid spread of the epidemic and the increase of deaths in many countries young people have stopped their education and stayed in their homes. Therefore, the likelihood of loneliness and depression increased in young people whose education process was negatively affected and their social relations were disrupted. Although they can continue their social relations through internet and social media applications, it is obvious that they will not be as healthy and high quality as social relations established face to face. This situation can be claimed to decrease the relationships and life satisfaction. At the same time, due to the development of technology, compared to other age groups young people can be exposed to negative flows caused by the COVID-19 epidemic around the world through internet and social media. This situation can be claimed to make young people psychologically more risky than other age groups.[5] Millions of agricultural workers—waged and self-employed—while feeding the world, regularly face high levels of working poverty, malnutrition and poor health, and suffer from a lack of safety and labour protection as well as other types of abuse. With low and irregular incomes and a lack of social support, many of them are spurred to continue working, often in unsafe conditions, thus exposing themselves and their families to additional risks. Further, when experiencing income losses, they may resort to negative coping strategies, such as distress sale of assets, predatory loans or child labour.

Review of Literature

1. **Debora MacKenzie** (2020) *Stopping the Next Pandemic: How COVID-19 Can Help Us Save Humanity.*[6] Debora MacKenzie has been reporting on emerging diseases for more than three decades, and she draws on that experience to explain how COVID-19 went from a potentially manageable outbreak to a global pandemic. Offering a compelling history of the most significant recent outbreaks, including SARS, MERS, H1N1, Zika, and Ebola, she gives a crash course in Epidemiology 101—how viruses spread and how pandemics end—and outlines the lessons we failed to learn from each past crisis. In vivid detail, she takes us through the arrival and spread of COVID-19, making clear the steps that governments knew they could have taken to prevent or at least prepare for this. Looking forward, MacKenzie makes a bold, optimistic argument: this pandemic might finally galvanize the world to take viruses seriously. Fighting this pandemic and preventing the next one will take political action of all kinds, globally, from governments, the scientific community, and individuals—but it is possible. No one has yet brought together our knowledge of COVID-19 in a comprehensive, informative, and accessible way. But that story can already be told, and Debora MacKenzie's urgent telling is required reading for these times and beyond. It is too early to say where the COVID-19 pandemic will go, but it is past time to talk about what went wrong and how we can do better.
2. **Wu, Yi-Chi, Chen, Ching-Sung Chan, Yu-Jiun** (March 2020) *Journal of the Chinese Medical Association. "The outbreak of COVID-19: An overview."* Currently, there is no validated treatment for COVID-19. The main strategies are symptomatic and supportive care, such as keeping vital signs, maintaining oxygen saturation and blood pressure, and treating complications, such as secondary infections or organs failure. Since there are no standard treatments for

COVID-19, it is important to avoid infection or further spreading. For healthcare workers, personal protective equipment should be put on and taken off properly while caring probable or confirmed patients. Stringent protection procedures should be conducted for high-risk procedures (such as endoscopy, Ambu bagging, and endotracheal tube intubation).

3. **Phumzile Mlambo-Ngcuka** (April 6, 2020*) Violence against women and girls: the shadow pandemic.*[7] With 90 countries in lockdown, four billion people are now sheltering at home from the global contagion of COVID-19. It is a protective measure, but it brings another deadly danger. We see a shadow pandemic growing, of violence against women. As more countries report infection and lockdown, more domestic violence help lines and shelters across the world are reporting rising calls for help. As the COVID-19 pandemic continues, this number is likely to grow with multiple impacts on women's well-being, their sexual and reproductive health, their mental health, and their ability to participate and lead in the recovery of our societies and economy. The increase in violence against women must be dealt with urgently with measures embedded in economic support and stimulus packages that meet the gravity and scale of the challenge and reflect the needs of women who face multiple forms of discrimination. The Secretary-General has called for all governments to make the prevention and redress of violence against women, a key part of their national response plans for COVID-19. Shelters and help lines for women must be considered an essential service for every country with specific funding and broad efforts made to increase awareness about their availability.

Objectives of the Study

The present study was carried out with the following objectives:

1. To analyze the impact of COVID-19 on people's lives;
2. The evaluation of the psychological and social effects of the pandemic on the society;
3. To highlight the economic issues facing by people due to COVID-19.

Research Methodology

The present study is basically descriptive and analytical in nature and is based on observation method. The data used in this study is purely from secondary sources.

Scope and Limitations of the Study

Scientific research on COVID-19 is of great importance in order to prevent the destructiveness of it in social, political, psychological and economic dimensions. In this context, a researcher may follow maximal scientific methods to come to the literal conclusions.

Conclusions and Recommendations

People with no home or shelter such as refugees, migrants or displaced persons will suffer disproportionately, both during the pandemic and in its aftermath. This might occur in multiple ways, such as experiencing limited moment, fewer employment opportunities, increased xenophobia, etc. The COVID-19 pandemic has disrupted every aspect of our lives. Even before the onset of the crisis, the social and economic integration of young people was an ongoing challenge. Now, unless urgent action is taken, young people are likely to suffer severe and long-lasting impacts from the pandemic. The social crisis created by the COVID-19 pandemic may also increase inequality, discrimination and medium and long-term unemployment if not properly addressed by appropriate policies. 2019-nCoV infection is a zoonotic disease with low to moderate mortality rate. Currently, there is no standard treatment for the disease and supportive treatment is the only strategy. Although many experimental trials are on the way, the best we can do to prevent a rampant outbreak is stringent infection control operation. First-line healthcare providers should be highly aware of appropriate infection prevention measures for suspected patients. Since women in India spend more hours caring for children, the elderly and sick family members, and masks and other personal protective equipments are often designed and sized for men; women may be at risk of more exposure to the virus. Physiologically and psychologically, the most affected people by the COVID-19 pandemic are those who suffer from this pandemic. Now is the time for global solidarity and support, especially with the most vulnerable in our societies, particularly in the emerging and developing world. The fight against the COVID-19 pandemic is global as well as on a national basis. Only together can we overcome the intertwined health and social and economic impacts of the pandemic and prevent its escalation into a protracted humanitarian and food security catastrophe, with the potential loss of already achieved development gains. Currently, humanity is in the middle of a process that must be rigorously managed. In this context, it is necessary to reveal scientific researches about COVID-19 and to discuss the short and long term effects of it on people.

Notes

1. Wu, Yi-Chi, Chen, Ching-Sung Chan, Yu-Jiun (March 2020): *Journal of the Chinese Medical Association. The outbreak of COVID-19: An overview,* Volume 83, Issue 3, pp. 217-220.
2. United Nations, https://www.un.org/development/desa/dspd/everyone-included-COVID-19.html (Accessed on January 20, 2022).
3. Coalition Secretariat (July 10, 2020): *Better Recovery, Better World: Resetting Climate Action in the Aftermath of the COVID-19 Pandemic.* https://www.financeministersforclimate.org/news/better-recovery-better-world-resetting-climate-action-aftermath-COVID-19-pandemic (Accessed on January 22, 2022).
4. UN Women (July 27, 2021): https://www.unwomen.org/en/news/stories/2021/7/faq-women-and-COVID-19-in-india?gclid=EAIaIQobChMIpfmUgYDF9QIVl5pmAh1NzQDNEAAYAiAAEgLR4_D_BwE (Accessed on January 22, 2022).
5. Akat Muhammed, Karatas Kasim (August 30, 2020): *Psychological Effects of COVID-19 Pandemic on Society and Its Reflections on*

Education, https://www.researchgate.net/profile/Kasim-Karatas/publication/343976009_Psychological_Effects_of_COVID-19_Pandemic_on_Society_and_Its_Reflections_on_Education/links/5f4b718192851c6cfd012dee/Psychological-Effects-of-COVID-19-Pandemic-on-Society-and-Its-Reflections-on-Education.pdf (Accessed on January 23, 2022).

6. MacKenzie Debora (2020). *Stopping the Next Pandemic: How COVID-19 Can Help Us Save Humanity,* Hachette Books.
7. Mlambo-Ngcuka Phumzile, Executive Director of UN Women, https://www.unwomen.org/en/news/stories/2020/4/statement-ed-phumzile-violence-against-women-during-pandemic?gclid=EAIaIQobChMIjPmb6fTE9QIVBpNmAh1lzQD_EAAYASAAEgKNMPD_BwE (Accessed on January 24, 2022).

12

The Changing Pattern of Sino-Indian Relations in South Asia

A Post-COVID Assessment

Sujit Kumar Datta

Introduction

South Asia is a word used to denote the southern part of the Asian continent, which comprises the South Asian Association for Regional Cooperation (SAARC) countries. South Asia is bounded on the South by the Indian Ocean and land by West Asia, Central Asia, East Asia, and Southeast Asia (World Bank, 2018). China always wants a peaceful and development-oriented relationship with South Asian counties. Besides, South Asian small counties need more economic cooperation from China as well as India. The peaceable growth of China has become more pertinent in the background of South Asia as it is perceived not as a threat to the neighbouring countries as the conventional International Relations theories argue concerning the rise of a hegemon; instead, the East Asian countries accommodated the rise of China than balancing it since this rise comes with an 'absence of fear' (Bijan, Z., 2005).

However, this has not been the case for China's immediate big neighbour, also vying to be a significant, influential authority in that region, India. The 'geopolitical centrality' of South Asia had recognized by mainly the British colonial administration. As a result, traditional geopolitical understanding of international relations has resurfaced where both the countries are set out for constructing their global identity as 'the Asian Power' (Srinivasan, T.N., 2005).

In this context, this chapter argues that the South Asian state has emerged as one of the main parts to transform the Sino-Indian relationship in South Asia after the Covid situation. With the rising effect of China and India as Asian giants, this chapter argues that the two powers are vying for geopolitical supremacy in that area though India is so behind China in all kinds of national and international components.

The Background of Research

The steady growth of China and rising India defines the Asian century with the corresponding impact on their domestic landscape and affecting the regional and global order. China has for centuries, maintained connections with South Asian nations, and Chinese travellers had written extensively about the region. China shares its boundary through five South Asian states named Afghanistan, Bhutan, India, Nepal and Pakistan. On the other hand, there is a geographical link with mountains and rivers with South Asian countries and China. While India is far behind China in the ranking of the world economy, democratic credentials of India happen to place New Delhi in good books of the great authorities, particularly the USA. However, South Asia does not appear central to Chinese global view. South Asia has not also been capable of creating a value chain for China in the worldwide market. China generally looks at South Asia for several perspectives. Nonetheless, geographically India promoted South Asian related diplomacy in the running century as neighbourhood policy towards South Asian nations. Even, India is a vital country of South Asia who can manage regional security.

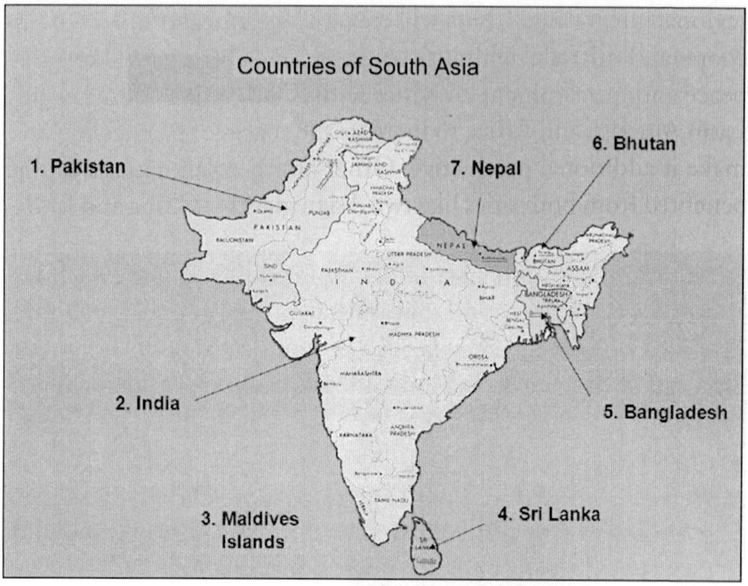

Map 12.1: Countries of South Asia.

Source: www. images.wisegeek.com

During the last seven decades, China has maintained excellent relations with South Asian nations to ensure South Asian harmony and safety, and China has followed "five principles of peaceful coexistence" policy which is more critical for Chinese foreign policy (Chung, C.P., 2009).

Nevertheless, China-India relations in South Asia has transformed into normal from 1988 to 2018. But, the two important Asian giants still have a challenging aspect of their bilateral relationship. Additionally, extra hegemonic perceptions of India in South Asia is a challenge for China to contain these kinds of hegemonic attitudes. For these reasons, South Asian small countries have maintained a decent relationship with China. In the context of South Asian politics, India's neighbouring countries underscored that peace and progress are the main features of 21st-century diplomatic vision. One the other hand, China wants to continue a close relationship with its neighbours to develop regional integration. China will create a local integration process to cooperate with its neighbour's countries. Even, China will focus its peace and development activities with South Asian countries like Latin America and Africa to increase the spaces of partnership and make it additional productive. Other South Asian nations can be benefited from both sides like two Asian giants—China and India.

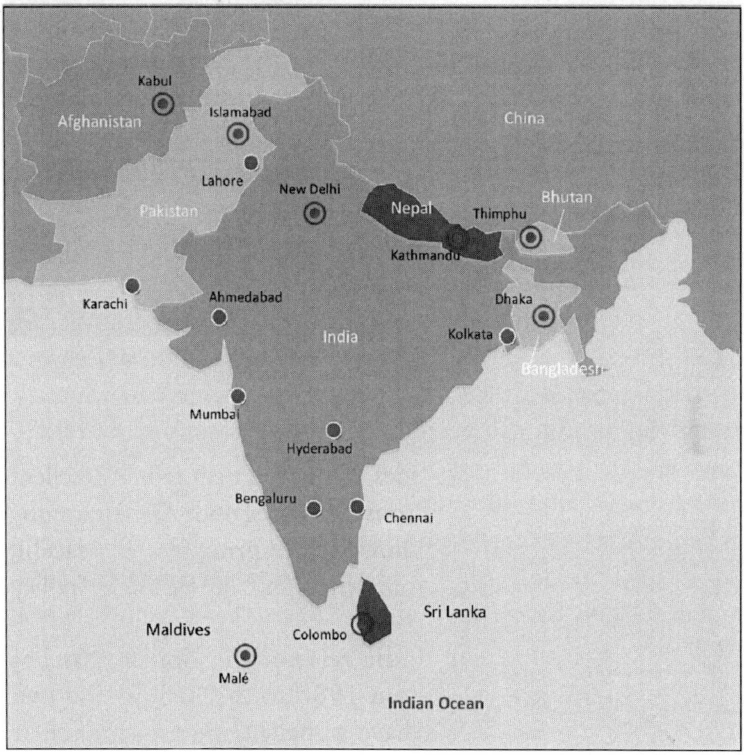

Map 12.2: China and South Asia.

Source: https://yourfreetemplates.com

This opportunity has been accomplished by completing administrative-political and structural constructions to bring low-tech Chinese factories to South Asian countries, making Chinese investment industrial-energy and infrastructure development, taking full advantage of the ocean-going blue economy. South Asian small states want to take advantage of these two Asian giants China and India rivalry or competition situation (Pant, H.V., 2013).

It is essential to overcome this situation that states of this region can come out with their national interest without being hurt, anyone. Increasing Chinese influence in South Asia is an excellent matter for India. India always wishes to lead the whole of South Asia, but some South Asian countries want to make good relations with China (Hall, I.). "Is a 'Modi doctrine' emerging in Indian foreign policy?" (Konwer, S., 2018). For these reasons, there is an unofficial conflict, cooperation as well as rivalry amid China and India in South Asian politics. The other South Asian countries should maintain a balanced foreign policy towards China and India (Holslag, J., 2010).

Research Question

This chapter will examine the difficulties and opportunities for transforming the Sino-Indian relationship in South Asia. Research questions related to why and how they change and what the underlying determinants are of the transformations in both states' behaviour in the context of South Asian politics. Thus, this chapter seeks to explain the transformation of the Sino-Indian relationship in South Asia for the following questions. The research question is:

"What factors have contributed to transforming the Sino-Indian relationship in the South Asian region in the post-Covid era?"

Research Methodology

Several research methods are usually employed in carrying out empirical social researches such as this research. The quantitative and statistical approach is used to conduct cross-national comparative studies based on aggregate data. Although the qualitative method is the primary tool to be employed in this study, quantitative and statistical method have used to get the public views regarding various issues and questions raised in different sections of this chapter. Thus, the techniques that I have followed here include both qualitative and interpretative analyses of primary as well as secondary data and materials such as books, articles, magazine, and government official documents, and survey data gathered through an email interview. To explore the involvement of China and India in South Asia, I have done library research combined with an examination of historical agreements and official documents, which included each government's publications, annual reports, defence white papers and interstate agreements, policy announcements and speeches to obtain primary sources of information. Secondary sources included academic journal articles, books, newspaper and information obtained from media and the Internet. To assess Sino-Indian transformation relationship in South Asia by using data from government documents, such as inter-state treaties and memorandum of understanding, legislative reports, and statistical compilations, which came in many formats, including books, periodicals, maps, and online databases, collected from Chinese, Indian and other South Asian countries governmental websites.

Theoretical Analysis

Regional transformation is the final category in Holsti's conceptualization of change in international politics. "It means quantitative changes which, when accumulated over a while, bring a new form to life. But, logically, the new forms must derive from old patterns. They can partly replace old forms, but by definition, they must include residues or legacies of the old. One cannot transform from nothing". *The Problem of Change in International Relations* (Holsti, K.J., 1964). In other words, transformation means that old ideas, practices and norms may remain reasonably similar over long periods, but the functions of the institutions change. The main interest in this study will be Holsti's final category transformation for explaining Sino-Indian transforming relationship in South Asia.

The reason for this is that while Holsti is more general and broad and explains transformation contextualizing International Relations theory, Paul, by contrast, is more specific and presents it in the context of a region. According to Paul, "regional transformation means 'serious alterations have occurred in relations among states, and in terms of their core national interests, strategies, behavioural patterns, perceptions, and institutional structures" (T.V. Paul. 2012). Three criteria stand out important in Paul's definition of regional transformation; first, meaningful alterations in the perceptions, core interests and strategies; second, fundamental alterations in behavioural patterns; and third, severe modifications in relations among states. Paul's criteria of regional transformation will help us to explain the changing way of conflict and cooperation in South Asia and whether the region has changed at the end of the Cold War. Three key areas are selected for closer scrutiny in this study: democracy, political economy and security.

As Paul argues: "Transformational change in a region could occur through the introduction of democratic order, robust economic interdependence, or an institutional framework among the core countries that constitute a region" (T.V. Paul, 2012). This issue primarily concerns the theoretical debate within International Relations about Sino-Indian transformative relationship in South Asia from 1988 to 2018 between neoliberalism and realism. Neoliberalism emphasizes the democracy, economic interdependence and institutions as a mechanism for regional peace and order (Bruce Russett and John R. Oneal, 1997). Realism argues that the fundamental source of regional order is the balance of power (T.V. Paul, James Wirtz and Michael Fortmann, 2004). While the liberalism sees regional transformation as a linear progression towards peace eventually heading towards a local security community and realism views peace as episodic.

There are three possible scenarios of transformative Sino-Indian relationship in South Asia. These are Cooperation Scenario, Competition Scenario and Competition with Cooperation Scenario. This thesis is going to test the hypothesis, arguing on which theoretical background is most appropriate to describe the transformation of the Sino-India relationship in South Asia. However, after reviewing the theory of Complex Interdependence and Benjamin Miller's view of significant power involvement in regional politics, this thesis aims to identify which hypotheses derive from this framework and to provide the best explanations of transformations of Sino-Indian relationship in South Asia.

At present, China and India in South Asia is the most robust demand for all South Asian nations. In recent time, China and India both are eager to enlarge their economy and power with their neighbours. Realist and neoliberals agree that countries are the maximum significant performers in the global scene and that egoist interests under the complex interdependence mainly influence their behaviours. However, they have different ideas regarding the attitudes of the state towards the distribution of cooperative gains. According to realists, states utility functions strongly consider how the benefits of cooperation are redistributed among countries, affirming that collaboration can fail if its services lead to a change in terms of power distribution. However, great powers have involved in South Asian politics from different dimensions. Finally, the Sino-Indian transformative relationship in South Asia is related to complex interdependence theory.

Historical Background of Sino-Indian Relations in South Asia

The history and background of Sino-Indian bilateral relationship in South Asia were mixed mistrust, cooperation and competition. "The 'peaceful rise' of China has become more pertinent in the context of Asia as it is perceived not as a threat to the neighbouring countries as the conventional International Relations (IR) theories argue concerning the rise of a hegemon; instead the East Asian countries accommodated the rise of China than balancing it since this rise comes with an 'absence of fear'" (Garver, John W., 2002).

However, "this has not been the case for China's immediate big-neighbour, also vying to become a leader in Asia, India. The 'geopolitical centrality' of Asia and the recognition of India and China as continental powers were long recognized by mainly the British colonial administration, especially about the British Raj's impending departure from the continent" (Peter John Brobst, Sir

Olaf Caroe, 2006). It is contended that "the term 'Great Game' was coined by a British Officer named William Connolly around 1840 and was later popularized by Rudyard Kipling to refer to the mastery of Asia" (Peter John Brobst, Sir Olaf Caroe, 2006). As a result, traditional geopolitical understanding of international relations has resurfaced where both the countries are set out for constructing their global identity as 'the Asian Power'. In the South Asian context, this chapter argues that the South Asia region has arisen as one of the critical areas of possible Sino-Indian strategic competitive location.

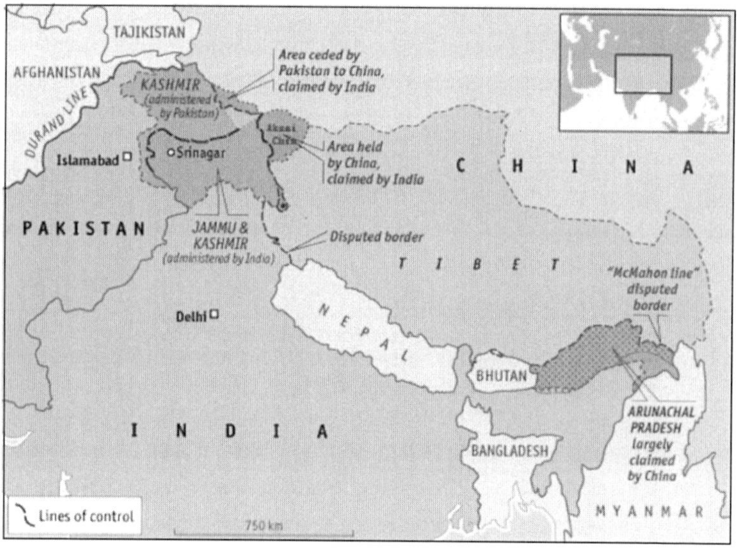

Map 12.3: The Line of Actual Control of the Sino-Indian border, 1959-to date.

Source: *The Economist* (2016).

China may not become part of South Asia on the ground of geographically, historically and culturally. But, "China is with South Asia on many grounds like political, strategic, economic and even cultural. China may not be geographically and historically part of South Asia, but its growing presence is being felt in South Asia, and it is going to keep its presence felt in the affairs of South Asian politics" (Brewster, David Gomà, 2018).

There are not many people in South Asia who bother much whether China geographically belongs to South Asia or not except India. There is a discernible difference of opinion about Chinese role in that region and its impression on same region politics among cross-sections of people in various South Asian countries. Most people in South Asian countries shape their views of China on differing threat perception of different South Asian counties and how China fits into their respective threat perceptions. India perceives China's greater involvement, especially its ties with Pakistan, Bangladesh, Sri Lanka and partly with Nepal as a threat to itself in terms of security which it tends to equate with its supremacy over the whole region. Thus, every Chinese step to make an inroad into South Asian politics is considered as a threat by India (Van Ness, Peter, 2018).

Besides this, all South Asian small countries welcomed China's role, presence, engagement and greater involvement in this region in all forms and manifestation as stabilizing, positive, necessary and geopolitical important, perhaps except Bhutan is the only India-friendly elements (Kumar, Pranav). "Sino-Bhutanese Relations: Under the Shadow of India-Bhutan Friendship" (China Report, 2010).

These tiny states of South Asia see China's existence in the area as a countervailing power to India and the West. It increases their autonomy *vis-à-vis* India and West too. Besides this, many of these countries lament China's 'lacklustre' attitude and response to Indian and USA moves to South Asia. These hardliners even urge for more forceful and multifaceted participation of China in South Asian politics. The Indian view on the Chinese involvement in South Asia is inquisitive and self-contradictory. Because Sino-Indian trade is increasing day by day and it is no problem at all. But, it is more problematic whenever China engages itself in economic and other activities such as trade, aid and investment, military assistance programme with smaller South Asian countries. Indian policy elites view that as a risk to the 'Common South Asian Identity'. But, the main reason is that China has much more offer to these smaller

South Asian countries where India can't match and doesn't want to offer. Either way, there are divergent views in South Asia regarding Chinese involvement in South Asian politics. Sometimes, it is the wonder why the Indian policy elites think that what is suitable for India may not or must not be right for other South Asian countries.

Smaller South Asian countries rightly or not perceive India as some sort of threat to them. Thus, it is just natural that they would welcome Chinese engagement is this region as that would give them an alternative source for development opportunities, more autonomy *vis-à-vis* India and the West. China also naturally wants to expand its market and investment and make more well-wisher. "India's policy of opposing Bhutanese attempt to establish diplomatic ties with China is ease point to understand Indian attitude towards China in the context of South Asian politics. India always fears that its smaller neighbours are a threat to it in one way or another and would pose a greater threat if they are in good terms with China" (Gupta, Prakash C., and Cecily S. Ray, 2003).

Indian policy elites have developed a habit of securitizing economic relations and development activities in other South Asian countries by China while it would not or could not offer economic benefits and investment to these countries. One wonders if the message is that you don't need to develop if that is going to be supported by China, the 'extra-regional' country—because then it will have 'security' implications for South Asia which for Indian policy elites means (Gonsalves, Eric, 2018).

The Indian policy elites considered not acceptable neighbourhood policy as espoused by a short time foreign minister and Prime Minister of India Inder Kumar (IK) Gujral, but interference and meddling into the internal affairs of its neighbours as the sure way to maintain its influence and dominance. South Asian affairs and undercut the basis of a cooperative, harmonious, shared South Asian identity, community and organization like the SAARC (Murthy, Padmaja. 1999). There is a strong feeling among many South Asian countries that the sub-region should move beyond present security fixation. The tendency of India, Pakistan and even others to securitize everything and judging everything from the realist security perspective must be amended, and they all should refocus on cooperative, prosperous economic development efforts together. But, that would not happen excluding China which is already in the affairs of the region. Whether we like it or not since China has a long border with five South Asian states and very close proximity with Bangladesh (Ali, Syed Muazzem, 2018). "The Current and Future State of India-Bangladesh Relations." Strategic Analysis, Vol. 42, No. 5, 2018, pp. 529-537.

As Sino-South Asia map shows that South Asia cannot develop itself excluding Chinese involvement and Chinese hydroelectric project on the river Tsang Po as the Brahmaputra is called in Tibet, China's cooperation should not be limited between China-India and China-Pakistan. However, all countries should have the win-win economic and other ties with China. Only the prosperous and secure neighbours can give India more sense of security and weak, poor, unstable, vulnerable and dominated neighbours would simply create more insecurity and will keep India itself down along with entire South Asia. China, it seems at least shortly does not want to challenge Indian preeminence in South Asia (Bosworth, Barry, and Susan M. Collins). "Accounting for Growth: Comparing China and India" (Bosworth, B., & Collins, S.M. 2008).

The best possible way for the whole of South Asia would be to forge a cooperative, stabilizing, development-based relationship with a rising China rather than ostracizing it or shying away from it and securitizing its involvement in the affairs of South Asian region. China has become a global actor as well as an actor in the South Asian sub-region. All should strive to find ways as to how to engage China in positive, stabilizing, development role in South Asia and how Sino-South Asian relationship can usher in a prosperous future for both South Asia and China.

Factors to Transform Sino-Indian Relations in South Asia in the post-COVID era

Sino-Indian transformative relations in South Asia have become increasingly involved in the last few decades. Though bilateral trade and cooperation has been growing, concerns have been increasingly strained by mutual suspicion and intermittent disputes. Given the vast influence, the two Asian giants have over the global strategic environment, a critical question that arises will be whether they can maintain a stable relationship amidst their growing distrust. This chapter will analyze the independent variables—Political and economic factors—which transform Sino-Indian relationship in South Asia with the help of Complex Interdependence theory in the case of their history of enmity; trade; strategic competition and cooperation in the case of great powers impact to transform Sino-Indian relationship in South Asia; especially USA's and Russian impact to South Asia. In general, Sino-Indian relations are influenced by several factors: (1) Historical legacy and Border Crisis; (2); Economy; (3) Soft power; (4) Indian nuclear test-1998; (5) Doklam standoff-2017; (6) Ladakh Crisis-2020; (7) Great powers impact. Related to another area of the world, South Asia has not been the top priority area for either the USA, Russia since the completion of the stony conflict (Gordon, Sandy, 1995).

Though in the 1990s, India's financial risk and its explosion of the nuclear bomb injected a new dynamism and complexity to the region, South Asia still has not acquired a significant devotion in the USA, Russian and Chinese external strategy perspectives. The breakdown of the Soviet Union that concluded the Cold War bipolar conflict between the USA and the USSR somewhat eased the safety situation in South Asia, thus reducing the significance of the region. But, a turnaround came after the 9/11 terror attacks that bought a decisive reorientation of the USA external strategy perspective on South Asian area. Concomitantly, it similarly refocused China's attention to South Asia. The 9/11 era brought a convergence of interest of great powers, especially the USA, Russia and China, on achieving stable South Asia. Specifically, these countries preferred a resilient and steady Pakistan and sought an end to terrorism in Afghanistan. These great powers were keen to avoid the area from flattering an atomic climax between India and Pakistan. However, despite this convergence of interests in the USA, Russia, and Chinese perspectives on South Asia, a critical area of divergence arose between the two on the issue of Indo-USA relations. Indo-USA relations altered the regional security balance. For China, in particular, this meant a grave security threat that brought the USA, Russia and China's doorsteps. Remarkably, the combined role of USA-India in the South Asian area is a significant risk for China. The major crisis of this region is not only Sino-India conflict nor India and Pakistan tension but also great powers in South Asia. As Indo-USA relations decisively impinge on China's security, South Asia has arisen as a new fulcrum of power competition among the USA, Russia and China in the post 9/11 era.

Discussion

By exploring the transformation of Sino-Indian relationship in South Asia, this chapter has focused on a principal question—"What factors have contributed to transforming the Sino-Indian relationship in the South Asian region?" The outcome of this research has generally borne out Complex Interdependence that the interconnection between the arguments and the empirical evidence corroborates the effects of independent variables. These factors have played a significant role to define the nature of Sino-Indian relations, which is not characterized by all the elements of rivalry as described in most of the literature, but as cooperation with deep engagement diplomatically and economically, cooperation in regional issues, and also competition in security arenas. This variable also offers competing explanations for local transformations.

This chapter has explored the underlying factors of transforming the Sino-Indian relationship in South Asia. Here, the independent variable is "factors to transform Sino-Indian relationship in South Asia", which refers to the changes from confrontation to cooperation. The main factors which transform Sino-Indian relationship in

South Asia are historical legacy, economy, soft power, Indian nuclear test-1998, Doklam standoff-2017, Ladakh Crisis-2020, joint employment and social challenges, significant powers impact (USA and Russia) impact on transforming Sino-Indian relationship in South Asia. The dependent variables comprise of two sets of variables, the one is "Sino-Indian transformative relationship in South Asia", and another is "Sino-Indian economic and strategic cooperation and competition in South Asia". The transformation of the Sino-Indian relationship in South Asia from 1988 to 2018 is about four stages. These are Recovery period (1988-1998), Frozen Period (1998-2003), Acceleration Period (2003-2013) and the Cooperative Period (2013-2018).

The areas of cooperation and competition of Sino-Indian transformative relationship in South Asia are trade and investment, security, the Indian Ocean, disaster management, anti-terrorism, energy, soft power, ICT etc. By analyzing both the variables of this chapter, it is clear that from several perspectives there exist a correlation between them. The independent variable has different impacts on dependent variables as it results in cooperation and competition both in Sino-Indian relationship in South Asia. The variables also indicate how the Sino-Indian relationship has been transforming in South Asia and mainly the factors of transformation that affect this transformation. The independent variable correlates with the dependent variables as it results in cooperation and competition both in Sino-Indian transformative relationship in South Asia. The independent variable of this present research is mentioned as the factors to transform the Sino-Indian relationship in South Asia, which have an impact on the dependent variables of the study. The transformation of the Sino-Indian relationship in South Asia has occurred in different stages.

On the other side, another set of the dependent variable on Sino-Indian strategic and economic cooperation and competition in South Asia portrays several fields where both the countries have collaboration and in some areas competition in the South Asian region. Here, it is clear that in South Asia, both India and China have several fields where they are cooperating each other and also maintaining an excellent strategic and economic relationship which even the result of several factors. Similarly, regarding the competition between these countries in South Asia, there are some specific areas too where both have own strategic and economic interests in this region and these competitions are also the effects of the independent variable of this research that is the factors to transform Sino-Indian relationship in South Asia. However, considering the independent variable and two sets of dependent variables, this research showed the correlation among them, and it depicted that the independent variables have a significant impact on the dependent variables.

In sum, the general framework of the research variables is as described above. The research hypothesis has examined these variables to test the theory of complex interdependence and Benjamin Miller's idea of significant power involvement in regional politics to understand the Sino-Indian transformative relationship in South Asia.

Future Challenges and Recommendations

There are some significant challenges for further transforming the Sino-Indian relationship in South Asia.

Firstly, a political consensus has not yet been translated into political reality. At the meeting in Wuhan, the two countries reached several vital agreements on the policy.

Secondly, the potential for economic and trade investment still has been more expressed. The China-India industrial structure has its characteristics, with software-hardware complementary advantages. As of November 2018, China was India's third-place export destination and the largest source of imports.

Thirdly, humanistic communication base is relatively weak. Like the two ancient civilizations, China and India have had a history of communication for more than 2000 years. They have become a significant word in the history of the exchange of civilizational civilizations, leaving rich strains and spiritual traditions for thousands of years. Indian song and dance, astronomy, calendar, literature, architecture and sugar technology have been introduced in China, with Chinese paper, silk, porcelain, tea and music, etc. The history of communication between the two peoples has been historical evidence of interconnect and mutual learning of their countries since ancient times.

Fourthly, third-party issues and historical legacies continue to interfere with relations between the two countries during the period. The impetus for advancing China-India relations comes from the intrinsic value of the relationship, and the two countries' relations can determine a third-party factor by no means.

There are some policy recommendations and potential areas which may sponsor an additional steady and supportive Sino-India two-sided relations in the context of South Asian politics in the future. These are:

1. China and India should solve the boundary issues and take Sino-Indian relationship to the heights, which is the most critical factor for China-India relations in South Asian politics. Both sides should realize that the minor adjustment of "Line of Actual Control (LAC)" will be an excellent initiative to relieve the border problem, which is the most critical limitation of Sino-Indian relations.
2. Eliminate negative impact from third-party factors by remaining strategically determined. Facing a rapidly evolving and complex domestic and international situation, China and India must stay strategically focused. They should not let short-term ups and downs cause tunnel vision. Both China and India have firmly followed the strategy of independence and non-violent progress and cherish their strategic autonomy. India enjoys great prestige in the Non-Aligned Movement, has a strong independent national character, and upholds its values and principles in foreign exchange without following others blindly. These national characteristics are much appreciated by Chinese people and

form an essential cornerstone for India to build its place in a multi-polar world.

3. China and India need to transform their financial model with international trade policy. Likewise, the current global system needs to change. There are many clauses in the country's import-export law, which are obstacles to South Asia countries to invest in China and India. By correcting these policies and regulations, China and India must create open conditions for South Asian countries.
4. Both countries should talk to each other on the matter of China-Pakistan relations because China-Pakistan relations is another crucial factor in China-India relations. Beijing will also assure New Delhi that China's continuing ties with Pakistan is only for economic cooperation which may serve as a helpful force to end subsidiary more extremist actions and to establish dogmatic clearance on the Kashmir matter.
5. China-India must express their misperceptions and mistakes on their strategical involvement in South Asia. Both have the nuclear ballistic development programmes Beijing and New Delhi have an avowed the policy of NO First Use (NFU). But India demanded China to using this strategy only for their two-sided NFU commitment which has been escaped by China. China grips enough amount of weaponry board entirely main Indian metropolises. India's present growth of the 'Agni' projectile goals to address that tactical inequity. By this period, likely Chinese replies to USA placement of projectile protection could in chance activate and the Indian accumulation of its atomic and projectile militaries. Like this background, tactical discourse and the overview of weapons regulator instrument a bi-lateral NFU would be one such measure could head off a needless weapons race.
6. The leaders of the two states ought to have the foresight to appear outside the safety prism. There are many zones in which China and India could collaborate in South Asia. Mutually two states care "Panchsheel or Five Principles of

Peaceful Coexistence" as the basis of foreign policy. On the other side, the two nations face control policy and intervention in national matters. As the two central Asian emerging states, China and India also pursue an extra reasonable, just and useful global financial direction so that worldwide South Asia can better advantage from the 21st century's global economic system.

7. South Asia is the furthermost significant market for both countries. China and India have great potential to enlarge trade to the South Asian countries, which is unhappily insufficient. China and India can acquire from each other on their limited areas which maybe helpful for the South Asian small countries.
8. China and India should realize their mutual interests and benefits which will cooperate in the coming decades as far as their mutual bilateral relations with other states.

Conclusion

There are ample signs that the transformation of the Sino-Indian relationship in South Asia have significantly changed in the present decade. Indian businesses are becoming busy trying to intensify economic relations with China, Chinese business people visiting Indian states to look for opportunities to invest, Chinese officials openly talking about wanting to invest a massive amount in South Asia. The smaller South Asian counties—like Bangladesh, Nepal and Sri Lanka—always wanted to have close relations with China. Although the prevailing discourses in international relations like to see this as attempts to balance India, it is much more than that as any perceptive observer can see. Chinese President Xi Jinping has attributed quite a high degree of importance to China's relationship with India and thinks that it is essential to have India walking beside China. His rhetoric makes one feel like the Nehru era friendship is back only this time, China is much more powerful and developed and far ahead of India. Xi thought that China and India should be direct trains pouring regional growth and twin announcers of provincial harmony and solidity.

When China and India join hands for collaboration, it will advantage not only the two nations but also the whole South Asian area. President Xi stated that "Chinese 'dragon' and the Indian 'elephant' should join each other in a duet, not a dual". "A duet, not a duel: China's worldview has evolved" (*The Hindustan Times*, 2018). Also Indian Prime Minister told that "When India and China work together, 1+1 is not two, but eleven". "I'm first Indian PM you came out of Beijing to receive: PM Narendra Modi to Xi Jinping in Wuhan" (*The Times of India*, 2018).

China and India have some striking similarities. Both the states are antique civilizations of the world having a magnificent past and again revived as new states in the mid-20th century. Demographically being the two most powerful nations in the world, "China and India are composed secretarial for more than a third of the world's total population. Today, China's economy is about five times larger than India's" (*The World Fact Book*, 2019). In the context of global politics, China's economic growth rates are so high rather than India. Both the nations have reemerged as major international and economic powers. This makes the Sino-Indian relationship in the South Asia serious not only for those existing in China and India but also for the entire world.

References

Ali, Syed Muazzem (2018). *The Current and Future State of India-Bangladesh Relations, Strategic Analysis*, Vol. 42, No. 5, pp. 529-537.

Bijan, Z. (2005). "China is rising in the 21st century", *Foreign Affairs*, Vol. 84, p. 18.

Bosworth, B., & Collins, S.M. (2008). "Accounting for growth: comparing China and India". *Journal of Economic Perspectives*, *22*(1), 45-66.

Brewster, David Gomà (2018). "China-India Relations in the Contemporary World", *Pacific Affairs*, Vol. 91, No. 3, pp. 553-554.

Bruce Russett and John R. Oneal. (1997). *Triangulating Peace: Democracy, Interdependence and International Organizations*, New York: W.W. Norton, pp. 37-41.

China Report (*2010*). Vol. 46, No. 3, pp. 243-252.

Chung, C.P. (2009). "The Good Neighbor Policy in the Context of China's Foreign Relations", *China: An International Journal*, Vol. 7, No. 01, pp. 107-123.

Garver, John W. (2002). "The security dilemma in Sino-Indian relations", *India Review*, Vol. 1, No. 4, pp. 1-38.

Gonsalves, Eric. (2018). "India, China, and the World: A Connected History", *Indian Foreign Affairs Journal*, Vol. 13, No. 2, pp. 177-181.

Gordon, Sandy. (1995). "South Asia after the Cold War: Winners and Losers", *Asian Survey*, Vol. 35, No. 10, 1995, pp. 879-895.

Gupta, Prakash C., and Cecily S. Ray. (2003). "Smokeless tobacco and health in India and South Asia", *Respirology*, Vol. 8, No. 4, 2003, pp. 419-431.

Holslag, J. (2010). *India and China: Prospect for Peace*, New York, Columbia University Press, pp. 221-225.

Holsti, K.J. (1964). "The concept of power in the study of international relations." *Background*, *7*(4), 179-194.

Konwer, S. (2018). "Hallmarks of Current Indian Foreign Policy". *Indian Foreign Affairs Journal*, *13*(3), 231-241.

Murthy, Padmaja (1999). *The Gujral doctrine and beyond: Strategic Analysis*, Vol. 23, No. 4, pp. 639-652.

Pant, H.V. (2013). "India and China Rising", *Cambridge Review of International Affairs*, p. 26.

Peter John Brobst, Sir Olaf Caroe (2006). *The future of the great game and India's Independence and the Defense of Asia*, Akron: The University of Akron Press, p. 12.

Srinivasan, T. N. (2005). "Productivity and Economic Growth in South Asia and China", *The Pakistan Development Review*, pp. 479-503.

T.V. Paul, James Wirtz and Michael Fortmann (2004). *The literature on Realism is vast. A relevant work for our purpose to Balance of Power Theory and Practice in the 21st Century*, Stanford: Stanford University Press.

T.V. Paul (2012). *International Relations: Theory and Regional Transformation*, Cambridge: Cambridge University Press, p. 5.

The Hindustan Times (2018). available at "https://www.hindustantimes.com/analysis/a-duet-not-a-duel-china-s-world-view-has-evolved/story-ODTbJPWvi4XUmzXgfKwieI.html" (Accessed on 17th June, 2020).

The Times of India (2018). "http://timesofindia.indiatimes.com/articleshow/63940029. cms?utm_source=contentofinterest&utm_medium=text&utm_campaign=cppst" (Accessed on 17th May, 2020).

The World Bank (2018) available at "http://www.worldbank.org/en/region/sar" (Accessed on 18th February, 2019).

The World Fact Book (2019). Central Intelligence Agency (US) available at www.cia.gov/library/publications/resources/theworldfactbook/geos/in.htm. (Accessed on 17th March, 2020).

Van Ness, Peter. (2018). "China and the Third World: patterns of engagement and indifference", In *China and the World,* Routledge, pp. 151-168.

13
India-Australia Relations
Post-Cold War to COVID-19 Era

Bimalendu Ghosh

Introduction

India's civilisation is one of the oldest civilisations of the world. For many millennia its society and culture have been moulded and influenced by the rise and fall of empire and the coming and going of invaders. With independence in 1947, India became largest democracy in the world and established relation with other countries independently. The relationship between India and Australia during the Cold War period includes divergent geopolitical perspectives, ideological differences and weak economic links. The post-Cold War India-Australia relations are multidimensional but it was gradually evolved. From the mid-19th century, particularly in Western Australia, horses were bred in large numbers for the Indian Army's cavalry units. The government of Prime Minister Ben Chifley was a strong supporter of India's independence movement after World War II. Chifley's successor, Robert Menzies, Australia supported the admission of India as a Republic to the Commonwealth Nations. In 1950, Menzies became the first Australian Prime Minister to visit India, where he met with the Governor-General Chakravarti Rajagopalachari and

Prime Minister Jawaharlal Nehru. Many Indian students came to Australia to study under the Colombo Plan in the 1950s and 1960s. One of the strongest links between Australia and India is a shared love of sport, particularly cricket and hockey. Cricket Test matches began almost immediately after India's independence in 1947 (Onslow, 2013). This has grown into an intense rivalry as Indian teams developed into highly skilled players. In recent times large numbers of Indians have come to Australia as students, mostly in universities. Recently deposed Australian Prime Minister Tony Abbott went as far as to argue for the benefits given to India through its colonization, emphasizing India's Westminster system of government and the English language as the primary evidence (Davis, 2015). So, they are well connected from the Cold War period to COVID-19 era.

India and Australia are founding members of the United Nations. India and Australia co-operate in various multilateral fora like, G-20, Commonwealth of Nations, Indian Ocean Rim Association for Regional Cooperation (IOR-ARC), ASEAN Regional Forum, Asia Pacific Partnership on Climate and Clean Development, and have participated in the East Asia Summits. Both countries have also been cooperating as members of the Five Interested Parties (FIP) in the WTO context. Australia is an important player in APEC and supports India's membership of the organisation. In addition, Australia supports India's candidature in an expanded UN Security Council. In 2008, Australia became an Observer in SAARC (India-Australia Relations, www.mea.gov.in). They share partnership in many international organizations and plan to extend their cooperation.

The Consulate General of India in Sydney was first opened as a Trade Office in 1941 and the High Commission in Canberra in 1945. The Consulate General of India in Melbourne was opened in 2006. The Consulate General of India in Perth was inaugurated in October 2011 (India-Australia Relations, www.mea.gov.in). Recent visits by Indian and Australian prime ministers, such as Tony Abbott's visit in 2014, and later the same year Narendra Modi's visit to Australia—the latter being the first by an Indian prime minister in 28 years, and Malcolm Turnbull's visit in 2017 have continued to progress the relationship. Australian PM Scott Morrison was scheduled to visit New Delhi in January 2020, but had postponed it due to the bush fires in Australia. The rescheduled plan for May and beyond was put on hold due to the outbreak of COVID-19. Prime Minister Narendra Modi has held his first virtual bilateral summit on 4 June, as he hopes to expand the strategic partnership with Australia in the backdrop of China's renewed efforts to step up aggression in the Indo-Pacific region. The summit is happening also amid new tensions between China and Australia over Canberra's call for a global inquiry into the origin of COVID-19.

However, India's nuclear status is now a non-issue following the mainstreaming of its programme, the lifting by Australia of its uranium ban, and the India-Australia civilian nuclear agreement. And people-to-people contacts have widened, with large numbers of Indian tourists, students, and immigrants contributing to Australia's economy and society. At the June 2020 Morrison-Modi virtual meeting, not unexpectedly, the bilateral defence and security partnership was elevated to a Comprehensive Strategic Partnership (CSP), both sides agreeing within the partnership to 'deepen and broaden' defence co-operation. Each has signed CSPs with a number of other countries, among the broad objectives of a collaborative approach to addressing the economic and social effects of COVID-19 (Weigold 2020). In spite of that, India-Australia relations present a paradox for mainstream international relations (IR) theories. Liberal theorists have argued that the growth in the relationship is natural, as the two are both liberal democracies. And yet, India and Australia have long been democracies, and this has not produced a close relationship. What little realist analysis has been done, however, has been just as problematic.

Bilateral Economic Relations

Australia and India have commercial ties dating back to the eighteenth century and the first recorded commercial transaction from the new British colony at Port Jackson was a 50 ton shipment of coal to Bengal in 1799 (Stuart, 2014). But the economic relationship between India and Australia has long been relatively weak. History shows, India and Australia have had divergent strategic trajectories, and their different commercial goals and strategies prevented the development of closer relations between the two countries. During the Cold War, their relationship was characterized divergent geopolitical perspectives, ideological differences and weak economic links.

But the end of the Cold War and India's decision to restructure its economy in 1991 produced a radically different strategic and commercial climate, one which is obviously far more helpful to the development of closer ties between India and Australia. As a result, relations between Australia and India began intensifying even before the emergence of China as a strategic concern for both countries. After 1990s, their economic relations significantly improved in all areas like trade, energy and mining, science & technology, information technology, education, defence etc. Australia's exports to India grew substantially in the first half of the 1990s, from about $530 million in 1989-1990 to $881 million in 1994-1995 (Grare, 2014). Bilateral trade with India grew quickly in the first decade of current century, reaching around $19.3 billion in 2008, but grew very little in the following decade, totalling only $27.4 billion in 2017 (Brewster, 2019), $30 billion in 2019 (Hundal, 2021). However, economic cooperation has continued to deepen since the turn of the century, with Australians increasingly seeing India as a rising global economic player and a potential export destination. Trade grew by 24.6 per cent per year between 2000 and 2009, making India Australia's tenth-largest two-way trading partner and fifth-largest export market (Grare, 2014). Major Australian exports to India in 2014-15 included coal ($5.5 billion), education-related travel ($2.21 billion) and gold ($903 million). Major Australian imports from India in 2014-15 were refined petroleum ($910 million), personal travel services ($561 million), business services ($481 million), medicaments ($247 million);

pearls and gems ($239 million) and passenger motor vehicles ($170 million) (Raghuramapatruni, 2017). Actually, Australia-India trade relationship has grown significantly in recent years which was absolutely absent in the past.

Like bilateral trade, bilateral investment has slowly grown. Several Australian resource companies are keen to invest in India but remain largely locked out of the market; while there are some planned Indian investments in Australia such as the Adani, Oswal Group, Aditya Birla Group, TATAs, Reliance, GVK Power and Infrastructure and few have come to fruition. Australian investment in India totalled $13.9 billion at the end of 2017, and Indian investment in Australia aggregated to $15.4 billion (Brewster, 2019). Thus, India is currently Australia's seventeenth-largest foreign investor, while Australia is the 22nd largest investor in India (Grare, 2014). It is expected, they achieve their desired economic goals in future.

India's main exports to Australia are gems and jewellery, machinery and textiles while India's major imports are non-monetary gold, coal, copper ores—the three products account for over 86 per cent of India's imports from Australia, with coal being the dominant import (Raghuramapatruni, 2017). India's main service exports to Australia are computer and information services and tourism. Main Australian service exports to India are education, education-related travel and tourism. India is Australia's largest export market for gold and chickpeas, second largest market for coal and copper ores and third largest market for lead and wool (India-Australia Relations, www.mea.gov.in). All the major Indian IT companies have a presence in Australia and are rapidly growing. These are Infosys; Satyam Mahindra; TCS; HCL; Polaris Software Lab Ltd.; Birlasoft; NIIT; ICICI Infotech; Wipro; Mahindra-British Telecom Ltd.; i-Flex; igate; among others.

The India-Australia Joint Ministerial Commission was established in 1989 and has held thirteen meetings to date, the last one in Canberra on 12 May, 2011. The Indian delegation for the JMC was led by Shri Anand Sharma, Minister for Commerce

& Industry. At the conclusion of the JMC, the two sides agreed to commence negotiations for a Comprehensive Economic Cooperation Agreement (CECA), which has now begun (India-Australia Relations, www.mea.gov.in). CECA helps to widen the opportunity of Free Trade Agreements between India and Australia.

The Australia-India Council (AIC) was established in 1992 by the Australian government to broaden the bilateral relationship through increasing levels of knowledge and understanding between the people and institutions of Australia and India. The annual Maritime Dialogue was agreed in November 2014 under the Framework for security co-operation. The other treaties and MoUs between India and Australia measure a range of areas. Notable areas of cooperation include Treaties and Memoranda of Understanding (MoUs) on Air Services; Civil Space Science, Technology and Education; combating International Terrorism; Customs; Defence Cooperation; Extradition and Mutual Legal Assistance in Criminal Matters; Intellectual Property; Civil Nuclear Cooperation; Skills Training Co-operation and Technical Vocational Education and Training (TVET); Social Security; Student Mobility and Welfare; Transfer of Sentenced persons; Arts and culture; Water Resource Management; Sports; Tourism and Wool and Woollen Products (Raghuramapatruni, 2017). Negotiations to conclude a comprehensive Economic Cooperation Agreement (CECA) between Australia and India were launched in 2011. There have been nine rounds of negotiations, the most recent of which was held in September 2015. During the official visits, the respective prime ministers of both the countries renewed their commitment to an early conclusion of an equitable, balanced, comprehensive and high quality agreement (Raghuramapatruni, 2017).

In July 2018, the Australian Government released a report by Peter Varghese, a former Secretary of the Department of Foreign Affairs and Trade; on Australia's economic strategy for India. The report points out that Australia's economic engagement with India will look very different from our engagement with East Asian partners. Rather than relying just on sales of commodities, as was often the case with China, our engagement with India needs to be led by services and investment, which will be the key to unlocking other economic opportunities. Varghese proposes some ambitious goals: by 2035, Australia should try to lift India into its top three export markets, with exports of around $45 billion (in constant dollars) and Australian investment in India of some $100 billion (Brewster, 2019). Varghese identifies key 10 industry sectors where engagement should be deepen in future. These includes: Education, Agribusiness, Resource generation, Tourism, Energy, Health, Financial services, Science and innovation, Infrastructure (urban and transport) and Sport.

Varghese also argues economic engagement should be focused on 10 Indian states and regions that are identified as having the most conducive business environment or being most relevant for Australia's sectoral focus: Maharashtra, Gujurat, Karnataka, Tamil Nadu, Andhra Pradesh, Telangana, West Bengal, Punjab, Delhi and Uttar Pradesh (Brewster, 2019). Varghese focuses strongly on the important role that the Indian diaspora in Australia could play in the economic relationship. While Australian state governments are already engaging with the diaspora, there is scope for greater engagement at the federal level. Overall, the Varghese report provides a valuable road map for enhancement of the relations between Australia and India (Brewster, 2019). Therefore, deeper integration may be possible between India and Australia.

The two economies can be seen as complementary in economic terms. From Australia's standpoint, India represents a huge and growing export market and an opportunity to provide greater balance to Australia's economic relationship with China. For India, Australia represents a politically stable and reliable source of energy and resource to help fuel its economic growth. Therefore, there is a large untapped potential for Australian firms to expand the size and scope of their business engagements with India and similarly India can tap the untapped market potential in Australia. Now, both the governments agree that there is significant potential for further cooperation across a broad range of areas. The two-way

Prime Ministerial visits in 2014 built significant momentum in the relationship and affirmed the Strategic Partnership agreed to in the 2009. This tradition is still continuing as we found the speech of Australian Prime Minister Scott Morrison. According to him, "India as a natural partner in the top tier of Australia's partnerships emphasises the continuing emergence of India as a key strategic partner" (White, 2020). However, their strategic culture has historically led India to shun 'natural partners', mechanisms such as the Quadrilateral Security Dialogue (the 'Quad') are gradually strengthening to provide some evidence of converging Australian-Indian geostrategic interests.

Uranium Export to India

Uranium is a continuing source of friction between India and Australia. Australia refuses to supply India with the uranium ore as it is not a signatory to the international Nuclear Non-Proliferation Treaty (NPT). But after a series of attempts by prime ministers of all parties John Howard, Kevin Rudd, Julia Gillard, Tony Abbott and Malcolm Turnbull, both Australian political parties opened the door for uranium exports to India.

Australia and India finalized their nuclear cooperation agreement in September 2014, after India ratified its additional protocol (Davenport, 2017). Australia is one of the world's largest exporters of uranium ore, but exports to India were banned because the country is not party to the nuclear Non-proliferation Treaty (NPT) and developed nuclear weapons. As a party to the 1986 Treaty of Rarotonga, which established a nuclear-weapon-free zone in the South Pacific, Australia is obligated to ensure that nuclear technology and materials are exported only to countries subject to safeguards required by the NPT. The Nuclear Suppliers Group (NSG), of which Australia is a member, also generally prohibits nuclear exports to countries outside of the NPT. The NSG is a voluntary group of 48 states that agreed to a set of guidelines for nuclear-related exports to help control proliferation. Despite not being a part of the NPT, India received an exemption from the NSG in 2008, which allows member states to export nuclear materials and technologies to India. India did negotiate a limited safeguards agreement with the International Atomic Energy Agency (IAEA) in 2008 and ratified an additional protocol to enhance its safeguards agreement in 2014 (Davenport, 2017). These steps, which India agreed to take to enhance its bid for an NSG exemption, mean that the IAEA has access to some but not all of India's nuclear facilities.

After three rounds of negotiations in mid-2014, a civil nuclear energy cooperation agreement was concluded during Tony Abbott's September 2014 visit to India. Further discussions took place in November, 2015 on the implementation of a uranium sale agreement to India, and by November 2015 the civil nuclear agreement had entered into force (Jaishankar, 2020). The consequences of civil nuclear agreement, Australia decides to sell or export uranium to India starting in 2017. According to the Australian Uranium Association, Australia can expect to sell some 2,500 tons of uranium annually to India by 2030, generating about $309 million per year at current prices (Grare, 2014). Now, Australia backed India's bid for membership of the Nuclear Suppliers Group (NSG).

India-Australia Education Cooperation

The Joint Working Group on Education & Training between the two countries has identified several key areas for co-operation, including collaborative research in education policy, research student exchange programmes, capacity building in vocational education and distance learning in higher education. The last meeting of the JWG was held in Canberra on 13-14 April, 2011 (India-Australia Relations, www.mea.gov.in). The number of Indian students studying in Australia rapidly increased from 20,512 in 2004 to over 1,20,000 enrolments in 2009 and Australia overtook the UK as the second largest destination for Indian students. However, following the tightening of student visa regulations, changes in the general skilled migration rules, negative impact of the string of student attacks in 2009-10, and the rising cost of Australian Dollar, the number of student enrolments from India declined significantly with enrolments at 1,00,310 and actual commencements at 42,576 during the year 2010 (-38% over 2009). The downward trend has continued in 2011, with 69,702 enrolments and 31,703 commencements during Jan.-Oct. 2011 (India-Australia Relations, www.mea.gov.in) but numbers remains significant, with over 38,000 Indian student visa holders in Australian tertiary institutions in 2011 (Stuart, 2014). Therefore, it is seen that considerable growth in tertiary education section having some ups and downs.

Growing Indian Community in Australia

There is a rapidly growing Indian community of nearly 4,50,000 in Australia. In addition, there are a sizeable number of people of Indian origin from countries such as Fiji, Malaysia, Kenya and South Africa. They are contributing significantly to the Australian economy as teachers, doctors, accountants, engineers and I.T. professionals. India is now the third largest source of immigrants to Australia, after UK and New Zealand and the second largest source of skilled professionals (India-Australia Relations, www.mea.gov.in). India now ranks fourth (behind the UK, New Zealand and China) in the list of the top 10 countries of birth of Australia's population. The India figure is nearly 4,00,000 people, or 1.7 per cent of Australia's population (Dobell, 2016). India's traditional view—when it thought of Australia at all—was of a racist White Australia. The new understanding of Australia is being created by Indians moving to Australia.

India-Australia Defence and Security Relations

India and Australia have a long history of military relations. Now their military relationship encircles almost every major area that includes: Firstly, strategic dialogues, coordination, and intelligence exchanges, including those involving third countries; Secondly, military exercises involving ground, air, and especially maritime forces; Thirdly, military-to-military exchanges and training; and

Fourthly, defence, commerce and technological cooperation. However, all four areas, and especially the fourth, are at a nascent phase of partnership with considerable scope for improvement.

Military exercises and engagements have proliferated by India and Australia and there has been an increase from 11 defence exercises, meetings, and activities in 2014 to 29 in 2017, and 38 in 2018 (Jaishankar, 2020). Naval engagement has been the most advanced, as is to be expected. The main bilateral exercise, AUSINDEX, was held every two years between 2015 and 2019. The 2019 edition of the exercise was particularly significant, representing a great degree of complexity and Australia's largest ever defence deployment to India. Linked to Australia's largest naval deployment, Indo-Pacific Endeavour 2019, the exercise involved four ships, Australian Army forces, and support personnel from all three services, with a total involvement of more than 1000 Australian personnel. The ships visited Chennai and Visakhapatnam and included both Indian and Australian P-8 maritime patrol aircraft, as well as submarines from the two countries in sophisticated anti-submarine warfare (ASW) exercises (Jaishankar, 2020). Most significant was the reality that US military personnel were observers in this exercise.

The Royal Australian Navy has been a regular participant in the *Milan* exercises since the early 2000s, including in the 2018 edition off the Andaman and Nicobar Islands. In 2018, for the first time, the Indian Navy took part in Australia's multilateral *Kakadu* exercise in Darwin. In addition, India took part as an observer in a submarine rescue exercise *Black Carillon* off Western Australia in 1918. India and Australia have also been involved in third country-led exercises, notably the United States' Rim of the Pacific Exercise (RIMPAC) and the Western Pacific Naval Symposium Multilateral Sea Exercise (WMSX) in the Singapore Strait and South China Sea (Jaishankar, 2020). This indicates they are engaged deeply in Maritime cooperation.

India and Australia air force engagement has also increased. A major threshold was crossed with the Indian Air Force's first involvement as a full participant in the *Pitch Black* exercise in Darwin in 2018. A multilateral exercise involving air forces from several Australian ally and partner countries, India deployed four Sukhoi Su-30MKI fighters, a C-17 heavy transport, and a C-130 tactical transport aircraft. The exercise was additionally significant for staging the first mid-air refuelling of an Indian combat aircraft (Su-30MKI) by an Australian aircraft (KC-30A), revealing a much greater degree of coordination than had been demonstrated previously (Jaishankar, 2020). Beyond exercises, subject matter expert exchanges involving flight controllers and safety and security have also taken place.

Army-to-army engagement of India and Australia is perhaps the least developed. In 2017 and 2018, the second and third editions of AUSTRA HIND, a Special Forces exercise, were held. Additionally, efforts at countering improvised explosive devices (IEDs) involving the two armies was jointly organised in India in 2018 (Jaishankar, 2020). The possibility of desert warfare exercises as well as Indian participation in a longstanding Australian jungle warfare school, have also been proposed.

Exercises are not the only reflection of interoperability, and a number of agreements have been finalised to improve the ability of the two militaries to work together. This began with Defence industrial cooperation—an area that India prioritises given its own equipment requirements—offers limited potential. A Joint Working Group on Defence Research and Materiel Cooperation meeting between India's Defence Research and Development Organisation (DRDO) and Australia's Defence Science and Technology Group (DSTG) met in 2018 (Jaishankar, 2020). Among other issues, India has expressed interest in certain Australian defence products, including the Bushmaster and Hawkei armoured mobility vehicles, maritime training simulators, mobile health stations, and water purifiers. Australia also has considerable expertise in radar and undersea technologies. The acquisition of diesel submarines from France by both India and Australia offers some opportunities for long-term technical collaboration between the three countries in that domain.

However, there are considerable opportunities for defence and security cooperation between India and Australia. Potential areas in maritime security include in naval exercises and training, greater cooperation in humanitarian and disaster relief operations and search and rescue, maritime border protection and maritime domain awareness. There are also opportunities for greater cooperation between the Indian and Australian armies and air forces.

Prime Ministers Abbott and Modi signed a landmark deal to increase their nations defence relationship in November 2014. Part of the framework for security co-operation includes annual Prime Ministerial meetings and joint maritime exercises. Areas of increased co-operation include counter-terrorism, border control and regional and international institutions. On 4 June, 2020, India and Australia signed an agreement to provide access to one another's military bases, in order to help facilitate joint military exercises. Known as the Mutual Logistics Support Agreement, it allows each country to use the other's bases for the refuelling and maintenance of aircraft and naval vessels. The agreement was reached over a virtual summit between Prime Ministers Narendra Modi and Scott Morrison due to the COVID-19 pandemic.

India-Australia Strategic relations

The relationship between India and Australia has gone through many ups and downs since India's Independence in 1947, often reflecting quite different ideological orientations and strategic perspectives—for several reasons neither country saw the other as a key strategic partner (Brewster, 2015). Traditionally, India-Australia relations have been marked by a considerable degree of distrust, a product of a number of historical, cultural, and economic factors. Nonetheless, the two countries have, since 2000, engaged upon a steadily growing defence and security partnership. Although the bilateral relationship was surprised by India's nuclear tests in 1998 and Australia's overzealous response, the 2000 White

Paper nevertheless expressed confidence in India's growing role in regional security and a desire to move beyond *ad hoc* conversations on defence and security issues towards more institutionalised discussions. This aim was soon achieved, in the form of the India-Australia Strategic Dialogue, first held in August 2001, which helped lay the groundwork for a series of bilateral security cooperation deals, notably the Memorandum of Understanding (MoU) on Combating International Terrorism, 2003, the MoU on Defence Cooperation, 2006, and the India-Australia Joint Declaration on Security Cooperation, 2009 (Hall, 2016).

As independent states, the political and strategic relationship between India and Australia has not been close. Their relations have often been characterised by long periods of indifference scattered with occasional political irritations. During the Cold War and for some time after, India was preoccupied with its immediate security problems in South Asia, while Australia traditionally focused on security concerns in East Asia and the Pacific. Australia rarely figured in New Delhi's security calculations except as a US stooge. Canberra considered India as difficult to deal with, anti-American, and too close to the Soviets (Brewster, 2014). But Australia and India's spheres of strategic interest are now converging and their strategic interests are coming into much greater alignment. The emergence of both China and India as major powers with strategic interests across the Indo-Pacific is bringing India and Australia closer together and forcing them to engage on security and defence issues much more than ever before. In addition, due to the COVID-19 pandemic, the world become more insecure than it has over the earlier few decades. In this perspective, the role of middle powers in global governance, the future of democracy, and the balance of power in the Indo-Pacific have all assumed greater relevance. So, the growing partnership between India and Australia—two democratic middle powers in the Indo-Pacific region—has become gradually more important. The size and location of India and Australia place them on the central axis of the Indo-Pacific region, along with the countries of Southeast Asia, namely, Indonesia, Singapore, Thailand etc. In addition to this, the facts that India and Australia are the largest maritime powers among the Indian Ocean's littoral states. Thus, has led to a series of bilateral agreements that provide a formal basis for cooperation on security and defence-related matters. Indo-US closer relationship and China fear also open the door of security cooperation between India and Australia. However, Australia and India share many strategic interests, including security within Southeast Asia, the stability of the Asia-Pacific region, combating international terrorism, non-proliferation of weapons of mass destruction, securing maritime lines of communication, and energy and resource security. They also share an interest in a range of transnational security challenges such as disasters, environmental degradation and international crime (Roberts, 2005). Today, defence and security partnership between India-Australia partnerships include close cooperation on Indian Ocean security, sophisticated bilateral naval exercises, high-level strategic dialogues, military exchanges and training, and some nascent defence technology cooperation.

In strategic terms, India-Australia has long treated one another as alien due to historical context and the negative public perceptions about the bilateral relationship. But that perspective has changed and now they co-operate each other in security matters. These developments provided the context for the evolution of strategic relations after 2000, when Prime Minister John Howard visited India, the first official visit by an Australian prime minister since 1989. At the same time, initial contacts between India and Australia began to address some of the lingering issues of the Cold War era. Defence talks between the two countries were held in May 2000, India's defence secretary visited Australia later in the year, and Australia returned its defence attaché to New Delhi for the first time after the 1998 nuclear tests (Jaishankar, 2020). A foreign ministers' dialogue was re-established in June 2001 along with an official strategic dialogue held in August of the same year. In 2003, members of India's National Defence College visited Australia, Australian observers participated in the *Milan 03* exercise, and a

Royal Australian Navy vessel visited Chennai. Between 2004 and 2006, military service chiefs from both countries made visits, and the period was marked by *ad hoc* cooperation between the two countries (along with the United States and Japan) in humanitarian assistance and relief operations following the 2004 Indian Ocean tsunami. An Indian frigate made port visits in Australia in 2006 and took part in exercises with Australian vessels (Jaishankar, 2020).

Strategic relations between Australia and India entered a more ambitious phase in 2006, coinciding with accelerated Indian engagement with both the United States and Japan. An India-Australia defence framework agreement—a Memorandum of Understanding on Defence Cooperation—was signed in March 2006 during John Howard's visit to India, amid a host of other agreements related to economics, trade, and technology. This placed a focus on terrorism, defence cooperation, information sharing, and extradition. As a consequence, the next two years saw a sudden acceleration in bilateral defence engagement. Australia's Minister for Defence Brendan Nelson visited India in July 2007, sandwiched between visits by Australia's Chief of the Defence Force and Chief of Navy, during which he signed an agreement on the protection of classified information (Jaishankar, 2020). During 2007, two parallel developments occurred that became linked in the public consciousness: the year's second *Malabar* naval exercise (*Malabar 07-02*), in which the US, Indian, Australian, Japanese, and Singaporean navies participated in the Bay of Bengal, as well as the first Quad meeting involving the foreign ministries of India, Australia, the United States, and Japan in Manila. *Malabar 07-02* was of significant scale, involving more than 25 ships, 150 aircrafts, and 20,000 personnel, including three carrier strike groups belonging to the United States and India. Australia's decision to withdraw in early 2008 from the Quad, following the election of Kevin Rudd's government, would prove contentious for some time.

Nonetheless, after about a year and a half of perceptible cooling, Prime Minister Kevin Rudd's visit to India in November

2009 produced a further breakthrough in defence relations. A Joint Declaration on Security Cooperation in 2009 by India and Australia which lead further cooperation in security matters. Key areas of cooperation identified in the Declaration, 2009 are Information exchange and policy co-ordination in regional affairs; bilateral cooperation within multilateral regional frameworks, particularly the East Asian Forum and the ASEAN Regional Forum; Defence dialogue and cooperation within the existing 2006 MOU on Defence Cooperation; Terrorism; Transnational organised crime; Disaster management; Maritime and aviation security and Law enforcement cooperation (Brewster, 2010). India has made analogous declarations only with the United States and Japan and Australia made analogous declarations only with the Japan and South Korea.

Defence Minister Stephen Smith visited India in December 2011, and that year also saw official bilateral dialogues on energy security, counter-terrorism, and for the first time, on East Asia and the Pacific. In late 2011, the ruling Australian Labor Party also reversed its policy of selling uranium only to signatories of the NPT (Grare, 2014). That paved the way for the new Prime Minister Julia Gillard during her 2012 visit to India to initiate negotiations towards a bilateral civil nuclear cooperation agreement. In 2013, despite a change in government, Foreign Minister Julie Bishop pledged Australia's support for India's membership to the Nuclear Suppliers Group (NSG). The most significant development in 2013 was A.K. Antony making the first ever official visit by an Indian defence minister to Australia. During his visit, a bilateral maritime exercise between Australia and India's navies was agreed, tentatively to take place in 2015. In early 2014, Australia participated in the *Milan* naval exercise hosted by India, and hosted the Indian Ocean Naval Symposium meeting in Perth (Jaishankar, 2020). The election of Indian Prime Minister Narendra Modi in 2014 and his overlap with the prime ministership of Tony Abbott offered an opportunity for another phase of Australia-India defence engagement. Prime Minister Abbott was one of the first leaders hosted for a state visit by Modi in September 2014. On Modi's return visit to Australia in November—the first by an Indian Prime Minister in 28 years—a Framework for Security Cooperation was signed, forming the underpinning of the current strategic relationship. The issues covered in that document include defence policy planning and coordination, counter-terrorism, border protection, nuclear non-proliferation, disaster management, and institutional cooperation, and feature marked changes in, among other things, the priority given to search and rescue operations and defence technology.

In June 2015, the first Australia-India-Japan trilateral senior official talks were held in New Delhi. A high-level Indian Coastguard meeting, involving Australia's Maritime Border Command (MBC), took place in August 2015, during the MBC chief's visit to India. And in September 2015, the first major bilateral naval exercise AUSINDEX was held in the Bay of Bengal. All of these developments were accompanied by the now-routine defence and foreign ministers' talks, the foreign ministry-led senior official dialogue, two-way military leadership visits, and a port call by two Indian naval vessels to Fremantle (Jaishankar, 2020). Early exploration of collaboration on defence science and technology occurred when the head of India's Defence Research and Development Organisation visited Australia in April 2016. Air force and naval cooperation also accelerated with Indian observers at the 2016 *Pitch Black* exercise, Indian naval observers at the *Kakadu* 2016 exercise, and India signing a White Shipping Agreement with Australia to improve information sharing for maritime domain awareness (along with similar agreements with France, Singapore, and the United States). In 2017, the Quad was revived in Manila, with a focus on coordination in the Indo-Pacific region. A second edition of AUSINDEX took place in 2017 off the coast of Western Australia, and a second and third round of Australia-India-Japan trilateral talks were held that year in Canberra and New Delhi, the last in parallel with the countries' first 2+2 dialogue. The first meeting of the Joint Working Group on Defence Research and Materiel Cooperation was held in India in October 2016 (Jaishankar, 2020).

The most recent major developments occurred following the 2019 re-elections of Scott Morrison and Narendra Modi, and their meeting at the G-20 Summit in Osaka. After several postponements due to the global corona virus pandemic, their virtual summit was held in June 2020 at which they announced a Comprehensive Strategic Partnership between the two countries. They concluded a framework agreement on maritime cooperation and on cyber technology cooperation. Most significantly on security matters, the two leaders announced the conclusion of a Mutual Logistics Support Agreement (MLSA), as well as an initial agreement on defence science and technology research. The two sides also agreed to upgrade their 2+2 dialogue to the rank of foreign and defence ministers, a level of official engagement that they have with only a few other countries, including the United States and Japan (Jaishankar, 2020). Over the last two decades or so, regular bilateral dialogues have significantly expanded opportunities for engagement on security and defence. These include annual meetings of Australian and Indian Foreign Ministers, regular meetings of Defence Ministers, annual Defence Policy Talks at senior official level, regular visits of Service Chiefs and regular staff talks between senior officers of the three services.

Major Defence Exercises between India and Australia

Exercise	Conducting/Hosting Entity	India/Australia's Participations
Exercise Kakadu	A joint-enabled, biennial exercise hosted by the Royal Australian Navy and Supported by the Royal Australian Air Force	India, Since 2016
Exercise Talisman Sabre	A bilateral combined training activity between Australian Defence Force and United States military	India, Observer in 2019
Rim of the Pacific (RIMPAC)	A biennial international naval exercise hosted by the US Navy	India, Since 2012
MILAN	A biennial multilateral naval exercise hosted by the Indian Navy	Australia, Since 2003

(*Contd.*)

Exercise	Conducting/Hosting Entity	India/Australia's Participations
Exercise AUSTRA HIND	A joint military exercise conducted between India and Australia	Held in 2016-2017 and 2017-2018
Exercise Pitch Black	A biennial multinational warfare exercise hosted by the Royal Australian Air Force	India, in 2018
AUSINDEX 2019	A biennial bilateral maritime exercise between India and Australia	Held in 2015, 2017, 2019

Source: Dr. Tejinder Hundal, *India and Australia in Indo-Pacific: Dynamics of Defence Diplomacy and Diaspora*, Notion Press, Chennai, 2021, p. 98.

India-Australia and Asia-Pacific

The idea of an Indo-Pacific region involves recognizing that the growing economic, geopolitical and security connections between the Western Pacific and the Indian Ocean regions are creating a single 'strategic system'. Today, around 80 per cent of China's oil imports, perhaps 90 per cent of South Korea's, and up to 90 per cent of Japan's are shipped from the Middle East and/or Africa through the Indo-Pacific region (Rozman, 2018). Thus, Indo-Pacific region has become hotspot of the region and world powers are engaged in this region. Being axis position of this region, India and Australia are active in the Indo-Pacific region. In addition, India and Australia, the largest maritime powers among the littoral states of the Indian Ocean, constitute the region's geopolitical poles (Grare, 2014). There are obvious commonalities in the Indian and Australian perceptions of the Indo-Pacific. This is increasingly seen by both Australia and India as a natural strategic space with Southeast Asia as a geographical centre. The significance of regarding the region as a strategic continuum, the importance of the maritime sphere, the rising profile of an under-governed Indian Ocean basin, and the recognition of the importance of normative standards in the governance of the region are reflected both in Australia's recent defence and foreign policy white papers, as well as in Indian Prime Minister Narendra Modi's 2018 keynote address at the Shangri La

Dialogue in Singapore. These sentiments are also reflected in similar actions, such as both countries continuing to sail their naval vessels in the South China Sea.

Important differences are seen between Australia and India regarding the Asia-Pacific region. The differences begin with their different geographies, histories, and strategic perspectives. In Australia, the Indo-Pacific concept has served two broad functions. The first is to elevate the Indian Ocean in Australia's strategic consciousness. The second is to widen its strategic scope to include India. For India, the Indo-Pacific represents the natural scope of its Act East policy, and has become a strategic reality with the increasingly active security footprint of China, the United States, Japan, and others in both the Indian and Pacific Oceans. For India, the entire Indian Ocean will take precedence, while for Australia it will be the southwest Indian Ocean, its immediate north, and vast stretches of the South Pacific.

Problem Areas

Firstly, India-Australia security relations is rhetoric, the road towards a closer security partnership is likely to be a slow and frustrating one for its proponents and this is because of their historical experience and cultures. Through their history as independent states, India and Australia have developed different strategic traditions and attitudes towards security cooperation, and this remains a significant issue in their engagement today. In short, Australia sees security alignments and cooperation as an important means of enhancing its influence while many in New Delhi effective see cooperation as reducing India's influence and inconsistent with a national objective of achieving strategic autonomy (Brewster, 2014). Australia always believed its security to be best insured by a close alliance with the United States, and it maintained a commitment to regionalism and multilateral dialogues that did not include India. New Delhi, by contrast, was the leading advocate of non-alignment and jealously preserved its strategic autonomy.

Secondly, another major challenge in developing the relationship is the very different perspective on the role and importance of defence forces as part of foreign policy. Australia sees its defence forces as playing an important foreign policy role. In contrast, India has a narrower view of the role of its armed forces, including the role of defence force relations with other countries. New Delhi does not see the Indian armed forces as being a principal foreign policy actor.

Thirdly, a mismatched capability of defence forces is another challenge for India-Australia relations. Australian and Indian naval forces have significantly differing capabilities. India has invested in carrier battle groups and nuclear-powered ballistic missile submarines, neither of which Australia seeks. The greater military divergence is reflected in the two countries' air and ground forces. The Indian Air Force has limited power projection capabilities and is still dependent on Russian platforms, although with considerable diversification underway. Outside of Special Forces, the two countries' armies are also of very different scales, making certain forms of interaction is difficult, such as large-scale exercises.

Fourthly, Australia and India face very different strategic circumstances, particularly in the context of their relations with the United States and China. Essentially, Australia is significantly more dependent on the United States for its security and on China for its prosperity than India, and that will likely remain so for the near future. India, by contrast, is much less integrated with the United States' security structures and much less integrated with supply chains linked to mainland China.

Fifthly, different priorities between the two countries are also constrained of their relations. For example, for Australia, the challenge of China relates to its own politics, society, and economy, as well as the security of its wider region. For India, China is a direct military threat on a passionately contested border. India and Australia have also expressed different functional priorities.

From Cold War, India and Australia still disagree fundamentally on many crucial global issues. India continues to support Iran, maintains close ties with Russia, resists the NPT, will not join the

Trans-Pacific Partnership and looks to BRICS for solidarity with the 'global south', while openly seeking a 'polycentric' world order. These positions all echo India's post-colonial identity, as seen in the early Cold War period. Australia has undoubtedly moved closer to Asia, long ago dismantled the White Australia policy and become a far more open and multicultural society since the period examined here. And yet, it maintains its links to the US and the UK and is broadly supportive of US hegemony over world order. Changing this aspect of India-Australia relations requires more than just the political will displayed by Narendra Modi and Tony Abbott. Rather, for the relationship to move forward there needs to be a shift in the ways in which India and Australia imagine world politics. Without this, India and Australia will continue to misunderstand one another regardless of how much desire there is to engage (Davis, 2015).

Beyond these natural differences in strategic perspectives, other factors may continue to constrain bilateral cooperation between India and Australia. They can be broadly divided into three categories: (i) lack of growth of trade relations, (ii) racism, and (iii) lack of people to people connection.

Future Opportunities

Although there are considerable challenges in developing the relationship between India and Australia but there are some potential areas for enhanced cooperation between India and Australia. In all these areas, cooperation is still at a nascent stage and much more can be done.

Firstly, Security dialogues contacts—with the 2+2 ministerial dialogue as the centrepiece—will make official engagements more routine and manageable, and thereby help consolidate the strategic partnership.

Secondly, cooperation in Indian Ocean regional institutions or further coordination at regional institutions and forums — such as the East Asia Summit, but especially groupings in which India and Australia play leadership roles, such as IORA—may be necessary, particularly in advancing a common agenda between like-minded partners.

Thirdly, Prioritisation may be required amid the proliferation of mini-lateral mechanisms (such as India-Australia-Japan, India-Australia-Indonesia, India-Australia-France, and India-Australia-Japan-United States) that will enhance their relationship.

Fourthly, Priority areas will remain in the maritime sphere, where interoperability is currently highest, but can deepen in terms of maritime domain awareness, search and rescue operations, and humanitarian assistance and disaster relief. In addition naval exercises and training, maritime piracy; maritime border protection and maritime domain awareness should be included in the priority list. Further, cooperation between other military services, such as closer air force and army cooperation might extend to more regular exercises, refuelling, and training in jungle and desert warfare.

Fifthly, Defence technology is an area that has lagged in the strategic relationship between India and Australia. There are unexplored opportunities, which might extend to the joint production or development of armoured vehicles, undersea sensors, radar systems, and various subsystems. Defence technology cooperation should be included in their bilateral cooperation. There is considerable scope for direct cooperation between the government defence research organisations, India's Defence Research and Development Organisation (DRDO) and Australia's Defence Science and Technology Organisation (DSTO) (Brewster, 2015).

Sixthly, bilateral relations will extend quite naturally to people-to-people ties, particularly given the burgeoning population of Australians of Indian origin. Tourism is significant role in promoting people-to-people relationship between India and Australia. Greater educational contacts in both directions will manifest themselves as well. Deepening and broadening trade and economic linkages as well as agribusiness would add further elements of trust, stability, and interest in the bilateral relationship in both countries. Energy partnership mainly, gas, coal and uranium and resource sharing can become an integral and inescapable aspect between India-Australia relations.

Finally, another area of potential cooperation is in Antarctic research and there has been relatively little interaction between India and Australia. While not directly security related, this area relates to the shared oceanic domain and can potentially create goodwill and a feeling of oceanic partnership. Australia's efforts in the Antarctic are conducted through the Australian Antarctic Division (AAD) based in Tasmania, since 1954 (now operates four permanent bases such as Davis Station), while India's are conducted through the National Centre for Antarctic and Oceanic Research (NCAOR), based in Goa, since 1984. India has two bases regarding the Antarctic research, namely, Maitri Station and Bharati Station. Australia claims more than 40 per cent of the continent as Australian territory (Brewster, 2014). Both organisations are wholly devoted to scientific research. India could potentially use the Australian logistical supply system operating through Tasmania, which is used to supply Davis Station. It is also notable that the potential for exchange of scientific personnel between the AAD and NCAOR is also unrealised.

Conclusion

Australia and India were historically entangled through the British Empire, colonial histories and their subsequent post-colonial identities have clearly been divisive in India-Australia relations. Both sides had ideational ambivalences towards one another on the basis of their colonial connections. This poor relationship was certainly not inevitable. However, the relationship was undermined repeatedly through different understandings about the nature of the post-colonial world, Colonial histories, and the identities they created, led to consistent misunderstandings.

The Australia-India relationship has come a long way over the last decade of previous century, but it will require significant political will on both sides to give it more substance. Bilateral trade has blossomed in recent years, although two-way investment is still relatively underdeveloped. A free trade agreement is under negotiation that would provide major benefits to both countries. There have been important developments in the political-security relationship over the last decade. There has been a significant expansion in dialogues but concrete co-operation is still nascent and needs more substance. India's new government is creating ample of opportunities for nurturing the two ways relationship between both the countries and a possible FTA between both the countries would be materialized which would drastically bring down the tariff levels accelerating the volume of trade between both the countries (Raghuramapatruni, 2017). In addition, Colonial history, cricket, English language have been positive in the India-Australia relations. The relationship between India and Australia now appears to be growing, after Modi's visit to Australia and the much-vaunted nuclear deal. India and Australia must understand that it can better achieve their strategic objectives in the Indo-Pacific in cooperation manner, than by acting alone. They will have to demonstrate that there are practical security problems that must be addressed in a cooperative manner (Brewster, 2014). It is expected that untapped potentiality in economy, military, as well as security will be achieved by India and Australia in near future.

References

Brewster, David (2019). "A New Engine for Growth: Australia's Second Sea-Facing our multi-polar future in the Indian Ocean", *Australian Strategic Policy Institute*, pp. 38-43.

Brewster, David (2015). "The Australia-India Framework for Security Cooperation: Another Step Towards an Indo-Pacific Security Partnership", *Security Challenges*, 2015, Vol. 11, No. 1, pp. 39-48.

Brewster, David (2014). "The India-Australia Security and Defence Relationship: Developments, Constraints and Prospects", *Security Challenges*, Vol. 10, No. 1, pp. 65-86.

Brewster, David (Autumn 2010). "The Australia–India Security Declaration: The Quadrilateral Redux?", *Security Challenges*, Autumn 2010, Vol. 6, No. 1, pp. 1-9.

Davis, Alexander E. (December, 2015): "A Shared History?: Post-colonial Identity and India-Australia Relations, 1947-1954", *Pacific Affairs*, Vol. 88, No. 4, pp. 849-869.

Davenport, Kelsey (September 2017). "Australia Ships Uranium to India", *Arms Control Today*, Vol. 47, No. 7, pp. 34-35.

Dobell, Graeme (2016). "Reaching for strategic convergence: Australia and India attempt strategic convergence", *Australian Strategic Policy Institute*, pp. 06-21.

Grare, Frederic (2014). "The India-Australia Strategic Relationship: Defining Realistic Expectations", *Carnegie Endowment for International Peace*, pp.1-43.

Hall, Ian (2016). "India in Australia's 2016 Defence White Paper", *Security Challenges*, Vol. 12, No. 1, pp. 181-186.

Hundal, Dr. Tejinder (2021). *India and Australia in Indo-Pacific: Dynamics of Defence Diplomacy and Diaspora*, Notion Press, Chennai.

India-Australia Relations (www.mea.gov.in), accessed on: 30/07/2021.

Jaishankar, Dhruva (2020). "The Australia-India Strategic Partnership: Accelerating Security Cooperation in the Indo-Pacific", *Lowy Institute for International Policy*, pp. 1-37.

Onslow, Elizabeth (2013). *India: The Story of the Nation* (Asia-Pacific Relations), published in electronic format by Trocadero Publishing, pp. 1-32.

Raghuramapatruni, Radha and D. Srinivasa Chary (2017). "Trends and Prospects of bilateral Trading Relations between India-Australia", *International Journal of Economic Research*, Vol. 14, No. 1, pp. 599-616.

Roberts, Frank and Varun Sahni (2005). "The Australia-India bilateral Security Relationship—Current Status and Outstanding Gaps", *Australian Strategic Policy Institute*, pp. 10-16.

Rozman, Gilbert and Joseph Chinyong Liow (2018). *International Relations and Asia's Southern Tier: ASEAN, Australia and India*, Palgrave Macmillan, pp. 10-11.

Stuart, David (2014). "The Australia-India Bilateral Relationship: A Practitioner's Viewpoint", in Amitabh Mattoo and Souresh Roy, (eds.), *India-Australia Relations in the Asian Century: Perspectives from India and Australia*, Manohar, pp. 69-83.

White, Martin (2020). "A Natural Partner? Intelligence Cooperation with India and Australia's Regional Interests", *Security Challenges*, Vol. 16, No. 2, Special Issue: Plan B for Australian Defence, pp. 88-105.

Weigold, Dr. Auriol (FDI Senior Visiting Fellow). *The Modi-Morrison Reset: Australia-India Relations 2020*, https://www.futuredirections.org.au/publication/the-modi-morrison-reset-australia-india-relations-2020 accessed on: 01/08/2021.

14

Renaissance of *Kirana* Stores during the Pandemic

A Perspective from the Consumer Shopping Experiences in Kerala, India

Anjali A. and *Bijith George Abraham*

Introduction

Shopping is an essential activity for every human being in the world for diverse reasons like staying trendy, spending essentials, and fulfilling one's needs. Shopping *vis-à-vis* consumption of goods and services enables heavy demand for the product/services powering the business opportunities and activities leading to production and distribution in the market and is also the key driving force in the quality of life, economic growth and development. An increase in consumption/shopping can benefit the Indian economy to grow by around 60 per cent as private consumption expenditure increases and also with favourable macroeconomic indicators are expected to continue the growth of the retail sector as a whole (*Financial Express*, 2019). The pandemic has fiercely disrupted the sector with the shock colliding massively between brick-and-mortar to the most modern shopping like essential to non-essential stores, online shops, and small to large retailers (OECD, 2020).

The Indian retail sector operates through a host of business models which are rapidly evolving with the changing trends and increased use of the internet and technology. The various retail models followed are Cash and carry/Wholesale trading, Single brand retail trading (SBRT), Multi brand retail trade (MBRT), and E-commerce (Marketplace model) (Deloitte, 2019). India is Asia's third-largest retail market and the world's fourth-largest after the US, China, and Japan (Deloitte-FICCI, 2018). The Indian food and grocery market are the world's sixth-largest, with retail contributing 70 per cent of the sales (India, 2019). The largest consumer segment with Indians spending more than 50 per cent of their monthly income is on groceries. According to the Deloitte-FICCI report (2018), food and grocery account for the majority share of the retail market in India followed by apparel and footwear, and consumer durables and IT segments. This consumer segment has tremendous growth potential due to the disposable income, rise in the young millennial generation, changes in lifestyles, spending patterns, and evolved family structures. India's retail industry is projected to grow at 9 per cent over 2019-2030, from US$ 779 billion in 2019 to US$ 1,407 billion by 2026 and more than US$ 1.8 trillion by 2030 (IBEF, 2022). Indian retail sector is appreciated as one of the fastest growing across the world and is the fifth-largest retail destination globally. India is among the highest in the world in terms of per capita retail store availability (India, 2022).

The Indian retail sector has seen tremendous growth from the Pre-1990s till the present day. In the early 1980s, the industry was dominated by the unorganised sector. In 1991 with Liberalization, Privatization, and Globalization, the organised sector started its expansion (Rani, 2013). There are many drivers that are leading to a strong growth in the Indian retail sector. One such strong driver is the consumption boom. The major things that will boost consumption are urbanization, income growth, favourable demographics, easy availability of credit, use of plastic money, technology and innovation, and evolving consumer attitudes (IBEF, 2022; WEF, 2018). The retail sector is expected to grow exponentially to reach USD 1,200 billion by 2021 and USD 1,750 billion by 2026 (FICCI, 2019). Domestic organised food and grocery retailers are expected to increase by 10 per cent Year over Year in FY22 (IBEF, 2022).

The Indian retail industry is divided into organized and unorganized sectors. The unorganised sector consists of all unincorporated private enterprises owned by individuals or households engaged in the sale and production of goods and services operated on a proprietary or partnership basis and with less than ten total workers (National Commision for Enterprises in the Unorganised Sector, 2007). Indian retail is dominated by a large number of unorganized retailers consisting of mom-and-pop stores named local *baniya* or the local *Kirana* stores run from generations to generations. These shops are operated by small family groups and thus it helps in creating familiarity with the local consumers. These unorganized retail stores are afflicted with various issues such as demand fulfilment, demand unpredictability, payment collection etc. And from the consumers' perspective some of the flaws are product availability, quality, variety, etc. remain chief areas of concern.

As World Health Organisation (WHO) declared the COVID-19 a pandemic, the world has changed completely. People are living differently, buying differently, spending differently, thinking differently, and behaving differently. The new normal has brought consumers to have a different derivation about surviving the crisis and their priorities have changed to safe health, better hygiene, safe place to buy from, and pocket-friendly products. The lockdown that was imposed due to the pandemic brought about changes in consumer buying behaviour. The types of goods purchased, the place of purchase, the way of payment, the adoption of new trends, were observed during the nationwide lockdown (Survey, 2020).

With the pandemic spreading, many restrictions were imposed by the Government as a step to curb the spread of the pandemic. Hypermarkets and shopping malls were not allowed to open, while neighbourhood mom-and-pop *Kirana* stores remained in business. Later permission was granted to the e-commerce companies to deliver essentials. The pandemic made ordinary *Kirana* stores to be noticed for their efficacy, value, and access to communities and customers. In contrast, new-age shopping malls located at a distance from residential areas and designed to operate with large footfalls were not open to mandated restrictions and norms of social distancing (Rustagi, 2020). The *Kirana* stores adapted quickly to the demands of the crisis to change themselves in terms of adapting to digital payments, changing operating models, delivering day-to-day supplies, and regaining customer faith. This was a boon for the *Kirana* stores (mom-and-pop stores) to regain the faith of the consumers for their daily or weekly essentials. The *Kirana* stores gained importance during the pandemic because of the reason of proximity, product availability, as well as home delivery services. The *Kirana* stores adapted quickly to this situation in terms of catering to the new consumer demand.

Hence, it is pertinent to understand the depth of transition that occurred to the mom-and-pop stores and also the changing pattern of the consumer's attitude during the new normal. Thus, the chapter focuses on the re-emergence of the traditional *Kirana* shops during the pandemic. It also tries to capture the change in the preference of the consumers from the multi-branded supermarkets to the local *Kirana* shops.

Review of Literature

Consumer buying behaviour is the scientific learning of how people buy, what they prefer to buy, when they need to buy, where they buy, and why they buy. Thus, it involves understanding various fields of psychology, anthropology, sociology, and economics (Deshpande, 2015). It also refers to the selection, consumption of goods and services for individual wants for sustainable consumption (Hansen & Schrader, 1997). Apart from individual factors, various other factors also influence the purchases such as social, cultural, economic, personal, and psychological (Ramya & Ali, 2016). While some influences are temporary and others are long-lasting, different factors affect how consumers behave during the purchase of a product, buy additional products, or buy nothing at all (Principles of Marketing, 2015). Consumer behaviour is a complex, dynamic, multidimensional process, and all marketing decisions are based on assumptions (Shukla & Shukla, 2013). Dynamic changes in taste, preferences, demographics, psychographics, lifestyles, and spending patterns of consumers, and many new business opportunities are also rising based on the local market condition (Cui & Liu, 2001).

The Indian grocery business has many distinctive ways due to consumers' diversity, and different distribution models in the sector such as mom-and-pop stores, giant supermarkets, hypermarkets, online grocery stores, malls, convenience stores, and branded stores (Sinha & Kar, 2007). The diversity of consumers has seen an increase in the channels of distribution. Some of them rely on the traditional mom-and-pop stores for their daily food and grocery needs, as these stores provide venue for personal connection, enhanced customer preferences, ample stock of locally relevant products, proximity, availability of credit, and the option to return/exchange products (Kumar, 2020).

India's retail sector is experiencing exponential growth with retail development taking place not just in major cities and metros, but also in tier II and III cities. Healthy economic growth, changing demographic profile, increasing disposable income, urbanisation, changing consumer tastes and preferences are some of the factors driving growth in the organised retail market in India (India, 2022). The change in consumer buying behaviour altered the format of consumer buying. Indian retail industry witnessed multi-store malls, huge shopping centres, and sprawling complexes which offer food, shopping, and entertainment all under the same roof. Increased urbanisation, amplifying disposable incomes, and lifestyle changes of the citizens transformed malls into retail destinations. The huge malls have become retail destinations with a wide variety of purchase options for goods, varied F&B options, and entertainment under one roof. These malls have evolved from shopping malls to entertainment centres that create experience zones for consumers to rejuvenate, socialize and entertain (Khullar, 2018).

The new age world consists of cash-rich, time-starved consumers who are empowered by technology to get what they want, when they want and where they want. And this has triggered a lot of changes in consumer buying behaviour. **Convenience** has become paramount consideration, followed by **healthy choices** and experiential shopping (Deloitte, 2019). The primary concerns of consumers are health, safety, and financial stability. The pandemic has instilled anxiety in consumers' minds that they are still hesitant about going to public places, such as malls, and restaurants (FICCI, 2020). The consumers are connected in a technology and internet-driven ecosphere, and it is critical for the retail players to engage with customers for a better connection, listen to the customers' voices, enhance service offerings, organise retail channels, and trade to provide seamless and integrated solution. They should ensure that consumers have a memorable experience irrespective of whether any products are bought or not (FICCI, 2019).

Consumers are provided with a wide choice of goods, more convenience, a better shopping environment, more offers, and other loyalty benefits. The organized retail thus has the ability to take different formats, from small neighbourhood stores in densely populated cities to large air-conditioned malls. Along with the benefits of convenience, to getting everything under one roof, the other benefits are it is spread in all local markets, providing the convenience of a neighbourhood *Kirana* store but with procurement on a mass scale that keeps prices low and provides greater variety (Reardon & Gulati, 2008).

While the share of organised retail and e-commerce is likely to increase, the traditional retail share of the Indian retail market is expected to continue in the foreseeable future (Dholakia, Dholakia, & Chattopadhyay, 2012). However, ease of access, locational proximity, local community knowledge, and personal relations with customers have given an edge to traditional retail stores over organised outlets (FICCI, 2019). Likewise, traditional mom-and-pop stores offer a unique experience of intimacy, ubiquity, and neighbourliness from the shopkeepers' interactions. Convenience in purchase makes *Kirana* stores still remain a sought-after place to shop. Unlike a developed market where consumers travel some distance for shopping, Indian consumers have the *Kirana* stores to service them on all days, all through the year (Shukla & Shukla, 2013).

The traditional *Kirana* stores in the Indian retail sector have a pertinent share of the total retail market with an approximation of 12 million *Kirana* stores (i.e., about 10 stores per 1,000 Indians). The low operating costs and extrinsic knowledge about the local community allow the *Kirana* stores to have limited product choices in the outlet while keeping their stock with distributor (FICCI, 2019).

Customers' shopping behaviours are not static in reality very dynamic in nature (Gowrisankaran & Rysman, 2012), hence, the consumers purchasing decisions can be affected by several factors based on their emergencies (Shi, Si, *et al.*, 2020). The COVID-19 pandemic has affected the daily life of all, and has brought direct and indirect consequences (Verma & Gustafsson, 2020), especially in the social, economic, cultural, and psychological aspects (Settersten, Jr., Richard, A., *et al.*, 2020). The pandemic has thus created lasting impacts on consumer culture, structure of the market, consumer purchasing decisions, and behaviours (Soares, João Coelho, *et al.*, 2022).

The exponential growth in coronavirus cases worldwide in the first half has reflected the adoption of restrictive measures (WHO, 2020). The pandemic has created a negative effect towards the behavioural intentions of consumers *vis-à-vis* changes in their consumption patterns (Brewer & Sebby, 2021). However, the safety concerns of the customers have considered various options for their shopping (Truong & Truong, 2022).

The pandemic and the associated restrictions have caused significant disruptions in consumer behaviour. The personal safety and safety of their belongings were marked high priority. However, the consumer has realised an alternative that is more convenient, affordable, and accessible for their shopping (Sheth, 2020). This has also been reflected in retailers' perspectives through personalized selling (Dixit & Dubey, 2022), safety measure (Mehra & Singh, 2016), embracing digitalization (Bendi & Ravindra, 2022), and several innovative practices. The new normal scenario has seen retailers much closer to the customers to promote their products by adopting new changing strategies. The retailers who embraced brick-and-mortar model have upgraded themselves by including health and safety features in their premises, physical distancing, contactless transactions, controlling the strength of customers in stores, speed services and self-service operations (Bendi & Ravindra, 2022).

The consumers felt a health risk in buying commodities during the pandemic. This has encouraged them to look for alternatives to their purchases. As a result, consumers have started relying on mom-and-pop stores (i.e., *Kirana* stores) instead of supermarkets and online shopping and there is an increase in trust in the relationship (EY, 2020). Hence, it is inevitable to understand the impact of the pandemic on the major things that will boost consumption in the urbanization, income growth, favourable demographics, easy availability of credit, use of plastic money, technology and innovation, and evolving consumer attitudes the consumer buying behaviour and their perception towards decision-making (Shim *et al.*, 2021). The studies on the re-emergence of the mom-and-pop stores during the pandemic and the associated changes in the attributes are scant. Identifying the gap in the research, the present study focuses on the re-emergence of mom-and-pop stores and the acknowledgement provided by consumers during the pandemic.

Data and Methodology

The study is a piece of exploratory-cum-empirical research. Altogether 300 samples were considered from the consumers of three zones in Kerala (south, central, and north) to embrace the consumer's perception of their change in the purchasing behaviour and adoption of local mom-and-pop stores. The data were collected when the pandemic was falling in many countries. However, the misery of the pandemic through government restrictions was still there with the mutated version of the virus. The Factor analysis is used to identify the underlying factors that nurture the shopping preference of the customers towards mom-and-pop/*Kirana* shops during COVID-19. A logistic regression model was developed with the selected variables through a literature scan.

Result and Discussion

As a result of the outbreak of the COVID-19 pandemic and the government role in curbing the spread of the pandemic, the consumers were not allowed to move around freely. The restrictions were brought in against the large gathering as part of the protocol. The consumers were affected the most with their income and livelihood along with the meeting daily essentials to meet their basic necessity. Gradually, the frequency of buying behaviour, shopping preferences, spending etc. affected to a large extent. The perception of the consumers on their consumption pattern during pandemic is described in this section.

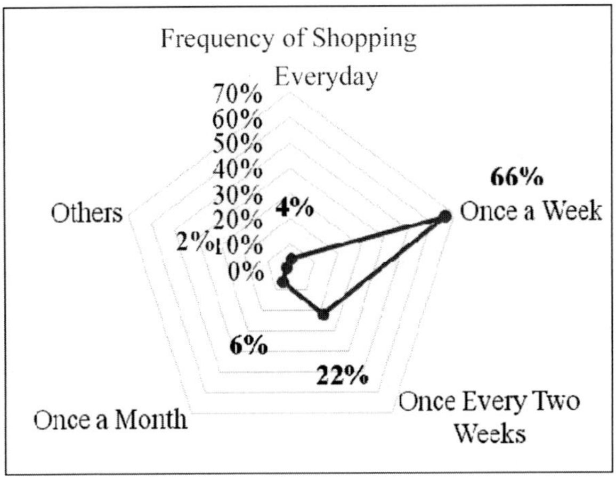

Fig. 14.1: Frequency of Shopping during COVID-19.

Source: Survey Data.

The pandemic decided the consumer's frequency of going out and this resulted in buying behaviour changes. Figure 14.1 shows the frequency of shopping during COVID-19. It is clear from the figure that majority of the consumers went out once a week out particularly for shopping with 66 per cent and followed by once every two weeks (22%). Though the food and essential goods are fragile it cannot be kept for long, thus, they normally prefer minimum a week gap for their purchase.

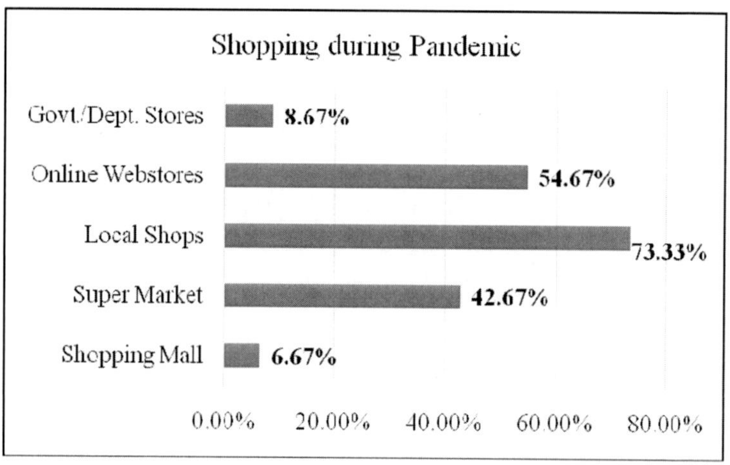

Fig. 14.2: Shopping preference during the pandemic.

Source: Survey Data.

As per the government orders, restrictions were high during lockdowns and defaulters were penalized with high fines and charges. The normal citizens had to produce affidavit to travel even to their neighbouring places. The consumer revealed that subsequent with the lockdown situation in their region they had to go out to buy goods and services citing with a sworn statement as per the protocol. Figure 14.2 explains that out of the main shopping options available to them, the consumer has the first and high preference for the nearest local shop (73.33%) to buy their daily essentials during lockdown periods followed by the second preference for the online web store/platforms and third preference with the supermarket (42.67%). However, the shopping preference for the government departmental stores and shopping malls didn't attract much of attention from the consumers.

The main reason for opting the local shops during the pandemic season are the easy accessible option available for the consumers. This is clearly represented in the Figure 14.3 amongst the different shopping centres the local shop is easily accessible, which is about 1 kilometre on an average. A state like Kerala with high density rates local shops are of high proximity of 1 to 2 kilometers. The others are placed approximately 3 kilometers and above. On the other hand, the reachability to the preferred shopping mall have approximate15 kilometers distance on an average.

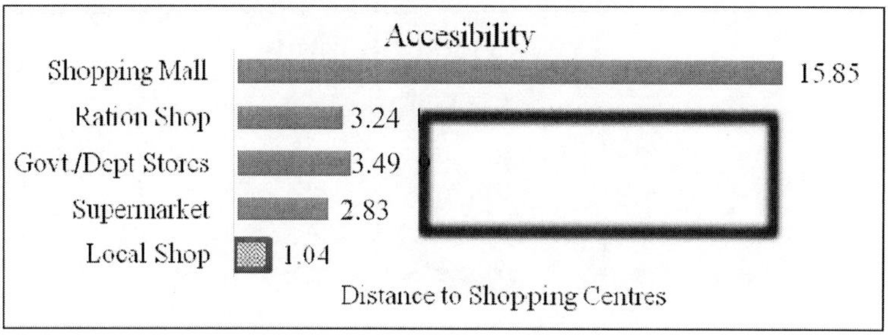

Fig. 14.3: Access to Shopping Centres.

Source: Survey Data.

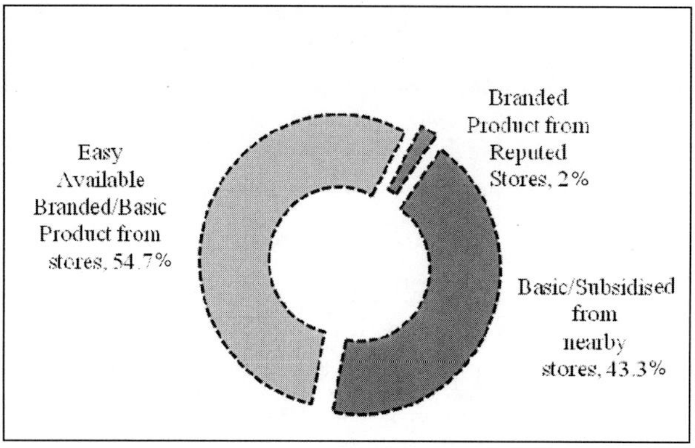

Fig. 14.4: Product preferred to buy in the current scenario.

Source: Survey Data.

The consumers place their purchases in consideration to the selected basket of good of their preference. However, the COVID-19, the subsequent lockdowns and restrictions apparently a lesson for them. Figure 14.4 share the feelings of the consumer's product preferences in the pandemic. The majority of the customers are happy with the easily available products (54.7%) whether it is branded or non-branded, on the other hand 43.3 per cent have preference to the basic and subsidized goods whichever is available in the nearby shops and a few still have preference to branded products from showrooms (2%). This implies the behavioural change in the mindset of the consumers from the branded to the easy access in the new normal scenario as a result of the pandemic.

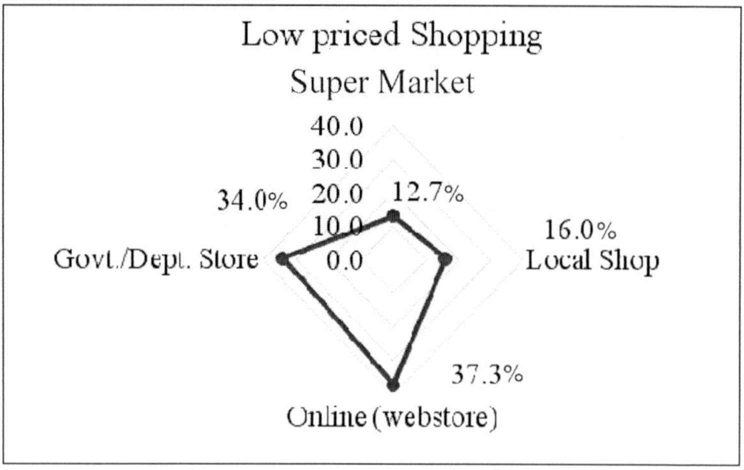

Fig. 14.5: Product available at low priced.

Source: Survey Data.

Mentioning the pricing of the products, the consumers have claimed (Fig. 14.5) that the products are comparably cheaper in the government department stores, followed by the online web stores, subsequently to the supermarkets and the local shops. However, during the pandemic, it seems that they are selecting the nearest shopping facility and easily accessible goods and services regardless to the price, brand and place of shopping (compare Fig.14.2, Fig. 14.3 & Fig. 14.4).

The COVID-19 severely affected the purchasing power of the consumers. The subsequent lockdown and stringent protocols put no less harm to the individual's income and livelihood. The common people struggled hard to meet their household needs and wants. Figure 14.6 (a) shows the consumers weekly shopping preference from their consumption basket during the pandemic. The consumers indicated that their weekly shopping includes vegetables and fruits (94%) followed by dairy products (76.67%); meat and fish (72.33%); provisions (62. 67%); home essentials (60.67%); and at last for ready to eat products (23.33%). Fig. 14.6(b) makes clear that the average weekly expenditure of the consumers are approximately Rs. 1624.67.

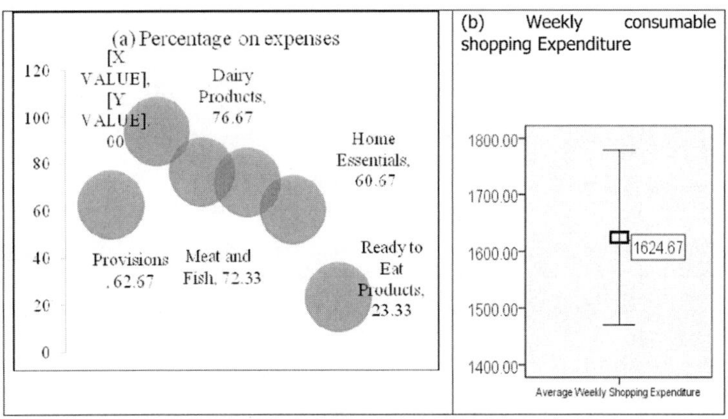

Fig. 14.6: Consumer's Expenditure and Consumption Basket.

Source: Survey Data.

Added to this, the preference of the consumers about their shopping was also considered based on the ranking (Fig. 14.7). The consumers responded that amidst the pandemic considering the safety, health and the societal value, they preferred the local *Kirana* Shops the most for their day-to-day necessities followed by the online web stores and supermarkets. Though the government operated shops are considerably cheaper they have given the rank 4th among the list. At last, once the favourite hangout place and the one stop shopping malls have given the last preference rank during the pandemic. This could be assimilated that the traditional shop once lost its delightful glimpse because of the most modern multi-outlet and shopping malls is recuperating as a result of the new normal scenario.

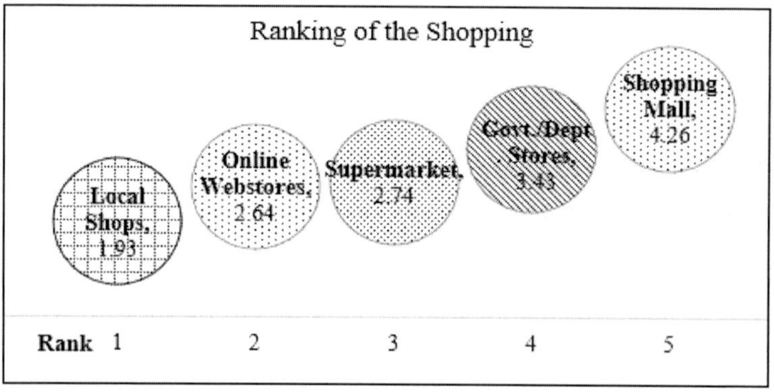

Fig. 14.7: Rank Preference of Shopping.

Source: Survey Data; (Scale 1 being the 1st rank; scale 5 being the 5th rank).

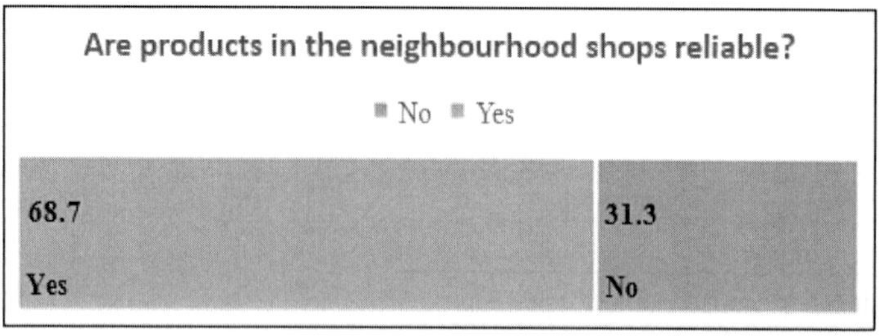

Fig. 14.8: Are products in the local shops reliable?

Source: Survey Data.

The study portrays the rebirth of the local *Kirana* shops during the pandemic. One and the only mode of buying goods and services lost the attraction, is regaining its importance and has become the need of the hour to the consumers. The consumers agree to the fact that the local *Kirana* shops are the most preferred which is very well reflected in their perception. The consumers also advocate that the local shops are very much reliable in the pandemic scenario (Fig. 14.8) as they provide the products in the neighbourhood with door-to-door provisions.

*Relevance of the mom-and-pop/*Kirana *Shops in the Pandemic*

Further to understand the underlying factor that supplement the re-emergence of the local *Kirana* shops, 17 statements were used in the factor analysis. The Cronbach's alpha coefficient of the selected variable was 0.816, which indicates high reliability since it exceeded the minimum standard of 0.70 (Tavakol & Dennick, 2011). To measure the strength of the relationship among variables, the Kaiser-Meyer-Olkin measure of sampling adequacy was 0.763, which is greater than the generally accepted minimum of 0.50 (Burns & Burns, 2008). The Bartlett's test was significant (approximate Chi-Square of 1875.299, df = 136, p <0.001). Therefore, it was appropriate to perform a factor analysis on these data.

Table 14.1: Reliability statistics, KMO and Bartlett's Test

KMO and Bartlett's Test		
Kaiser-Meyer-Olkin Measure of Sampling Adequacy		.763
Bartlett's Test of	Approx. Chi-Square	1875.299
Sphericity	df	136
	Sig.	.000
Reliability Statistics Cronbach's Alpha		N of Items
	.816	17

The factor analysis revealed five factors with Eigen value greater than 1; these factors accounted for 62.99 per cent of the total variance (Table 14.2). Initially in the extracted sum of squared loadings, the first factor explained about 31.42 per cent, the second factor explained about 10.32 per cent, the third factor explained

Table 14.2: Total Variance Explained

Component	Initial Eigen values			Extraction Sums of Squared Loadings			Rotation Sums of Squared Loadings		
	Total	% of Variance	Cumulative %	Total	% of Variance	Cumulative %	Total	% of Variance	Cumulative %
1	5.343	31.427	31.427	5.343	31.427	31.427	2.911	17.122	17.122
2	1.753	10.315	41.742	1.753	10.315	41.742	2.385	14.029	31.152
3	1.308	7.693	49.435	1.308	7.693	49.435	2.312	13.601	44.753
4	1.176	6.917	56.352	1.176	6.917	56.352	1.677	9.866	54.619
5	1.129	6.642	62.994	1.129	6.642	62.994	1.424	8.375	62.994

Extraction Method: Principal Component Analysis.

7.69 per cent, the fourth factor explained 6.91 per cent, and the last factor explained about 6.64 per cent of the total variance. Later, the total amount of variance accounted in the extracted solution was redistributed over to the five extracted factors in the rotated sum of squared loadings with the percentage of variance for the first factor at 17.12 per cent, the second factor at 14.0 per cent, the third factor at 13.6 per cent, the fourth factor at 9.86 per cent, and the last factor at 8.37 per cent of the total explained (Table 14.3).

Table 14.3: Factors, variables and factor loadings

Factor	Variables	Factor Loadings	Variance explained
Convenience and Adaptability factor	Accessible shopping Convenient to buy products Easy/digital payment methods Necessity goods available Comfortable purchasing time	.808 .734 .665 .619 .561	17.122
Quality and safety factor	Safety practices and measures Maintain social distancing Decent quality of products Local procured fresh products	.758 .686 .650 .538	14.029
Price flexibility and credit availability	Affordable price Discounts and price adjustments possible Credit facility available	.796 .637 .631	13.601
Personalized Shopping services factor	Well-known shop for years Personalized services Care for aged	.734 .627 .587	9.866
Safe home delivery factor	Online home delivery partner options Safe door to door delivery	.749 .595	8.375

*Compiled from the Rotated Component Matrix.
Extraction Method: Principal Component Analysis.
Rotation Method: Varimax with Kaiser Normalization.

Table 14.3 represented the rotated factor loading which shows the correlation between the variables and the factor. These factors were explained based on the factor loadings of 0.5 and above.

The first factor was labelled "Convenience and Adaptability Factor" since it included variables relevant to the current scenario like "Accessible Shopping", "Convenient to Buy Products", "Easy/ Digital Payment Methods", "Necessity Goods Available", and "Comfortable purchasing time". As lockdown engaged in different parts of the state, the consumers preferred to buy their day-to-day products from the nearest accessible shops with a comfortable purchasing time. Moreover, the availability of necessity goods and the digital money exchange through internet banking, mobile banking, wallet payments etc. are also preferred by the consumers in the scenario.

The second factor was labelled "Quality and Safety Factors" as it included variables such as "safety practices and measures", "maintain social distancing", "decent quality of products", and "local procured fresh products" which shows the assurance on safety measure adopted by the shops against the pandemic spread, ensuring the quality and freshness of the products which are locally procured.

The third factor was labelled "Price flexibility and Credit availability factor" since it included variables such as "affordable price", "discounts and price adjustments possible", and "credit facility available". One of the main characteristics of the traditional *Kirana* shops are providing credit facility to their customers which is not there in the most modern shops. As COVID-19 impacted the income and livelihood of the citizens, they have limitation to arrange immediate payments for what they buy. Moreover, they round off the price of the goods in mutual concerns too. The *Kirana* shops have that facility which is equally preferred by the consumers in the current context.

The fourth factor was "Personalized Shopping Services Factor" since the variables such as "Well Known Shop", "Personalised Services" and "Care for Alone/Aged" which clearly depict the personal touch and support to benefit the consumers. The *Kirana* stores are known for the personalised shopping experiences. The shopping dilemma caused by the pandemic has supported by the traditional local *Kirana* stores to some extent with their personalised support to the consumers.

The last factor was "Safe Home Delivery Factor" which included variables such as "Online home delivery partner options" and "Safe Door to Door Delivery". The consumers also preferred to take orders through the phone/online delivery partners of the shop and expected a safe door to door home delivery.

Thus, the result of the factor analysis brought in the underlying factors for the renaissance/re-birth of the *Kirana* Shops during the pandemic.

Acceptance of Local Kirana *Shops during the Pandemic*

Further, a logistic regression model was also used to estimate the predicted depended variable preference of 'local mom-and pop store', i.e., 'Acceptance of *Kirana* Shops' during the global pandemic and the pertinent independent variables associated in the model. As the logistic regression calculates the probability of an event occurring over event not occurring, hence it is explained in terms of odds (Park, 2013).

$$logit(y) = \ln(\text{odds}) = log\left(\frac{p}{1-p}\right) = \text{a} + \beta\chi \qquad ...(1)$$

The model is to predict the logit, i.e., rate of change in the "log odds" as *X* changes. The calculated exp (B) is the expected effect of the independent variable on the "odds ratio", which is the probability of the event divided by the probability of the non-event and they are in log-odds units.

The prediction equation is:

$$log\left(\frac{p}{1-p}\right) = b_0 + b_1 \times x_1 + b_2 \times x_2 + b_3 \times x_3 + b_4 \times x_4 + b_5 \times x_5 \quad ...(2)$$

where, p is the predicted probability of preferring 'local mom-and pop store' during the pandemic and x are the predictor variables included in the model, i.e., "convenience", "quality and safety", "price flexibility and credit availability", "personalized shopping services" and "safe home delivery".

Table 14.4: Variables in the Equation

	B	S.E.	Wald	df	Sig.	Exp(B)	
Step 0	Constant	1.012	.131	60.036	1	.000	2.750

As a precondition to use the logistic regression model for model prediction, it was important to test the hypothesis whether the constant term is significantly different from zero. The Wald Chi-square test in Table 14.4 examines the null hypothesis that "the constant is equal to 0". From the test it was evident that the constant in the equation was significant with *p*-value <0.000 and thus we rejected the null hypothesis.

Next, we determined the overall fit of the model using the Hosmer and Lemeshow test (Table 14.5). Because the *p*-value (0.312) is higher than the significance level (0.05), we conclude than the model fits the observed dataset. Hence, the model predictions could be determined with the given variables.

Table 14.5: Hosmer and Lemeshow Test

Step	Chi-square	df	Sig.
1	9.375	8	.312

Table 14.6: Model Classification Table—Acceptance of *Kirana* shop

Observed			Predicted		
			Shopping preference of Local Shops during Pandemic		Percentage
			No	Yes	Correct
Step 0[a,b]	Shopping preference of Local Shops during Pandemic	No	0	80	.0
		Yes	0	220	100.0
	Overall Percentage				*73.3*
Step 1[b]	Shopping preference of Local Shops during Pandemic	No	10	70	31.7
		Yes	6	214	94.2
	Overall Percentage				*74.7*

a. Constant is included in the model.

b. The cut-off value is 0.500.

Table 14.6 shows the per cent of cases that were correctly predicted by the model increased from 73.3 per cent in the constant model to 74.7 per cent in the full model.

Table 14.7 exhibits the variables, variable codes and description of the variables used in the logistic model. Altogether five independent variables were selected in the model to predict the relationship between predictors and the predicted variable.

Table 14.7: Variables used in the model

Variable	Variable Code	Name of the Variable	Description
Dependent (y)		Local Shop Preference	Customers shopping preference of Local mom-and-pop or *Kirana* Shops during Pandemic as a predicted variable.
Independent (x1)	CAF	Convenience	Convenience of shopping including easiness in access and payment at the shop as a predictor variable.
Independent (x2)	QS	Quality and Safety	Quality of the products available and safety measures at the shop as a predictor variable.
Independent (x3)	PFCA	Price flexibility and Credit availability	Price easiness/flexibility and the availability of credit facilities at the shop as a predictor variable.
Independent (x4)	PSS	Personalized Shopping Services	Extend of personalised or customised services from the shop as a predictor variable.
Independent (x5)	SHD	Safe Home Delivery	Safe and door-to-door delivery provided by the shop as a predictor variable.

Source: Compiled for logistic regression analysis.

At the desired significance level of less than 0.05. in Table 14.8, the variables of the model Convenience (CAF), Quality and Safety (QS) and Personalized Shopping Services (PSS) positively contributed to the model, whereas Price Flexibility and Credit Availability (PFCA) and Safe Home Delivery (SHD) were considered less important in the model.

Table 14.8: Regression Model

		B	S.E.	Wald	df	Sig.	Exp(B)
Step 1[a]	CAF	.779	.276	7.928	1	.005	2.178
	QS	1.024	.313	10.740	1	.001	2.785
	PFCA	-.626	.298	4.394	1	.036	.535
	PSS	.660	.229	8.320	1	.004	1.934
	SHD	-.276	.146	3.565	1	.059	.759
	Constant	-3.021	1.839	2.699	1	.100	.049

a. Variable(s) entered on step 1: CAF, QS, PFCA, PSS, SHD.

As there is an increase in the independent variable "*xi*" by one unit, i.e., "*xi+1*" keeping all other factors remaining constant, the odds of the dependent variable increase by a factor exp (i), which is the odd ratio (Boateng & Abaye, 2019). For every one-unit increase in the predictor variable, the outcome variable will increase by the beta coefficient value (Park, 2013). The coefficient for CAF says that keeping other variables constant, for every one-unit increase in CAF will have a 117 increase in the odds of being included in the predicted variable. Similarly, the coefficient for QS would see a 178 increase for every one-unit increase. Further, the coefficient for PSS would see an increase of 93 for every one-unit increase. However, every one-unit increase in the variable PFCA (-46) and SHD (-24) is resulting in a negative effect in the model.

The fitted logistic regression equation was;

$$\log (p/ (1-p)) = -3.021 + 0.779 \times CAF + 1.024 \times QS - 0.626 \times PFCA + 0.660 \times PSS - 0.276 \times SHD \quad \ldots (3)$$

Hence, the model establishes that the consumers have given "Convenience", "Quality and Safety" and "Personalized Shopping Services" with prior importance to shopping from the local mom-and-pop/*Kirana* shop during the pandemic.

Conclusion

The changing Indian consumer is now seeking more value in terms of improved shopping experience, easy availability, good quality, pleasant shopping ambience, good competitive prices, easy payment options, and quick delivery. All these factors have created a rapid growing opportunity for retail formats to emerge and grow at a fast pace. The retail market witnessed big retailers dominating and building strong customer base. The 'stay-at-home' mandate and 'lockdowns' changed the Indian consumer attitude and behaviour. The change in the shopping pattern of consumers are because of the change in the taste and preferences of consumers resulting in a great transformation in lifestyles and spending patterns. These restrictions actually gave a lifeline to the *Kirana* stores, the unsung heroes, who served everyone. *Kirana* shops were able to reach out to people and supply essentials to the people and get back the trust. Understanding the buying behaviour of consumers and adapting to the needs is the key to success. The pandemic helped *Kirana* shops to understand the need of the customers and change the way of working. Thus, the *Kirana* (mom-and-pop store), known for serving people in a particular area, became a forever trusted choice of buying.

During the pandemic rolling customers have identified the prominence of the local mom-and-pop/*Kirana* stores returning in action through their rejuvenated services like convenience, quality and safety, price flexibility and credit availability, Personalized shopping services and safe home delivery. It is relevant to see that the logistic regression model with predictor variables like "Convenience", "Quality and Safety" and "Personalized Shopping Services" has given prior importance to the predicted variable shopping from the local mom-and-pop/*Kirana* shop during the pandemic.

References

Ablett, J., Baijal, A., Beinhocker, E. & Bose, A. (2007). *The 'bird of gold': The rise of India's consumer market.* [Online] Available at: https://www.mckinsey.com/featured-insights/asia-pacific/the-bird-of-gold#

Anon (2015). *Principles of Marketing.* Minnesota: University of Minnesota Libraries Publishing.

Anon (2020). *Retail and Consumer.* [Online] Available at: https://www.pwc.in/industries/retail-and-consumer.html

Bendi, D., & Ravindra Babu, S. (2022). "Sustainable Marketing Models with Changing Customer Mindset." *AIMS Journal of Management,* 244. https://aimsjm.s3.ap-south-1.amazonaws.com/AIMS_Journal_of_Management_Jul_2022.pdf#page=254

Blythe, J. (2008). *Consumer Behaviour.* London: Thomson Learning.

Boateng, E.Y. & Abaye, D.A. (2019). "A Review of the Logistic Regression Model with Emphasis on Medical Research." *Journal of Data Analysis and Information Processing,* 7(4), pp. 190-207.

Brewer, P., & Sebby, A.G. (2021). "The effect of online restaurant menus on consumers' purchase intentions during the COVID-19 pandemic." *International Journal of Hospitality Management, 94,* 102777.

Burns, R.P., & Burns, R. (2008). *Business research methods and statistics using SPSS.* Sage.

Chappelow, J. (2018). *Consumer Spending.* [Online] Available at: https://www.investopedia.com/terms/c/consumer-spending.asp [Accessed 13 July, 2020].

Cui, G., & Liu, Q. (2001). "Executive insights: emerging market segments in a transitional economy: a study of urban consumers in China." *Journal of International Marketing, 9*(1), 84-106.

Deloitte-FICCI (2018). *Consumer Leads,* s.l.: s.n.

Deloitte (2019). *Unravelling the Indian Consumer,* s.l.: RAI.

Deshpande, P.P. (2015). "Consumer Behaviour as a Synthesis of Different Social Science Approaches." *Journal of Socialomics, 4*(2), pp. 1-4.

Devi, K. & Gerald, D.J.W.A. (2016). "Unorganised Sector Particularly Focus Only Retailers: A Study on its Strength and Weakness." *Indian Journal of Applied Research,* pp. 14-16.

Dholakia, N., Dholakia, R.R., & Chattopadhyay, A. (2012). "India's emerging retail systems: coexistence of tradition and modernity." *Journal of Macromarketing, 32*(3), 252-265.

EY (2020). *Sentiments of India—Pulse of the country, Kiranas,* s.l.: EY.

FICCI, D. (2019). *Evolve for Consumer,* Global: Deloitte-FICCI.

FICCI, D. (2020). *FMCG and retail (e-commerce),* s.l.: FICCI.

Gowrisankaran, G., & Rysman, M. (2012). "Dynamics of consumer demand for new durable goods". *Journal of Political Economy, 120*(6), 1173-1219.

Hansen, U., & Schrader, U. (1997). "A modern model of consumption for a sustainable society". *Journal of Consumer Policy, 20*(4), 443-468.

IBEF (2022). *Retail,* s.l.: IBEF.

Ila Dixit & Archi Dubey (2022). "Impact of Integrated Marketing Communication on Brand Performance: A Study of Ornament Industry in Chhattisgarh." *AIMS Journal of Management,* 113. https://aimsjm.s3.ap-south-1.amazonaws.com/AIMS_Journal_of_Management_Jul_2022.pdf#page=254

India (2022). *Indian Retail Industry Analysis.* [Online] Available at: https://www.ibef.org/industry/indian-retail-industry-analysis-presentation#:~:text=The%20modern%20retail%20market%20in,%24%2060%20billion)%20by%202020. [Accessed 3 August 2022].

India, I. (2019). *Indian Food Processing.* [Online] Available at: https://www.ibef.org/industry/indian-food-industry.aspx#:~:text=The%20Indian%20food%20and%20grocery,per%20cent%20of%20the%20sales.&text=It%20contributes%20around%208.80%20and,cent%20of%20total%20industrial%20investment. [Accessed 13 July 2020].

Khullar, P. (2018). *How Indian malls are transforming into retail destinations.* [Online] Available at: https://www.financialexpress.com/money/how-indian-malls-are-transforming-into-retail-destinations/1397953/

Kumar, A. (2020). *Rise: The Economic Times.* [Online] Available at: https://economictimes.indiatimes.com/small-biz/sme-sector/indian-kirana-stores-will-continue-to-be-dominated-by-standalone-shops-this-time-around-with-an-online-avatar/articleshow/79692171.cms?from=mdr

Mehra, P., & Singh, R. (2016). "Consumer preferences and purchase decision-making for micro-packs—an empirical study." *Vision, 20*(3), 224-236.

National Commision for Enterprises in the Unorganised Sector (2007). *Report on the conditions of work and promotion of livelihoods in the unorganised sector,* s.l.: Dolphin Printo Graphics.

OECD (2020). *COVID-19 and the retail sector: impact and policy responses,* Paris: OECD.

Online, F. E. (2019). *Economy.* [Online] Available at: Shopping more can help India's GDP growth as the private consumption expenditure will continue to drive around 60% of the nominal GDP in the current financial year. [Accessed 13 July, 2020].

P. Singh, T. (2017). "Organised Retailing—A SWOC Analysis." *International Journal of Business and Management Invention,* pp. 10-12.

Park, H. A. (2013). "An introduction to logistic regression: from basic concepts to interpretation with particular attention to nursing domain." *Journal of Korean Academy of Nursing, 43*(2), 154-164.

Ramya, N. & Ali, D.S.M. (2016). "Factors affecting consumer buying behaviour." *International Journal of Applied Research, 2* (10), pp. 76-80.

Rani, E. (2013). "Supermarkets vs. Small kirana stores." *IOSR Journal of Business and Management, 10*(1), pp. 1-7.

Reardon, T. & Gulati, A. (2008). *The Rise of Supermarkets and their Development Implications: International Experience Relevant for India,* New Delhi: IFPRI.

Rustagi, D.N. (2020). *Corona, kirana and the convergence model for Indian retail.* [Online] Available at: https:// www.cnbctv18.com/retail/corona-kirana-and-the-convergence-model-for-indian-retail-5883431.htm

Settersten, Jr., R.A., Bernardi, L., Härkönen, J., Antonucci, T.C., Dykstra, P.A., Heckhausen, J. & Thomson, E. (2020). "Understanding the effects of COVID-19 through a life course lens." *Advances in Life Course Research, 45*, 100360.

Sheth, J. (2020). "Impact of COVID-19 on consumer behaviour: Will the old habits return or die?" *Journal of Business Research, 117*, 280-283.

Shim, J., Moon, J., Song, M. & Lee, W.S. (2021). "Antecedents of purchase intention at Starbucks in the context of COVID-19 pandemic." *Sustainability, 13*(4), 1758.

Shi, S., Wang, Y., Chen, X., & Zhang, Q. (2020). "Conceptualization of omnichannel customer experience and its impact on shopping intention: A mixed-method approach." *International Journal of Information Management, 50*, 325-336.

Shukla, A. & Shukla, A. (2013). "A Study of Changing Consumer Behaviour Towards Convenience Stores by Entrance Malls in India." *ZENITH International Journal of Business Economics & Management Research, 3*(4), pp. 287-302.

Sinha, P.K. & Kar, S.K. (2007). "An Insight into the Growth of New Retail Formats in India". *IIMA W.P. No. 2007-03-04,* pp. 7-10.

Soares, J.C., Limongi, R., De Sousa Júnior, J.H., Santos, W.S., Raasch, M. & Hoeckesfeld, L. (2022). "Assessing the effects of COVID-19-related risk on online shopping behaviour." *Journal of Marketing Analytics*, 1-13.

Survey, L. (2020). *News: The Economic Times.* [Online] Available at: (https:// economictimes.indiatimes.com/news/ economy/indicators/lockdown-brings-change-in-buying-behaviour-more-older-people-hop-onto-digital-tech-survey/articleshow/75656615.cms?from=mdr).

Tavakol, M., & Dennick, R. (2011). "Making sense of Cronbach's alpha." *International Journal of Medical Education, 2*, 53.

Truong, D., & Truong, M.D. (2022). "How do customers change their purchasing behaviours during the COVID-19 pandemic?." *Journal of Retailing and Consumer Services, 67*, 102963.

Verma, S., & Gustafsson, A. (2020). "Investigating the emerging COVID-19 research trends in the field of business and management: A bibliometric analysis approach". *Journal of Business Research, 118*, 253-261.

WEF (2018). *Future of Consumption in Fast-Growth Consumer Markets: India,* Switzerland: World Economic Forum.

WHO (2020). *Coronavirus disease 2019 (COVID-19), Situation Report 99,* Paris: WHO.

Index